SHORTCAKE CAKE

STORY AND ART BY

suu Morishita

10

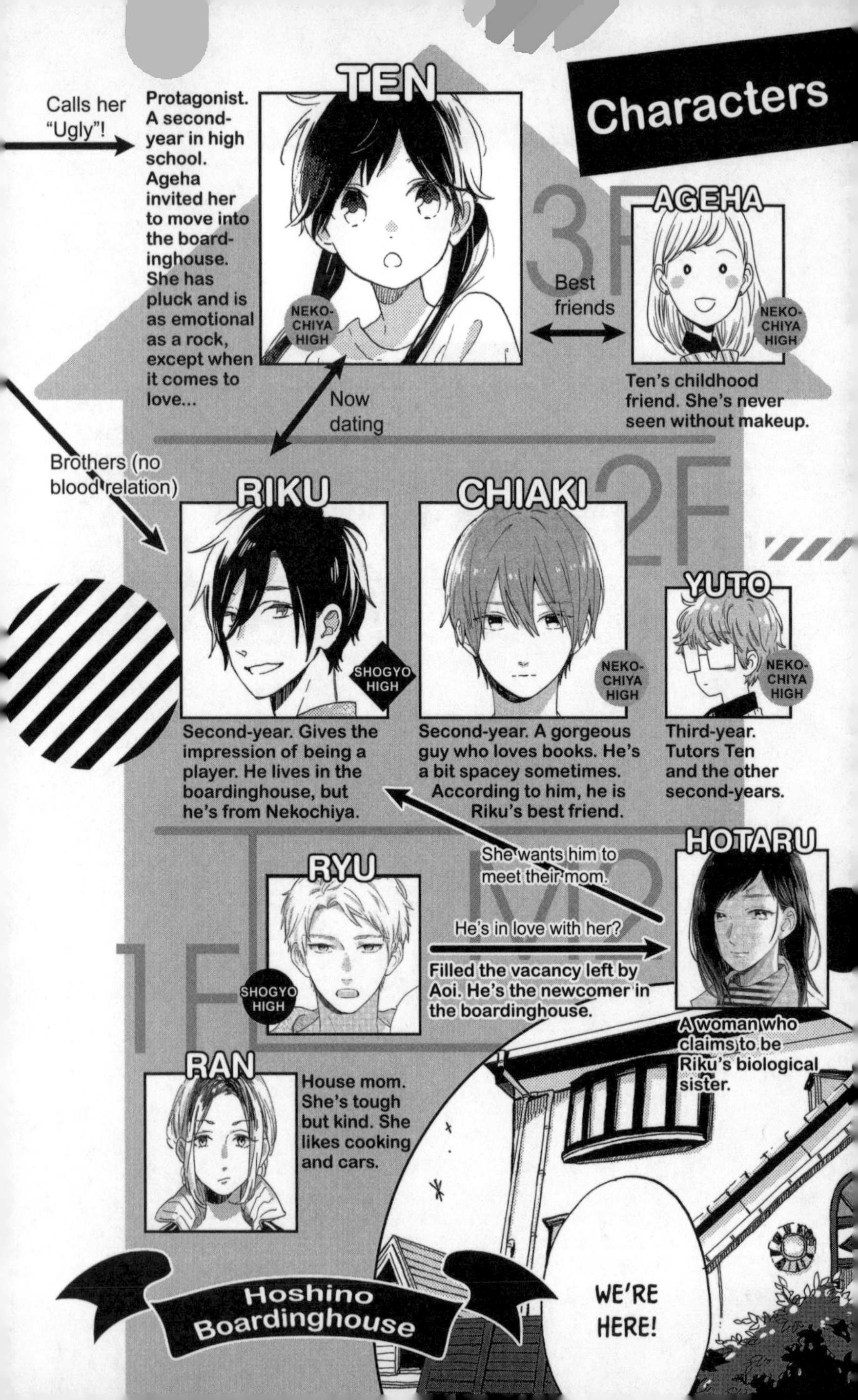
Characters
TEN
Calls her "Ugly"!
Protagonist. A second-year in high school. Ageha invited her to move into the boardinghouse. She has pluck and is as emotional as a rock, except when it comes to love...
NEKO-CHIYA HIGH
3F
AGEHA
Best friends
NEKO-CHIYA HIGH
Ten's childhood friend. She's never seen without makeup.
Now dating
Brothers (no blood relation)
2F
RIKU
SHOGYO HIGH
Second-year. Gives the impression of being a player. He lives in the boardinghouse, but he's from Nekochiya.
CHIAKI
NEKO-CHIYA HIGH
Second-year. A gorgeous guy who loves books. He's a bit spacey sometimes. According to him, he is Riku's best friend.
YUTO
NEKO-CHIYA HIGH
Third-year. Tutors Ten and the other second-years.
HOTARU
She wants him to meet their mom.
M2
RYU
SHOGYO HIGH
He's in love with her?
Filled the vacancy left by Aoi. He's the newcomer in the boardinghouse.
A woman who claims to be Riku's biological sister.
1F
RAN
House mom. She's tough but kind. She likes cooking and cars.
Hoshino Boardinghouse
WE'RE HERE!

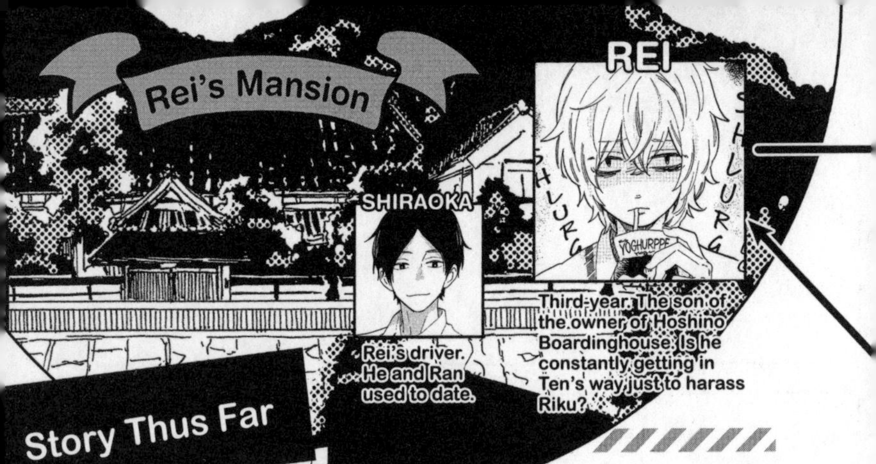
Rei's Mansion
REI
SHLURG
SHLURG
YOGHURPPE
Third-year. The son of the owner of Hoshino Boardinghouse. Is he constantly getting in Ten's way just to harass Riku?
SHIRAOKA
Rei's driver. He and Ran used to date.
Story Thus Far

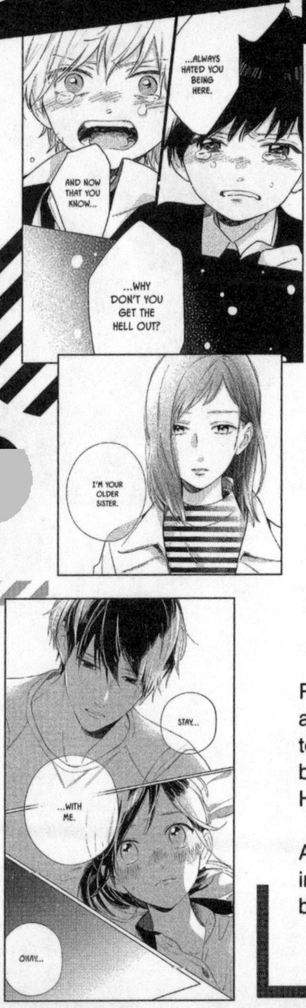
...ALWAYS HATED YOU BEING HERE.
AND NOW THAT YOU KNOW...
...WHY DON'T YOU GET THE HELL OUT?
I'M YOUR OLDER SISTER.
STAY...
...WITH ME.
OKAY...

Ten was commuting two hours each way to school by bus until her friend Ageha invited her to move into the Hoshino Boardinghouse. The place is full of characters, and it's there that she meets Riku and Chiaki. Ten and Riku start dating, but they keep their relationship secret at the boardinghouse. Ten struggles at first as she's never been one to keep secrets, but the relationship blooms thanks to Riku's kindness and support from Chiaki.

Ten is determined to learn more about the past that Riku refuses to talk about. She and Chiaki reach out to Shiraoka, and say nothing about it to Riku.

They learn from Shiraoka that Riku never knew his biological parents, and that he was raised by Rei's parents. Riku was eventually kicked out of the Mizuhara household by Rei after their parents died. After Shiraoka relates this crushing family history, he asks Ten and Chiaki to please put an end to the ongoing sibling feud.

Ryu moves into the boardinghouse in April, accompanied by a woman named Hotaru who claims to be Riku's older sister. She asks Riku to meet his biological mother, but Shiraoka refuses to let it happen. He takes Riku back to live with him at his place.

At Shiraoka's urging, Ten visits Riku and finds herself in an embrace more intense than she's experienced before...

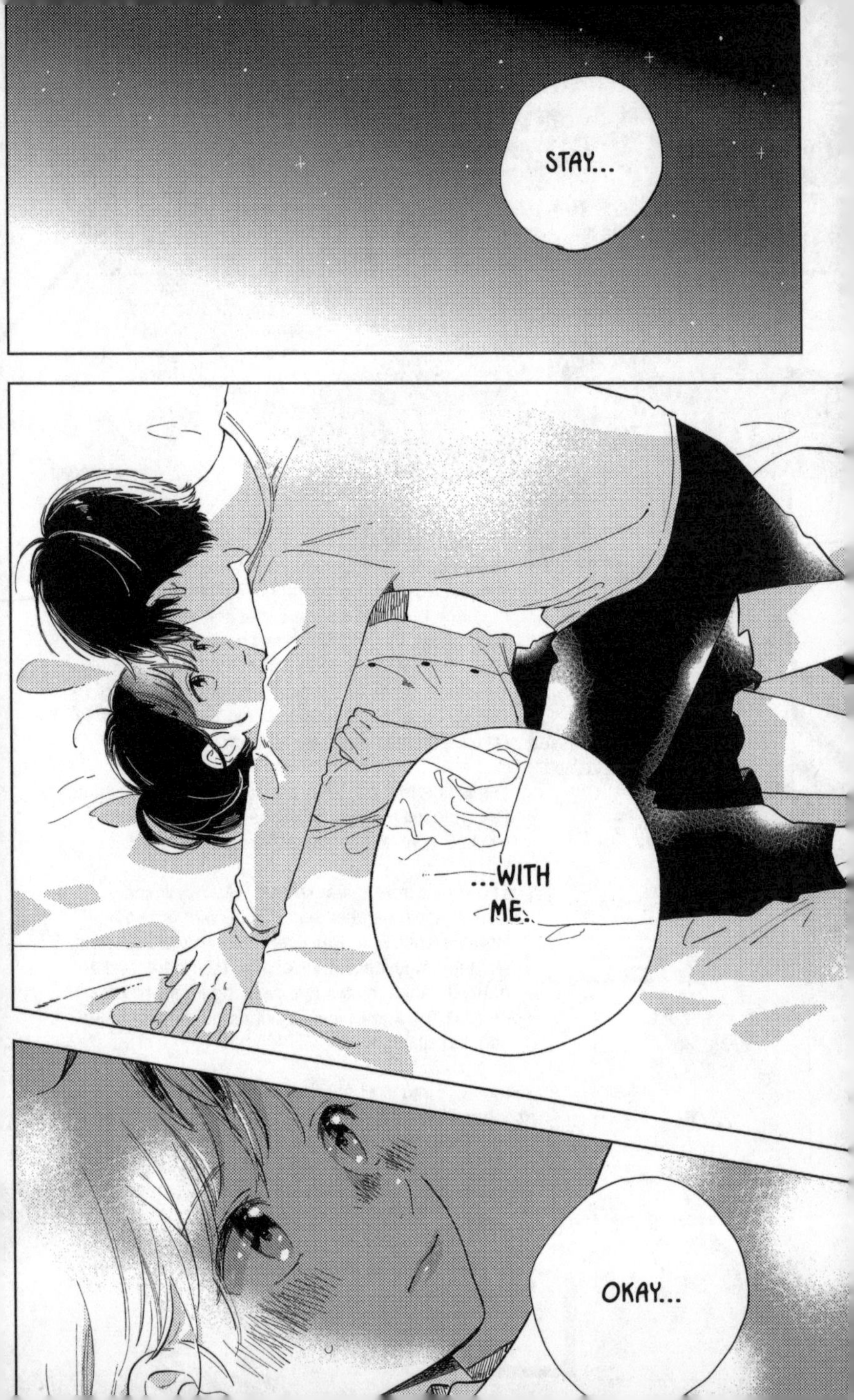
STAY...
...WITH ME.
OKAY...

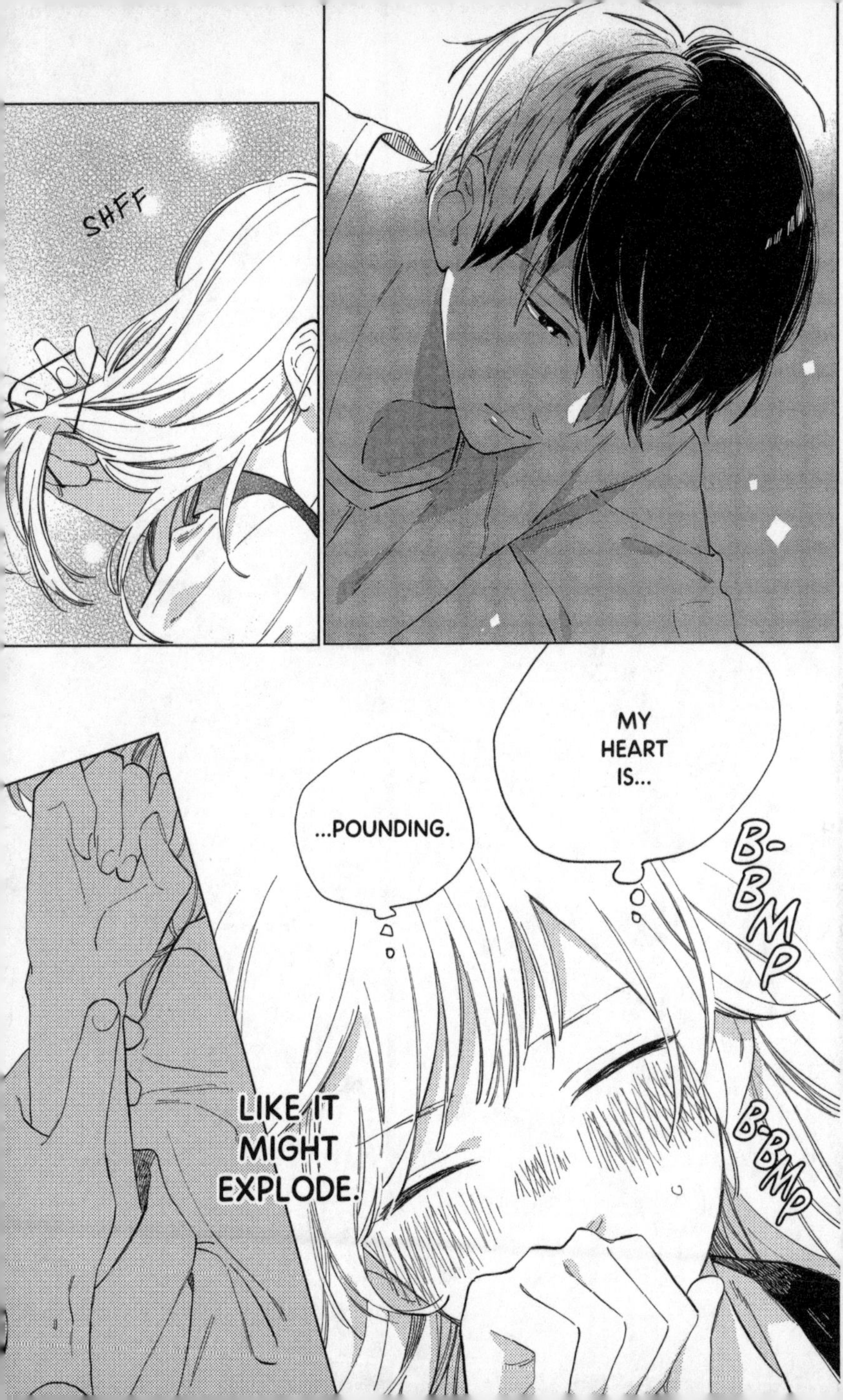
SHFF
MY HEART IS...
...POUNDING.
B-BMP
B-BMP
LIKE IT MIGHT EXPLODE.

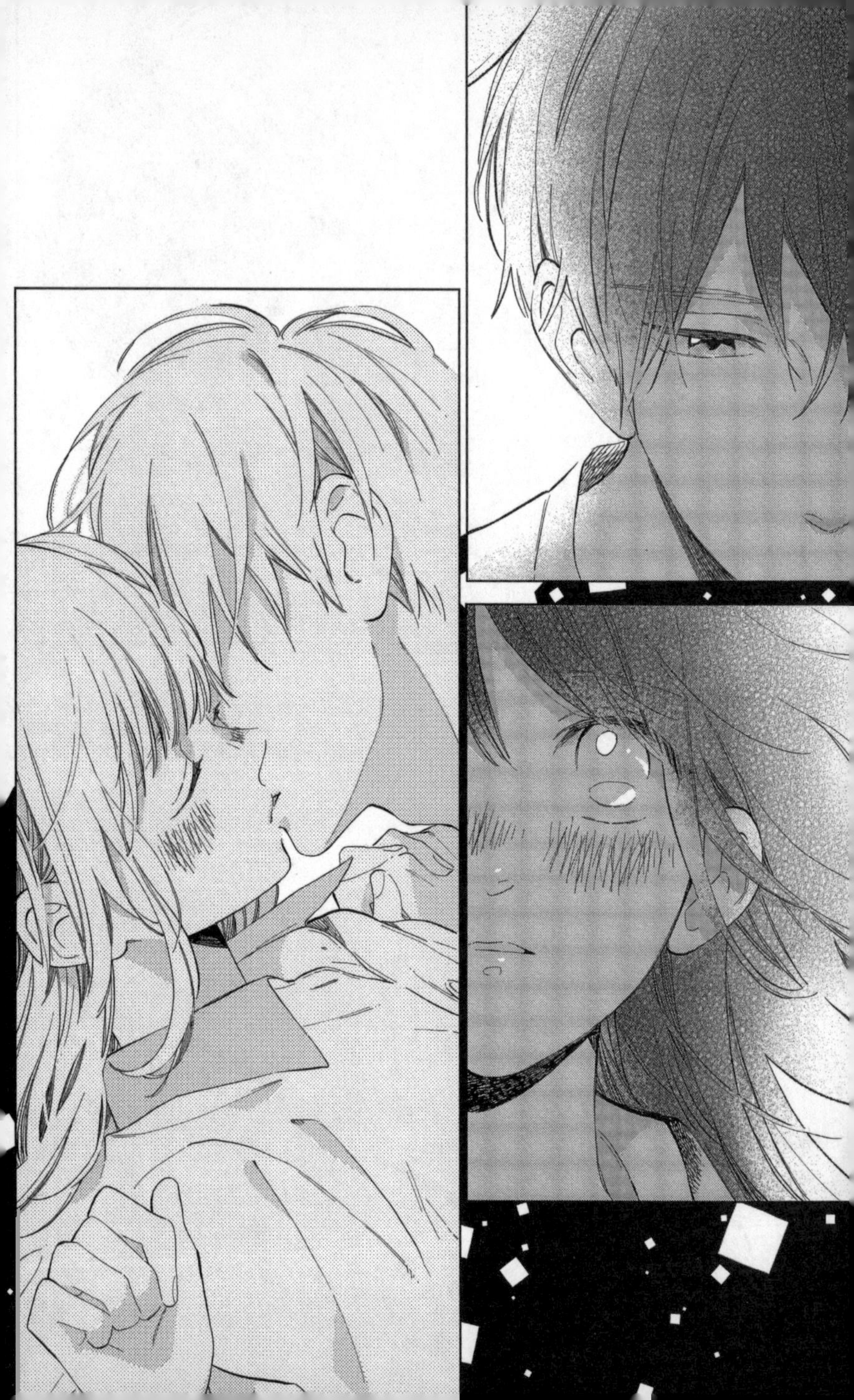

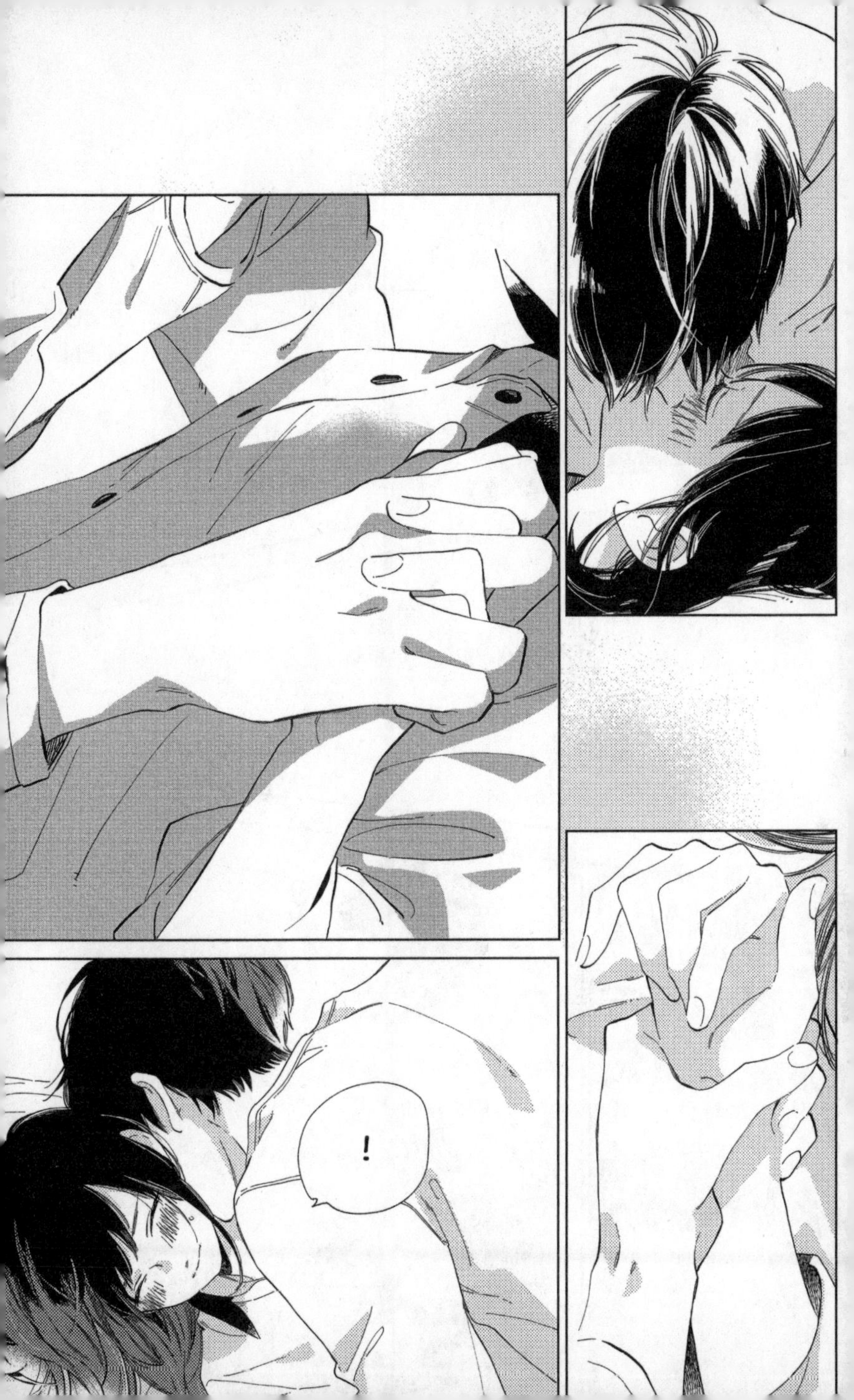
!

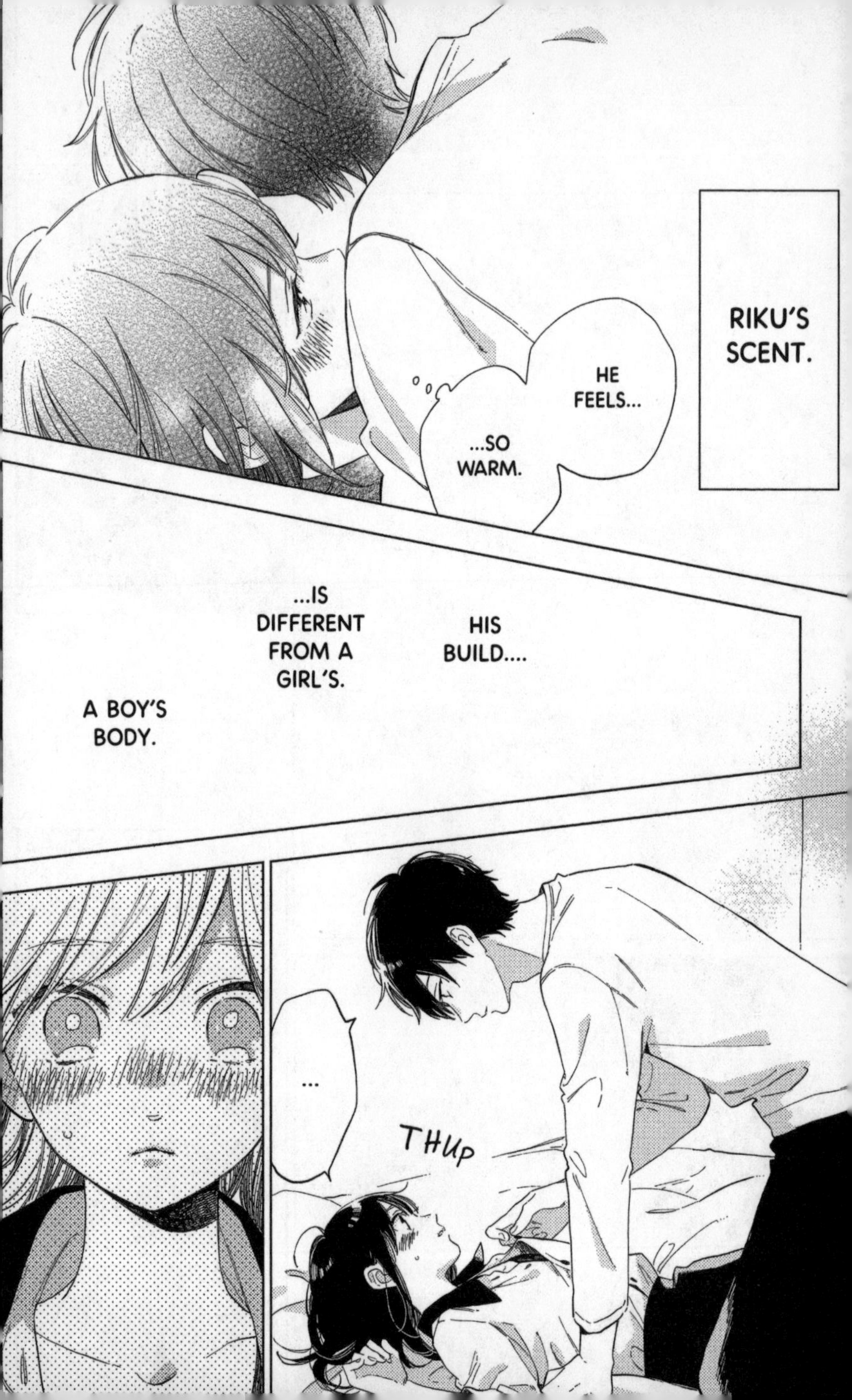
RIKU'S SCENT.
HE FEELS... ...SO WARM.
HIS BUILD....
...IS DIFFERENT FROM A GIRL'S.
A BOY'S BODY.
THUP
...

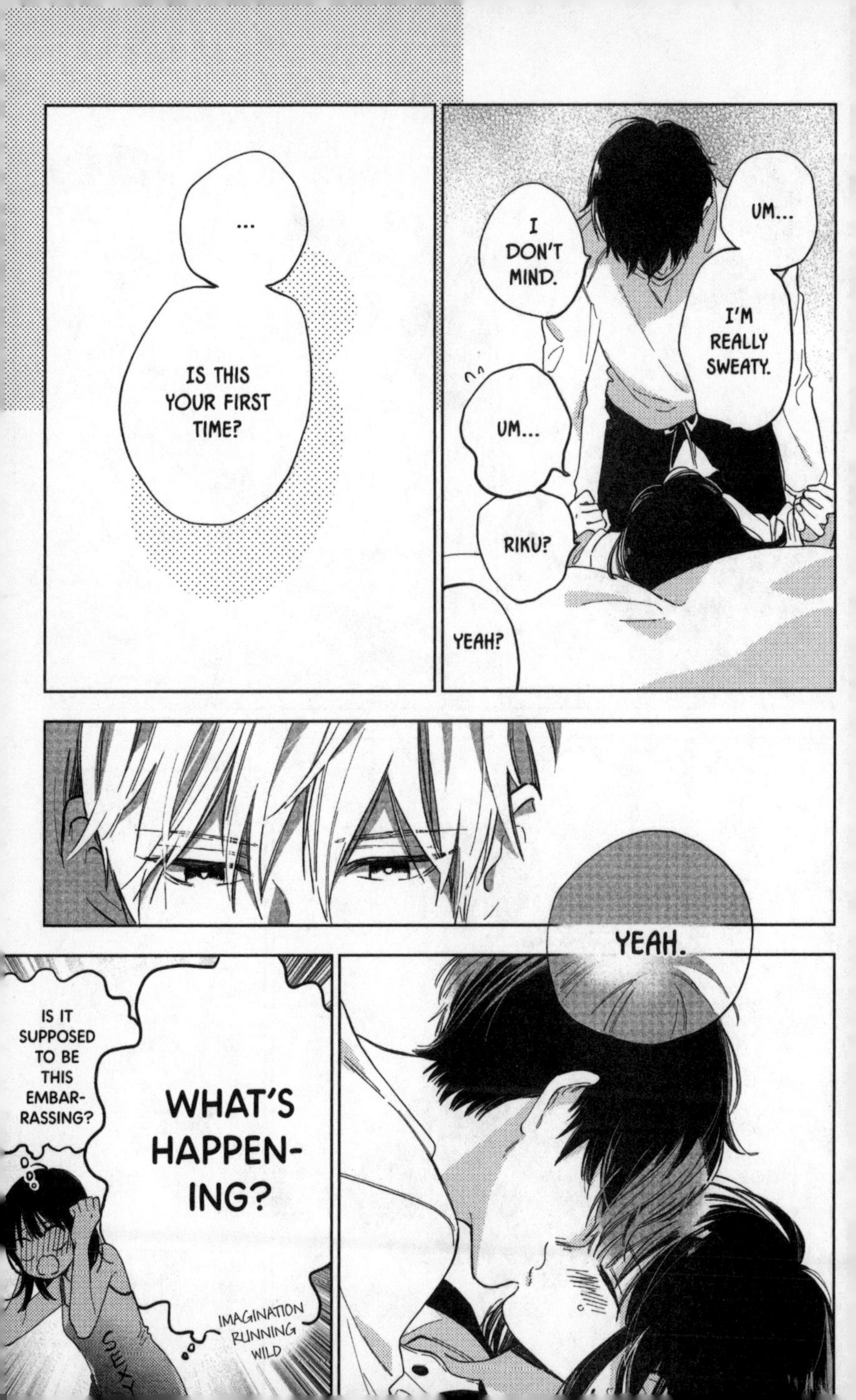
UM...
I DON'T MIND.
I'M REALLY SWEATY.
UM...
RIKU?
YEAH?
...
IS THIS YOUR FIRST TIME?
YEAH.
WHAT'S HAPPEN-ING?
IS IT SUPPOSED TO BE THIS EMBAR-RASSING?
IMAGINATION RUNNING WILD

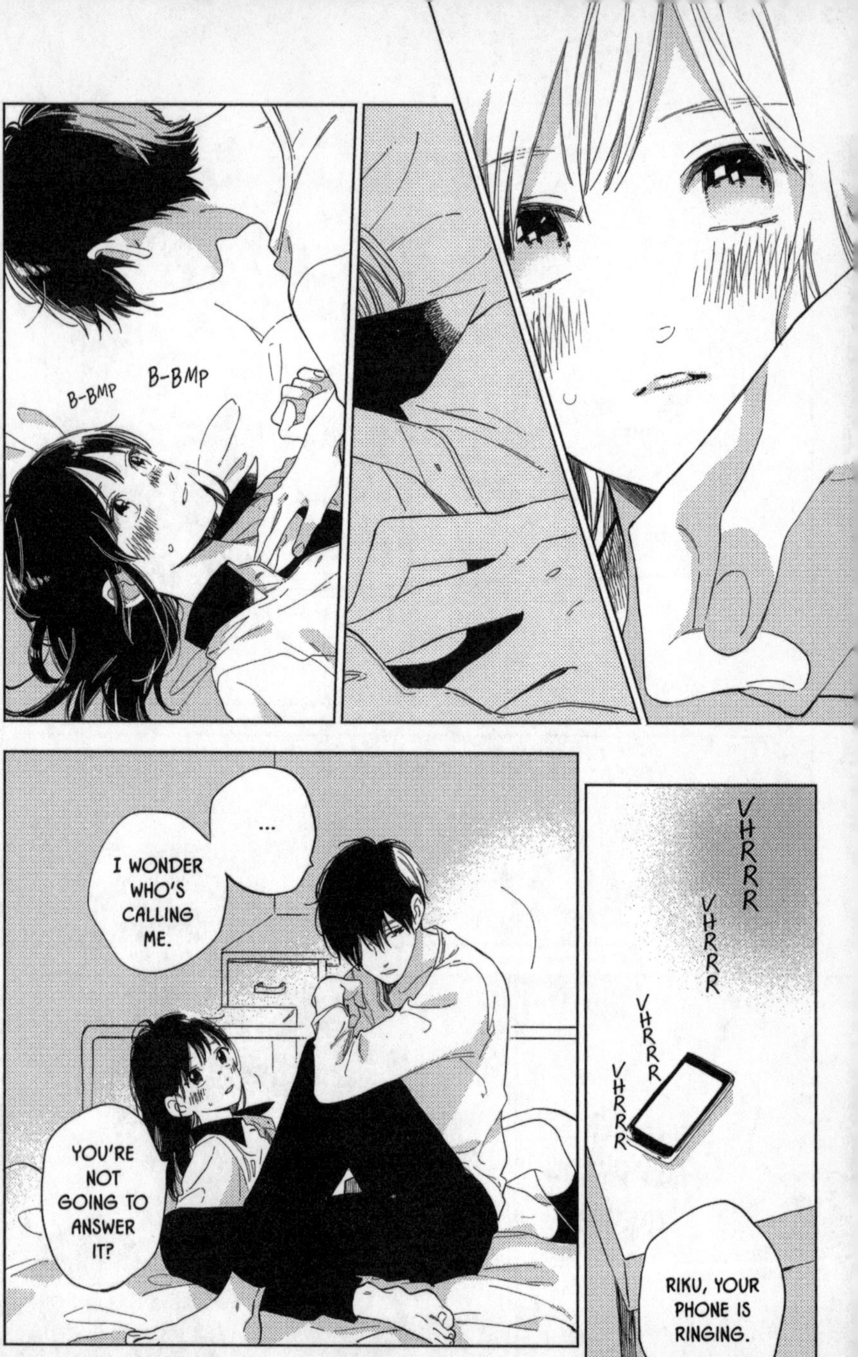
B-BMP
B-BMP
VHRRR
VHRRR
VHRRR
VHRRR
RIKU, YOUR PHONE IS RINGING.
...
I WONDER WHO'S CALLING ME.
YOU'RE NOT GOING TO ANSWER IT?

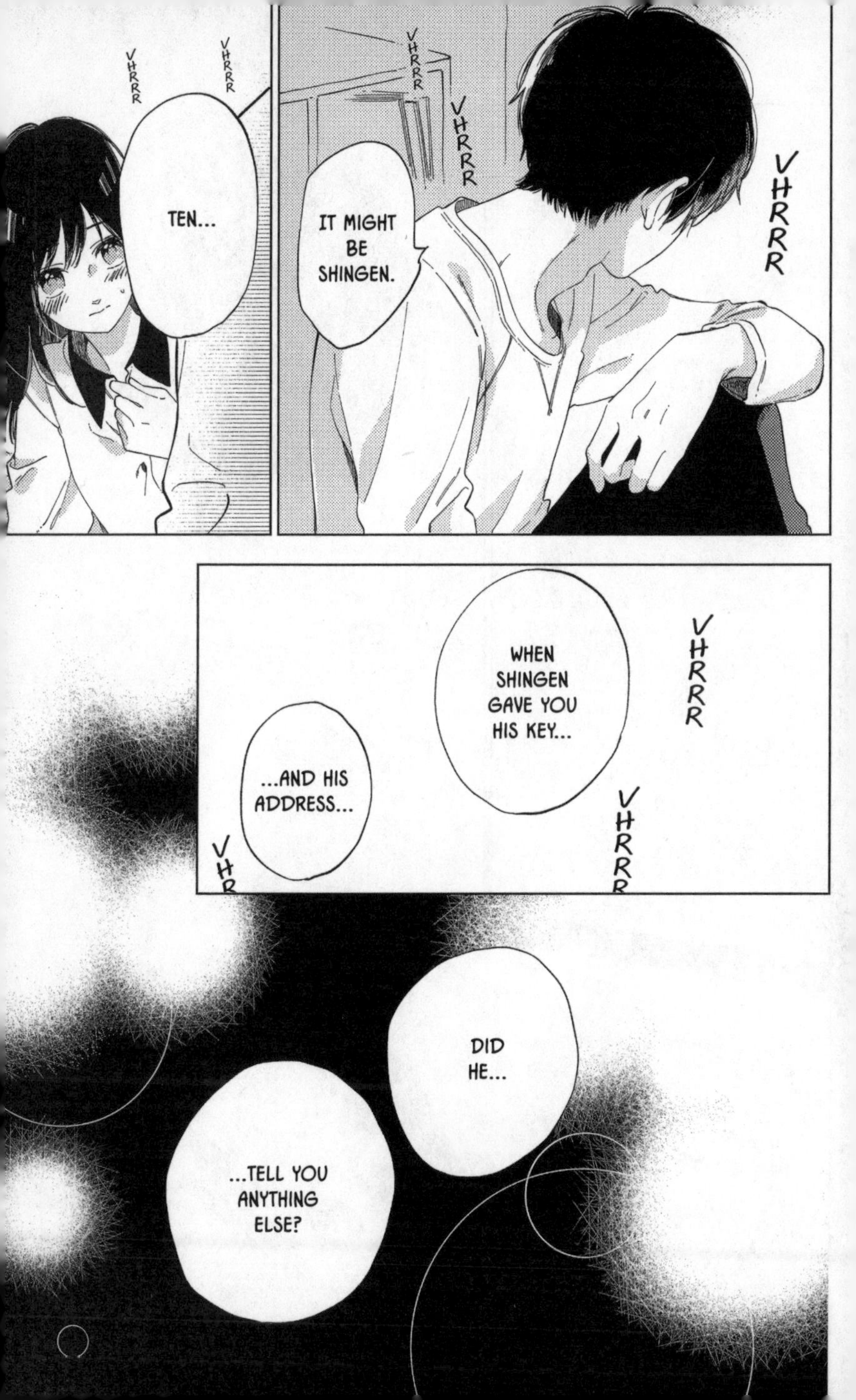
VHRRR
VHRRR
VHRRR
IT MIGHT BE SHINGEN.
VHRRR
VHRRR
TEN...
VHRRR
WHEN SHINGEN GAVE YOU HIS KEY...
VHRRR
...AND HIS ADDRESS...
DID HE...
...TELL YOU ANYTHING ELSE?

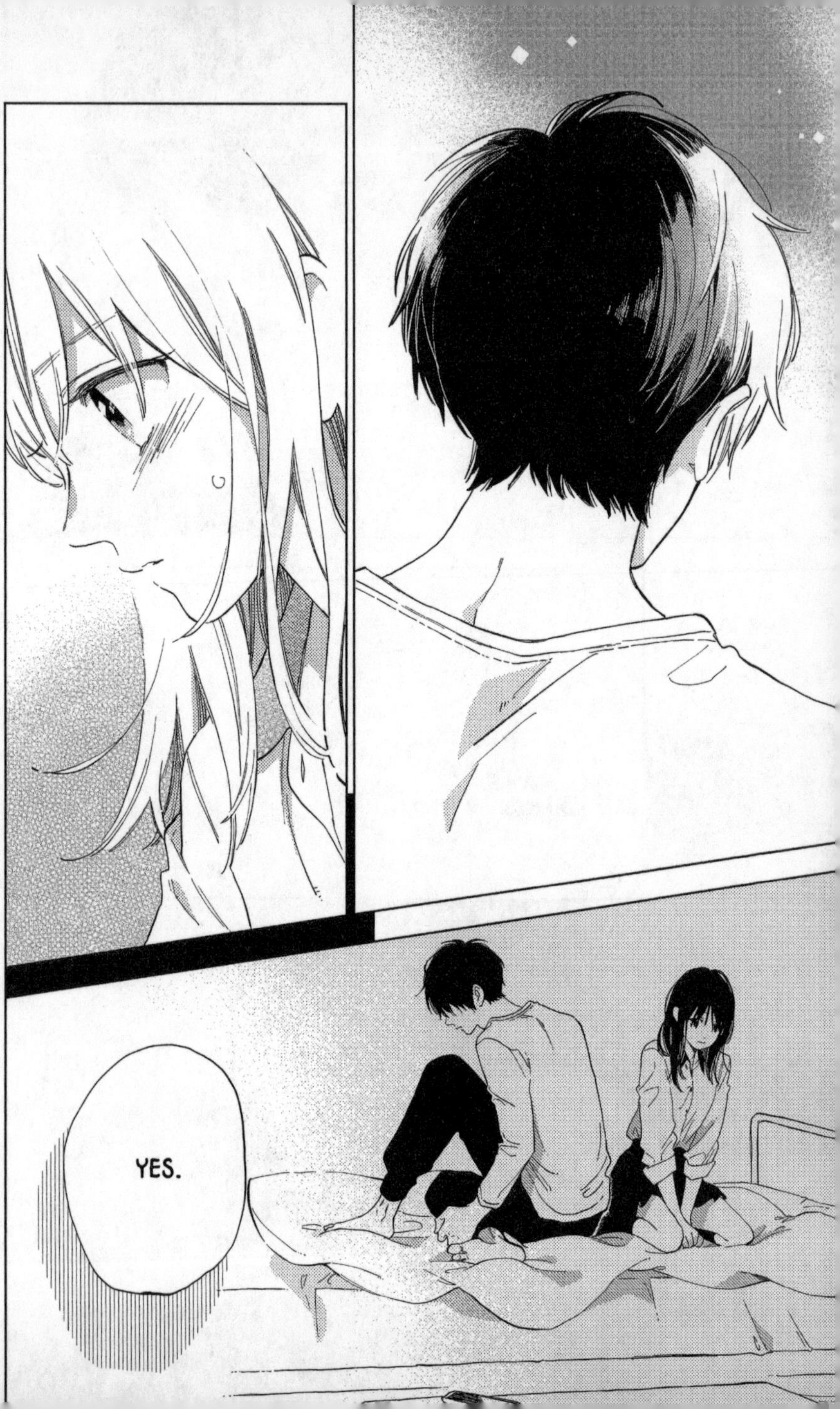
YES.

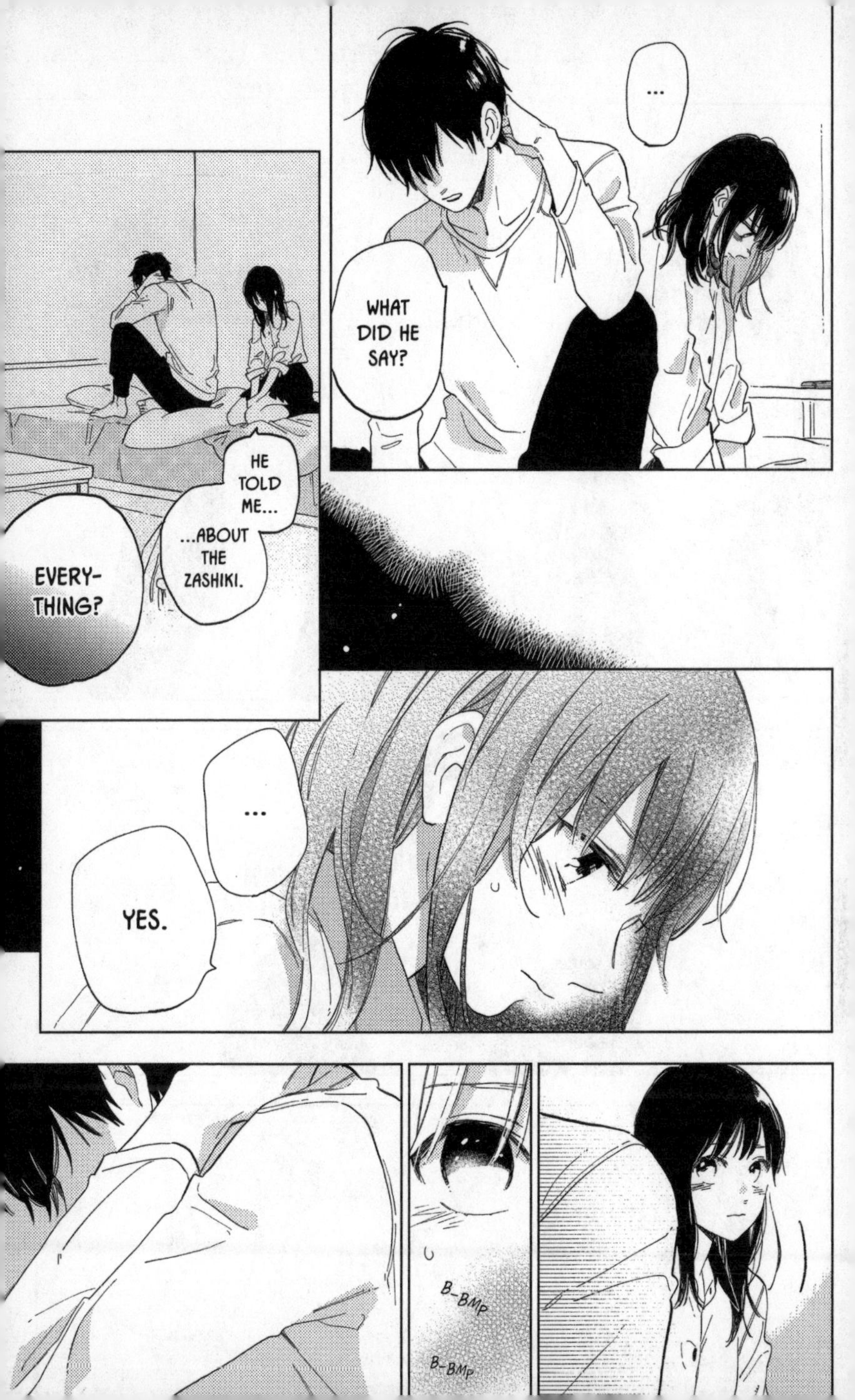
...
WHAT DID HE SAY?
HE TOLD ME...
...ABOUT THE ZASHIKI.
EVERY-THING?
...
YES.
B-BMP
B-BMP

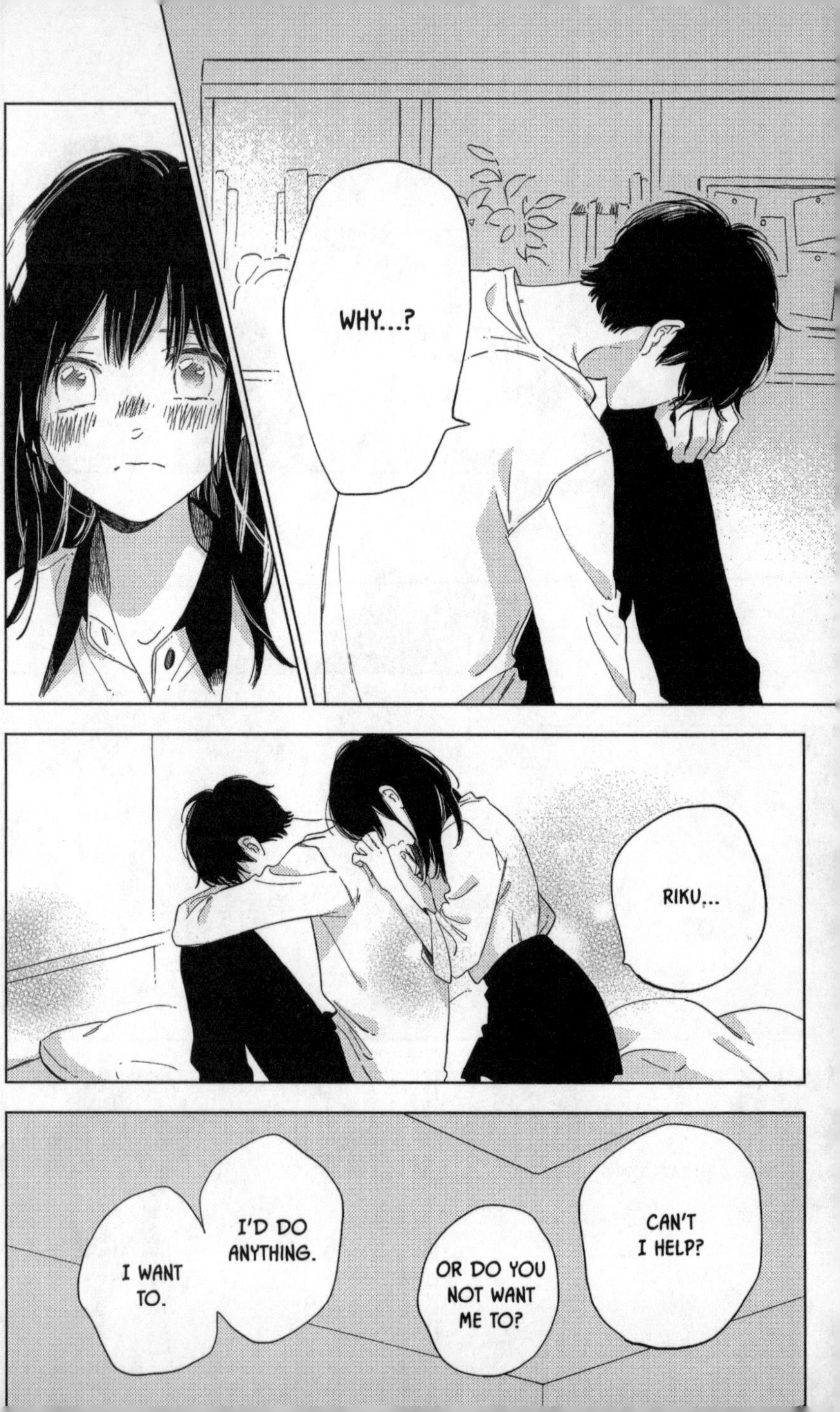
WHY...?
RIKU...
CAN'T I HELP?
OR DO YOU NOT WANT ME TO?
I'D DO ANYTHING.
I WANT TO.

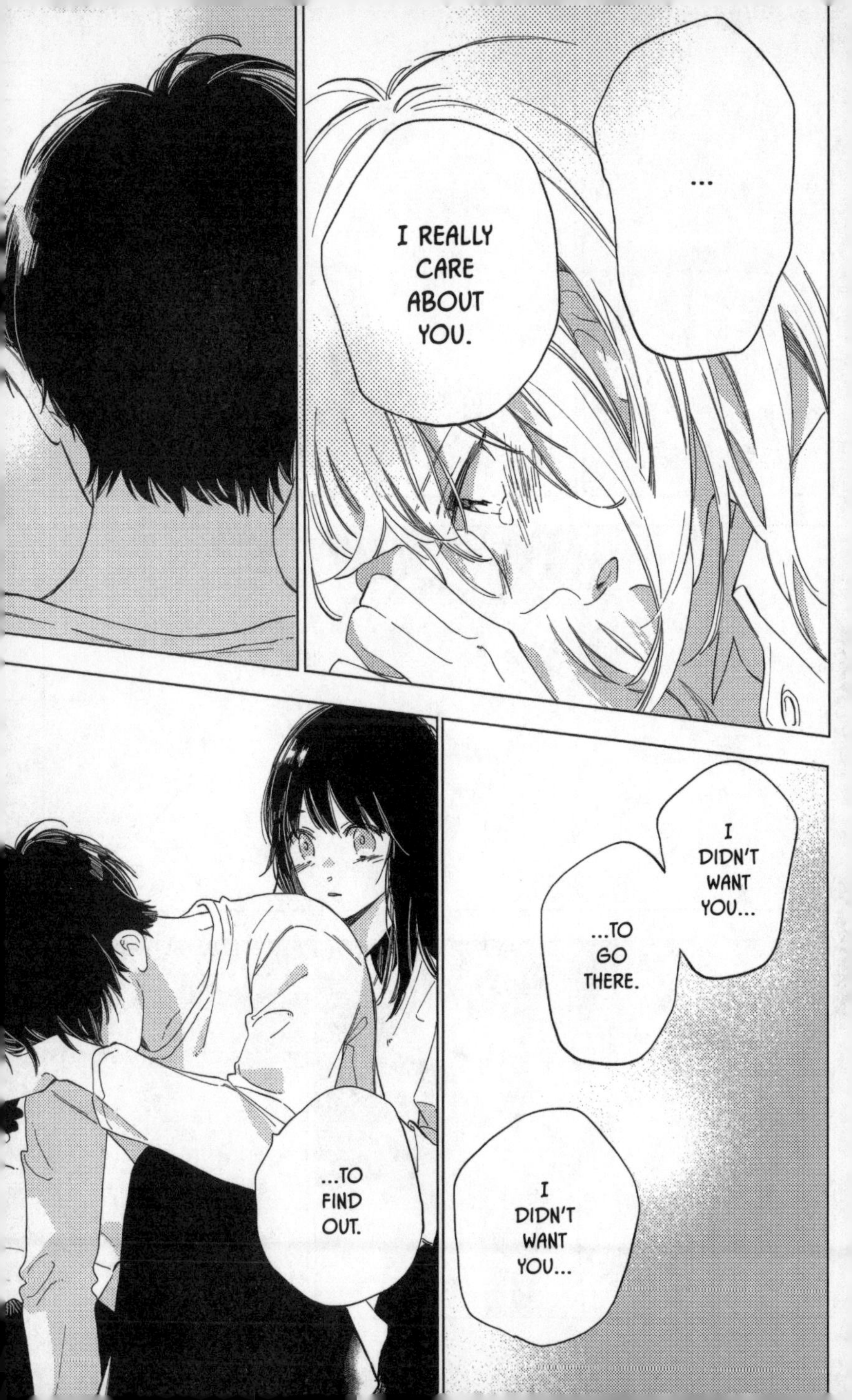
...
I REALLY CARE ABOUT YOU.
I DIDN'T WANT YOU...
...TO GO THERE.
I DIDN'T WANT YOU...
...TO FIND OUT.

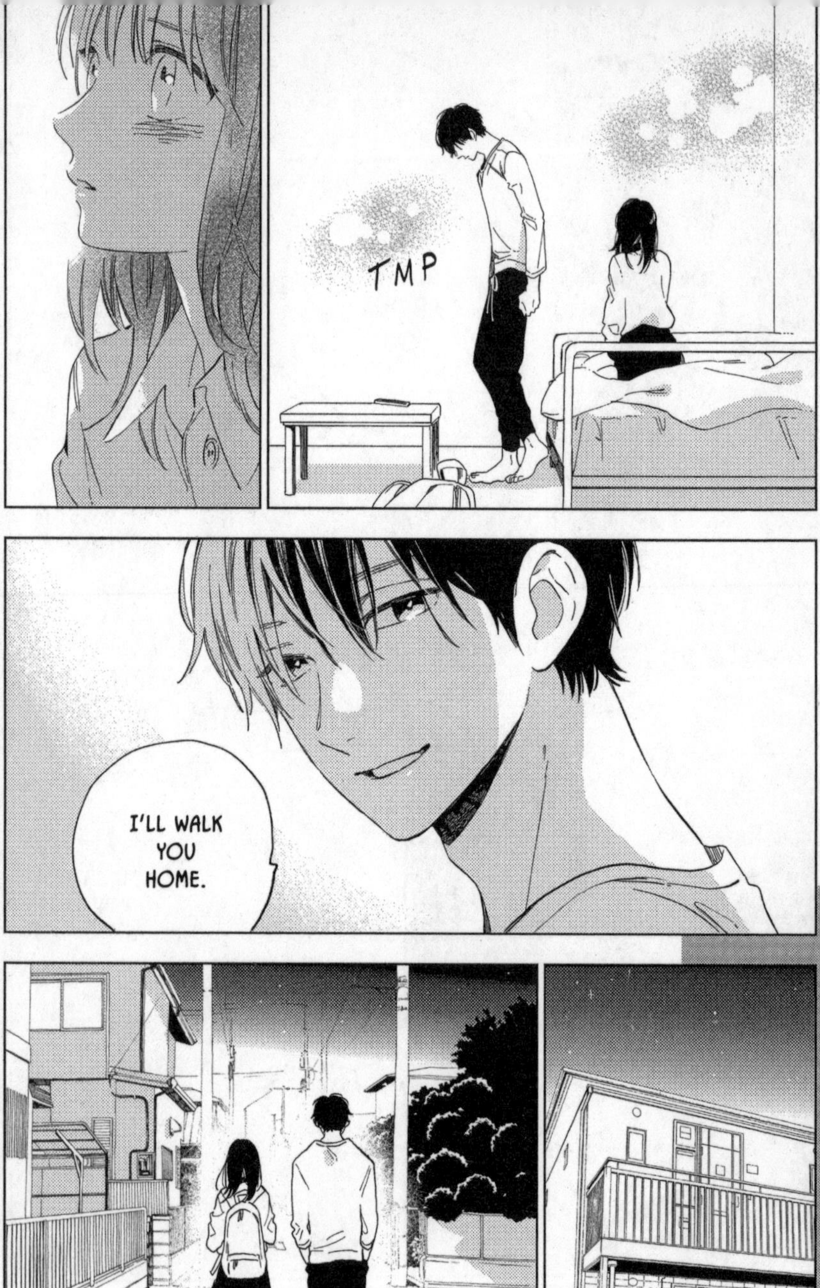
TMP
I'LL WALK YOU HOME.

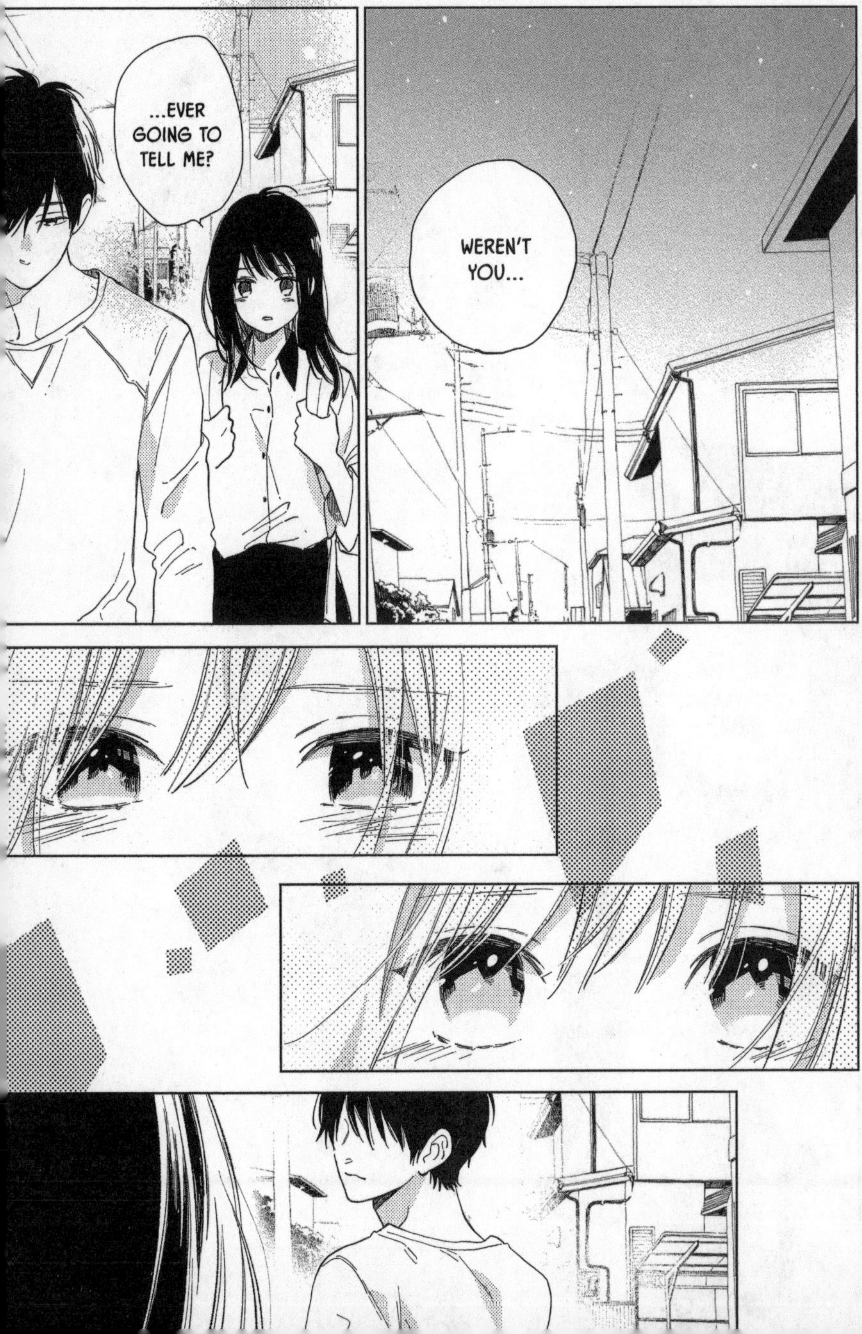
WEREN'T YOU...
...EVER GOING TO TELL ME?

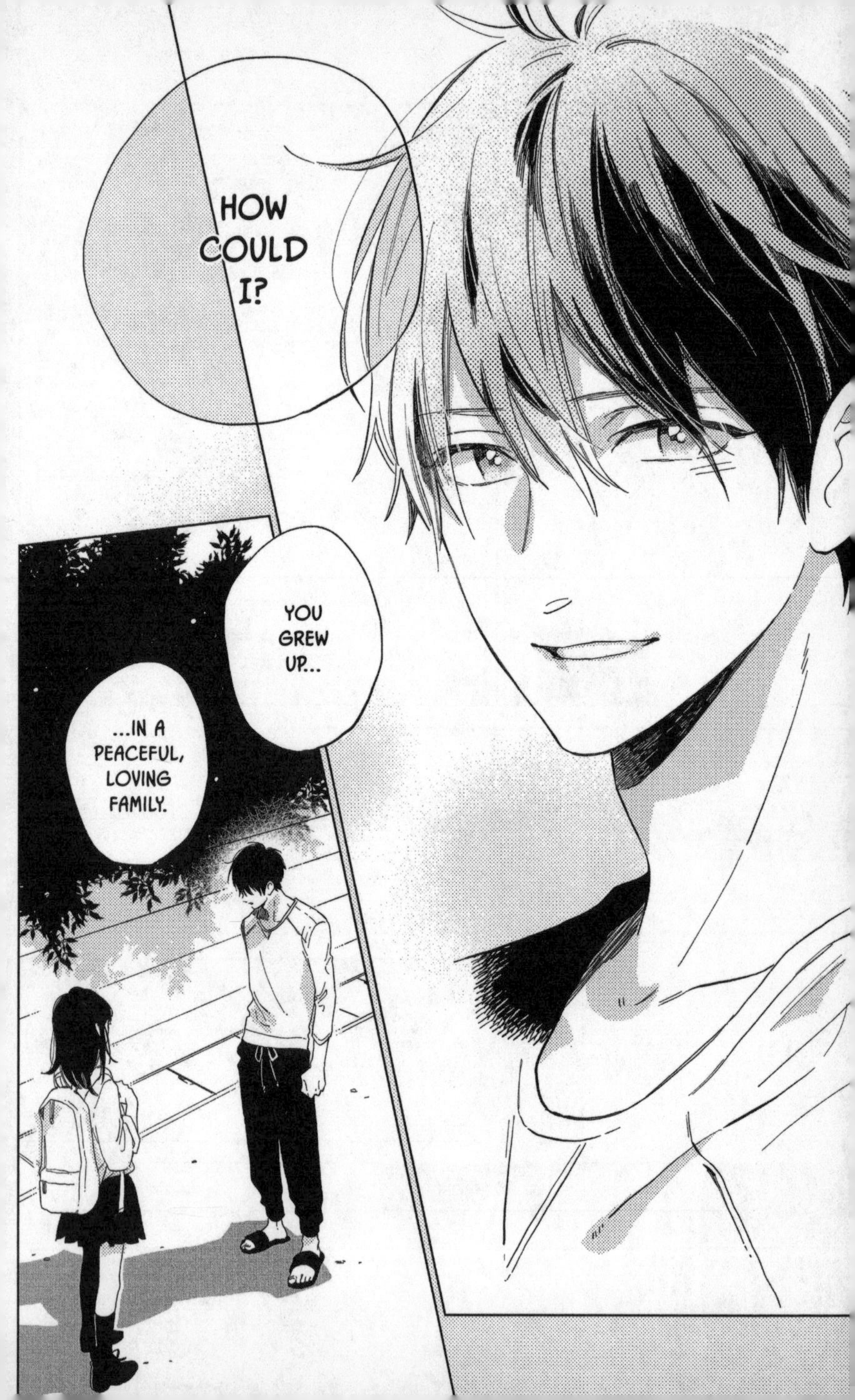
HOW COULD I?
YOU GREW UP...
...IN A PEACEFUL, LOVING FAMILY.

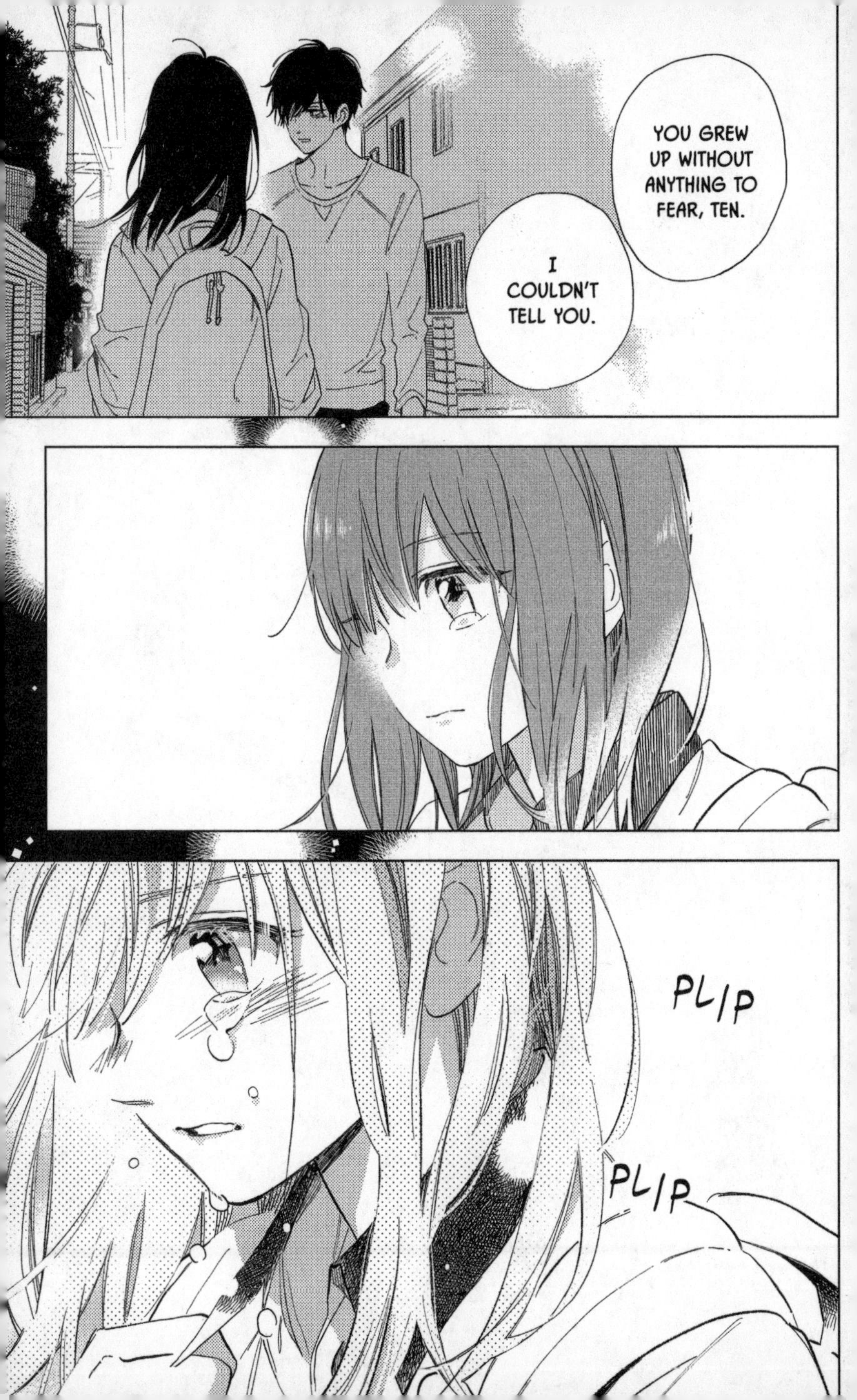
YOU GREW UP WITHOUT ANYTHING TO FEAR, TEN.
I COULDN'T TELL YOU.
PLIP
PLIP

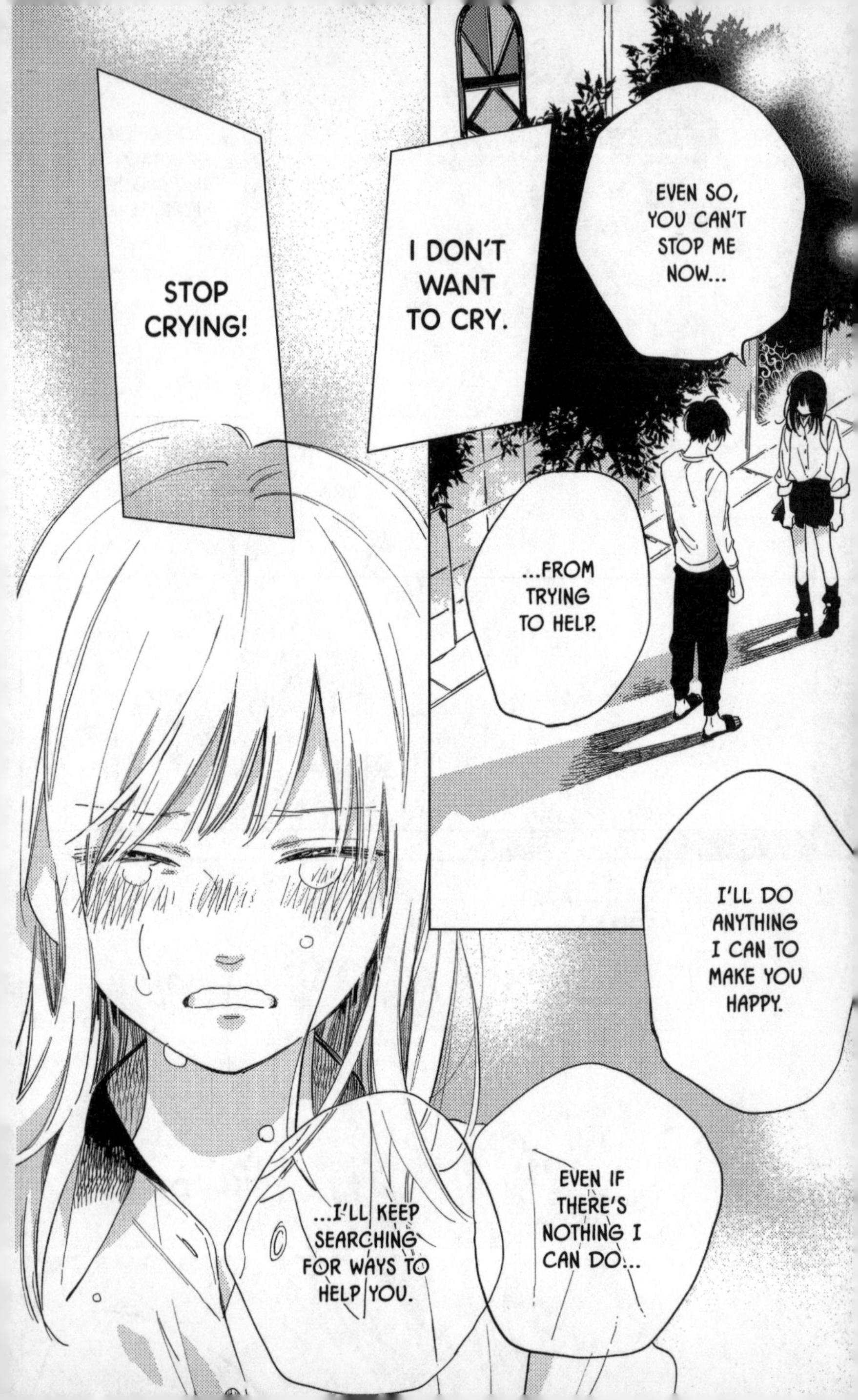
EVEN SO, YOU CAN'T STOP ME NOW...
...FROM TRYING TO HELP.
I DON'T WANT TO CRY.
STOP CRYING!
I'LL DO ANYTHING I CAN TO MAKE YOU HAPPY.
EVEN IF THERE'S NOTHING I CAN DO...
...I'LL KEEP SEARCHING FOR WAYS TO HELP YOU.

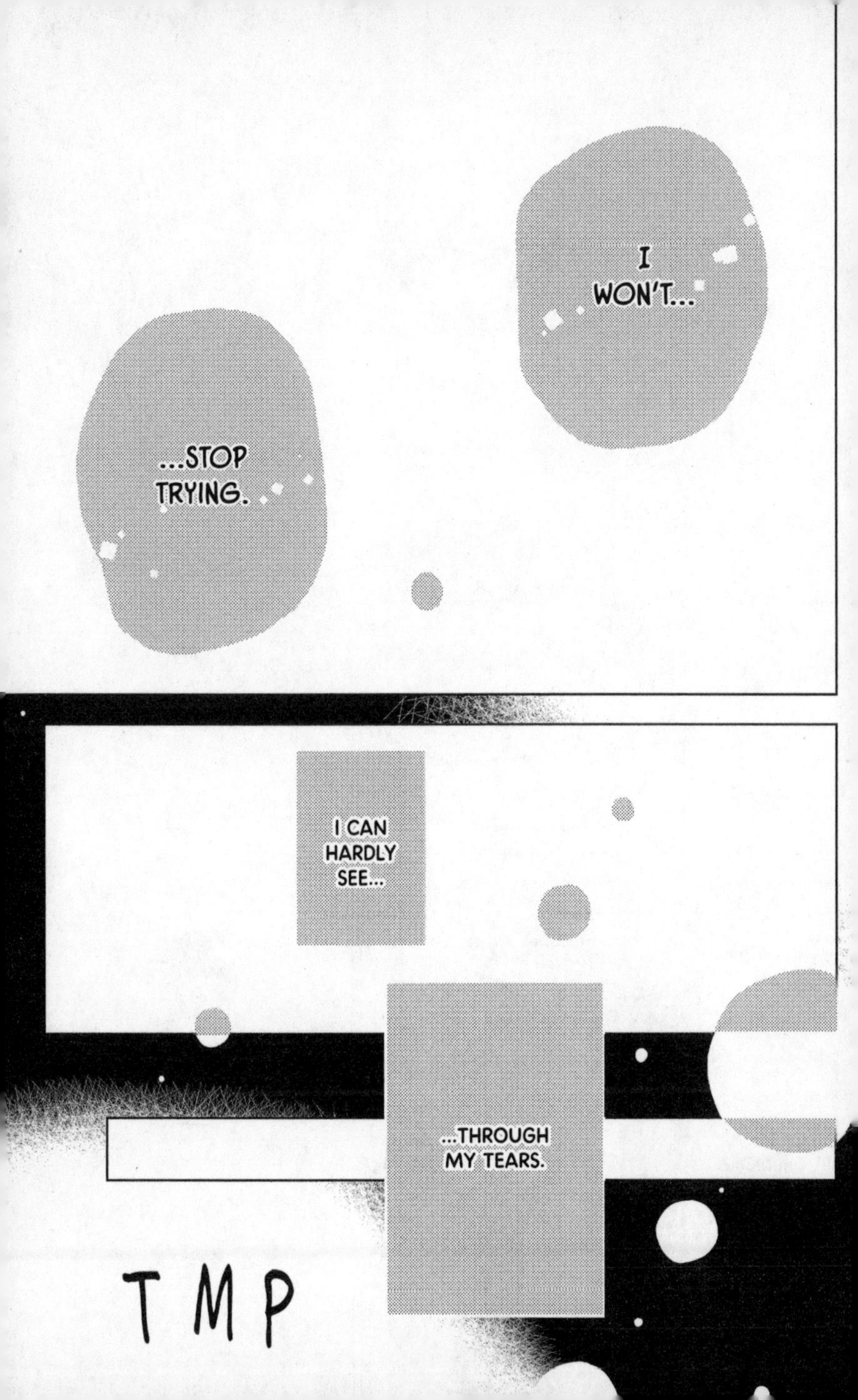
I WON'T...
...STOP TRYING.
I CAN HARDLY SEE...
...THROUGH MY TEARS.
TMP

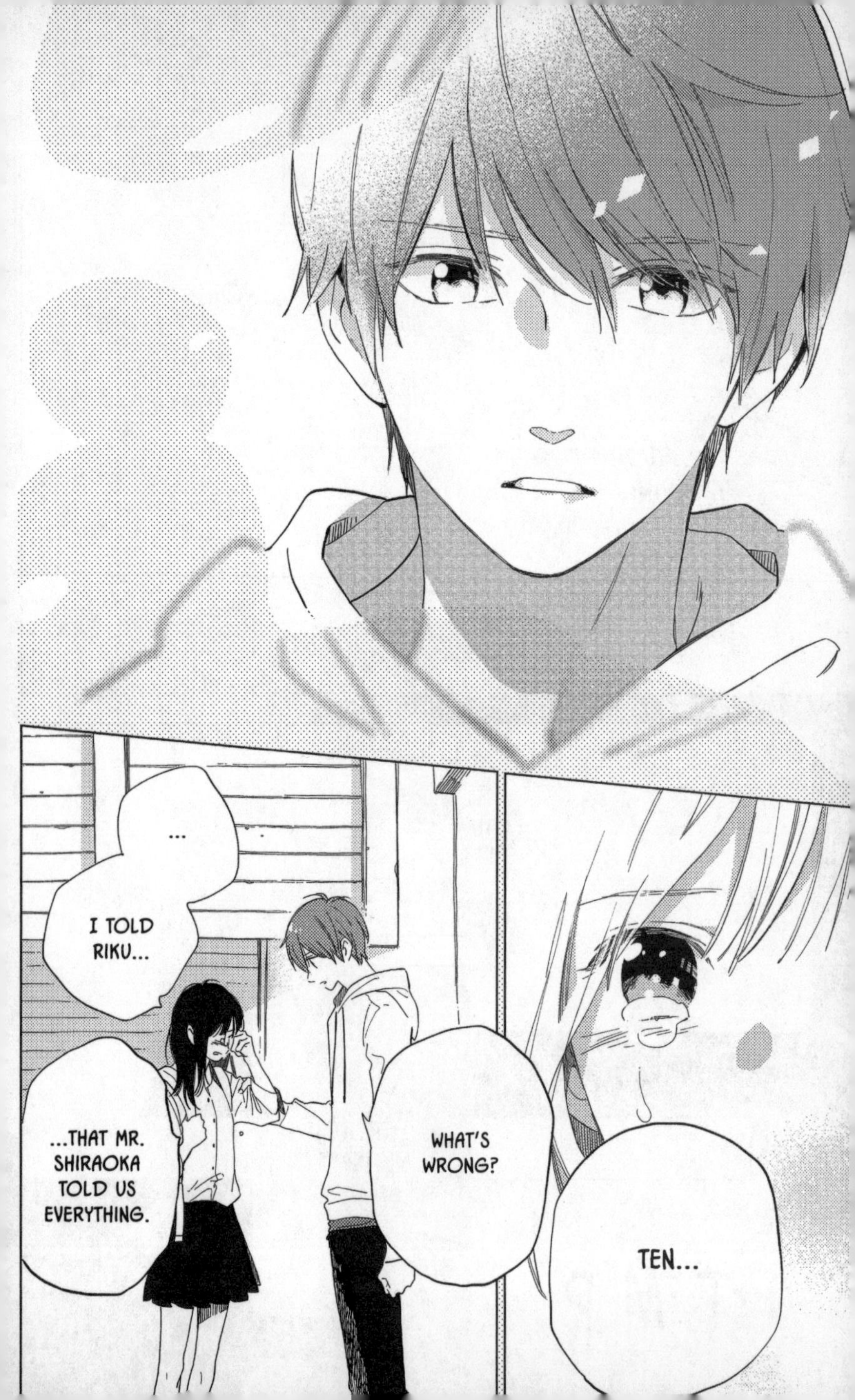
TEN...
WHAT'S WRONG?
...
I TOLD RIKU...
...THAT MR. SHIRAOKA TOLD US EVERYTHING.

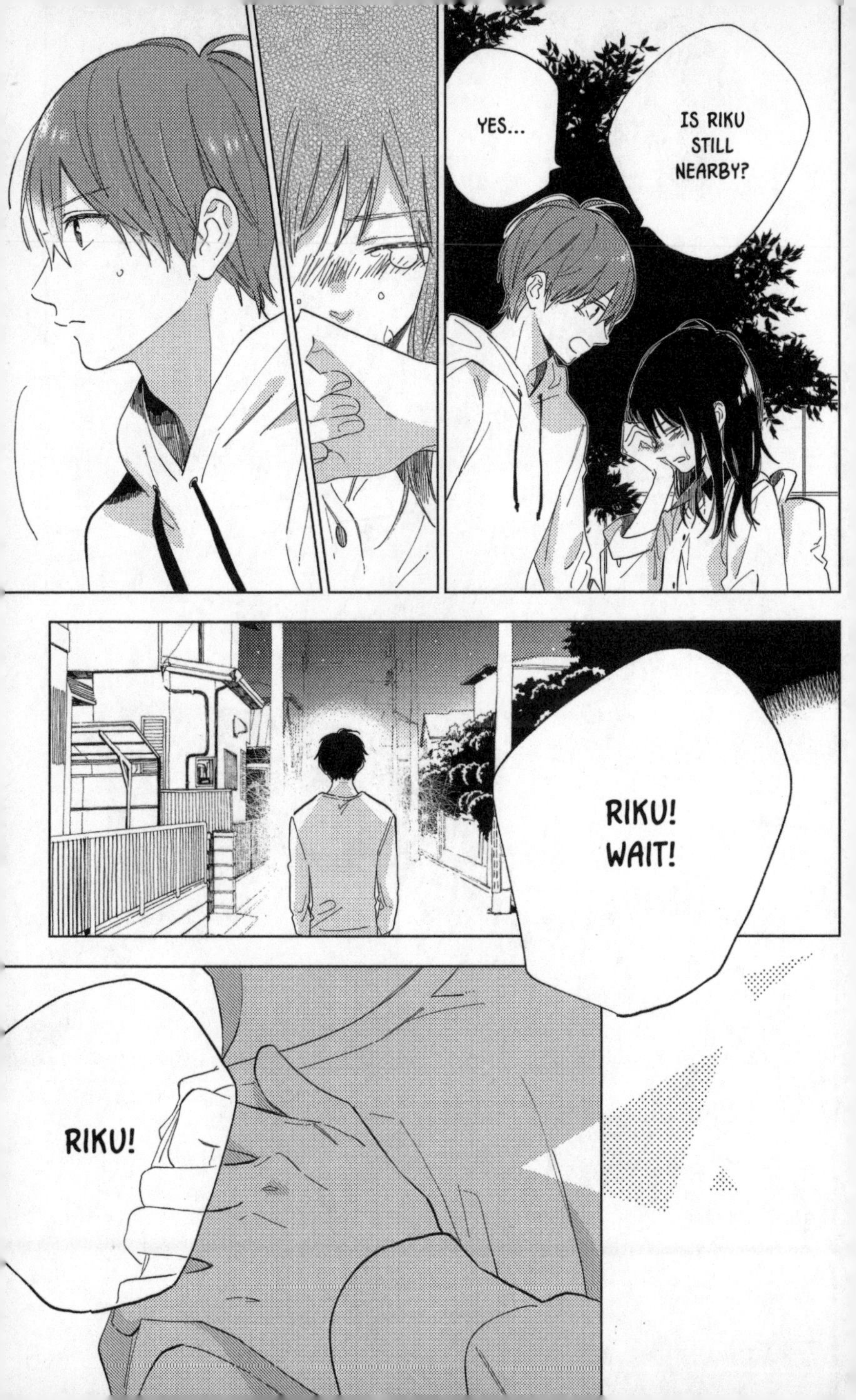
IS RIKU STILL NEARBY?
YES...
RIKU! WAIT!
RIKU!

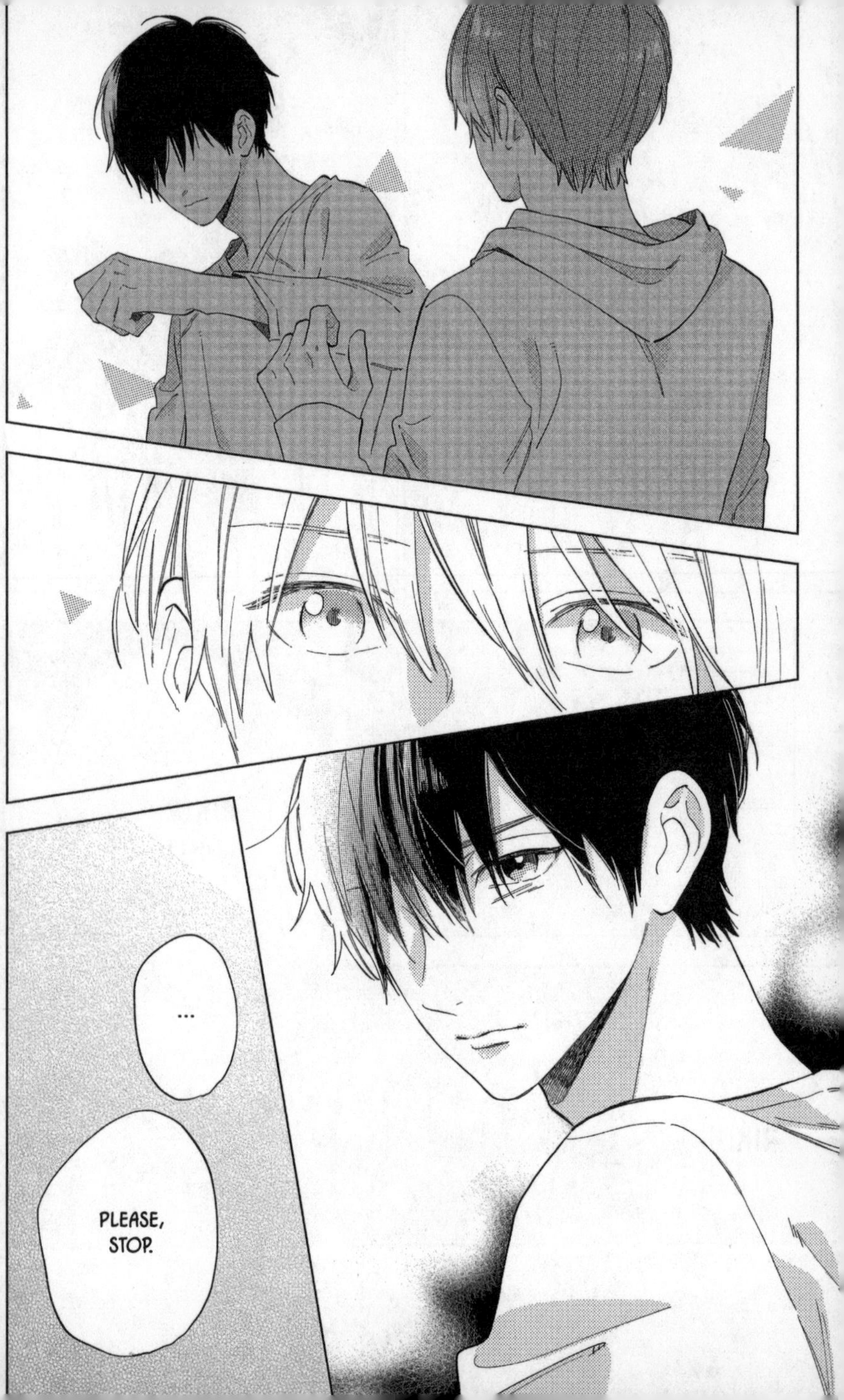
...
PLEASE, STOP.

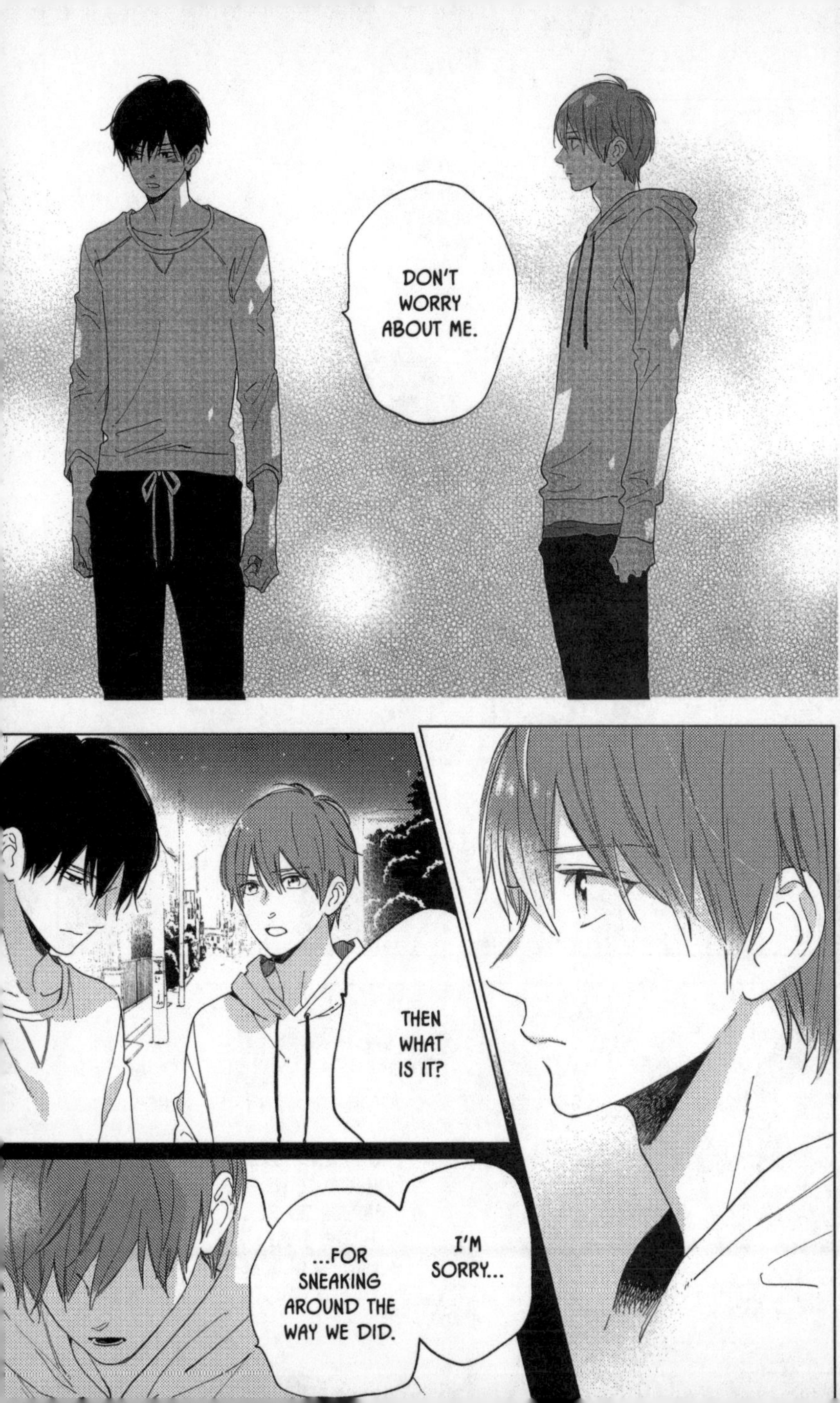
DON'T WORRY ABOUT ME.
THEN WHAT IS IT?
I'M SORRY...
...FOR SNEAKING AROUND THE WAY WE DID.

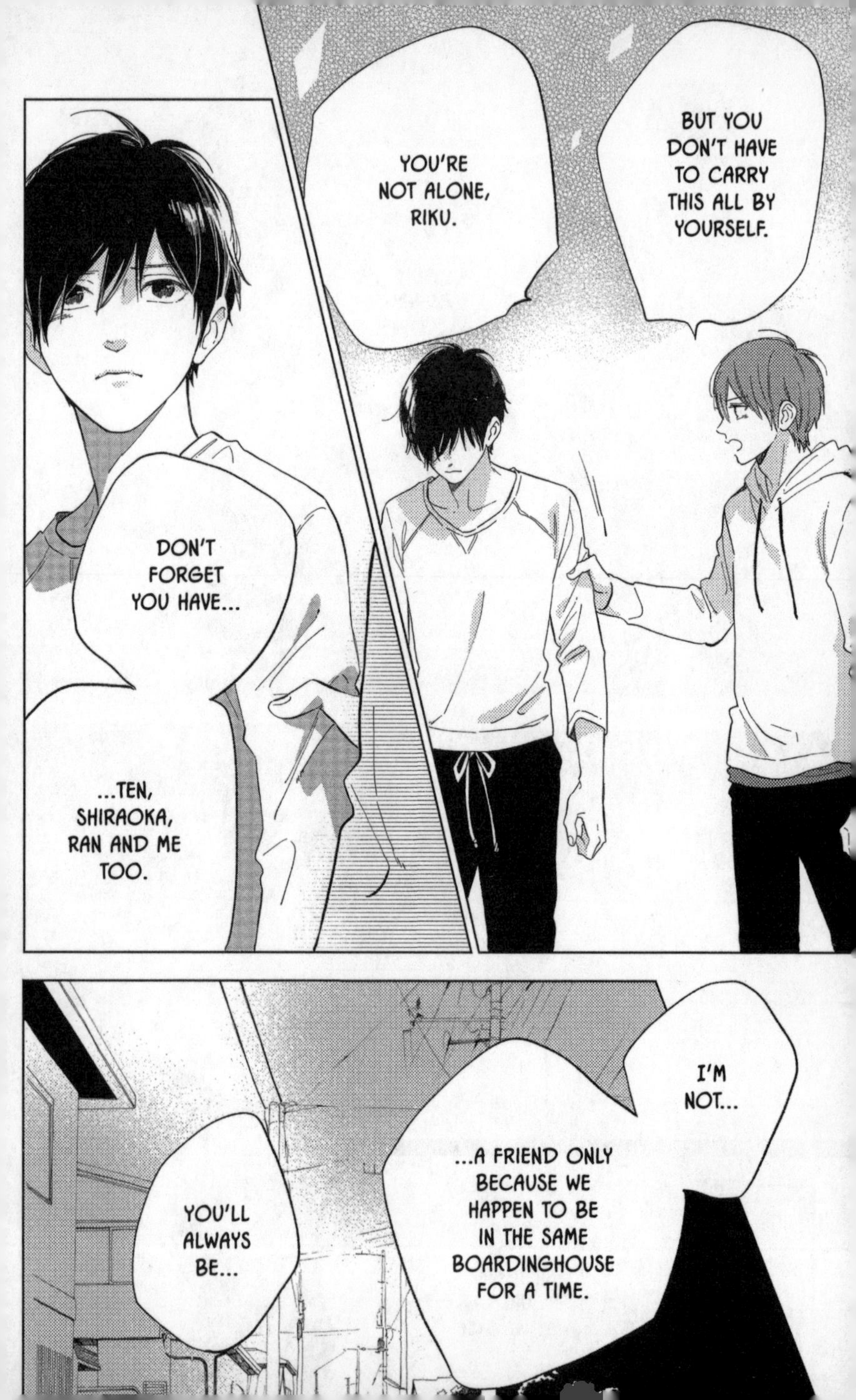
BUT YOU DON'T HAVE TO CARRY THIS ALL BY YOURSELF.
YOU'RE NOT ALONE, RIKU.
DON'T FORGET YOU HAVE...
...TEN, SHIRAOKA, RAN AND ME TOO.
I'M NOT...
...A FRIEND ONLY BECAUSE WE HAPPEN TO BE IN THE SAME BOARDINGHOUSE FOR A TIME.
YOU'LL ALWAYS BE...

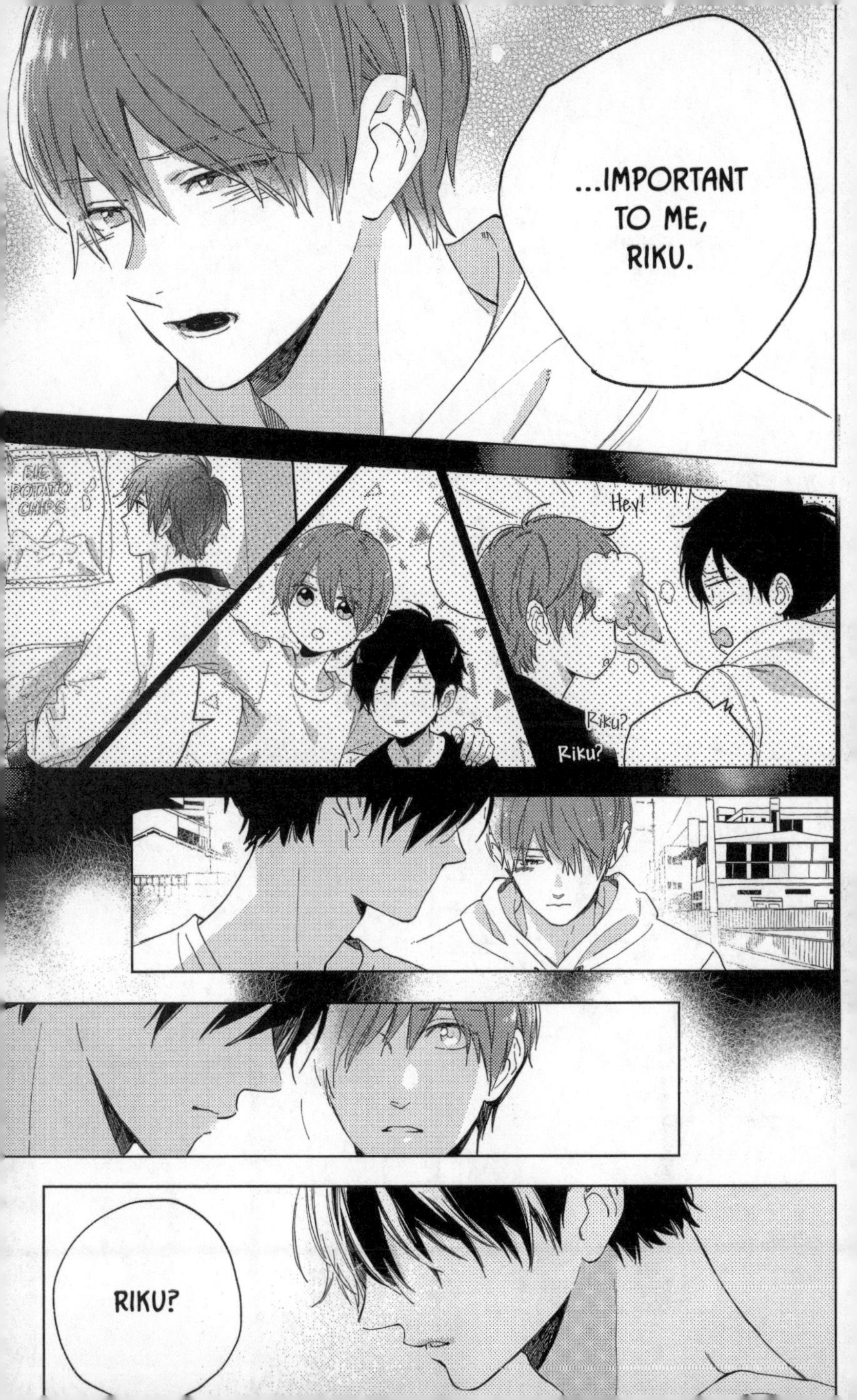
...IMPORTANT TO ME, RIKU.
Hey!
Hey!
Riku?
Riku?
BIG POTATO CHIPS
RIKU?

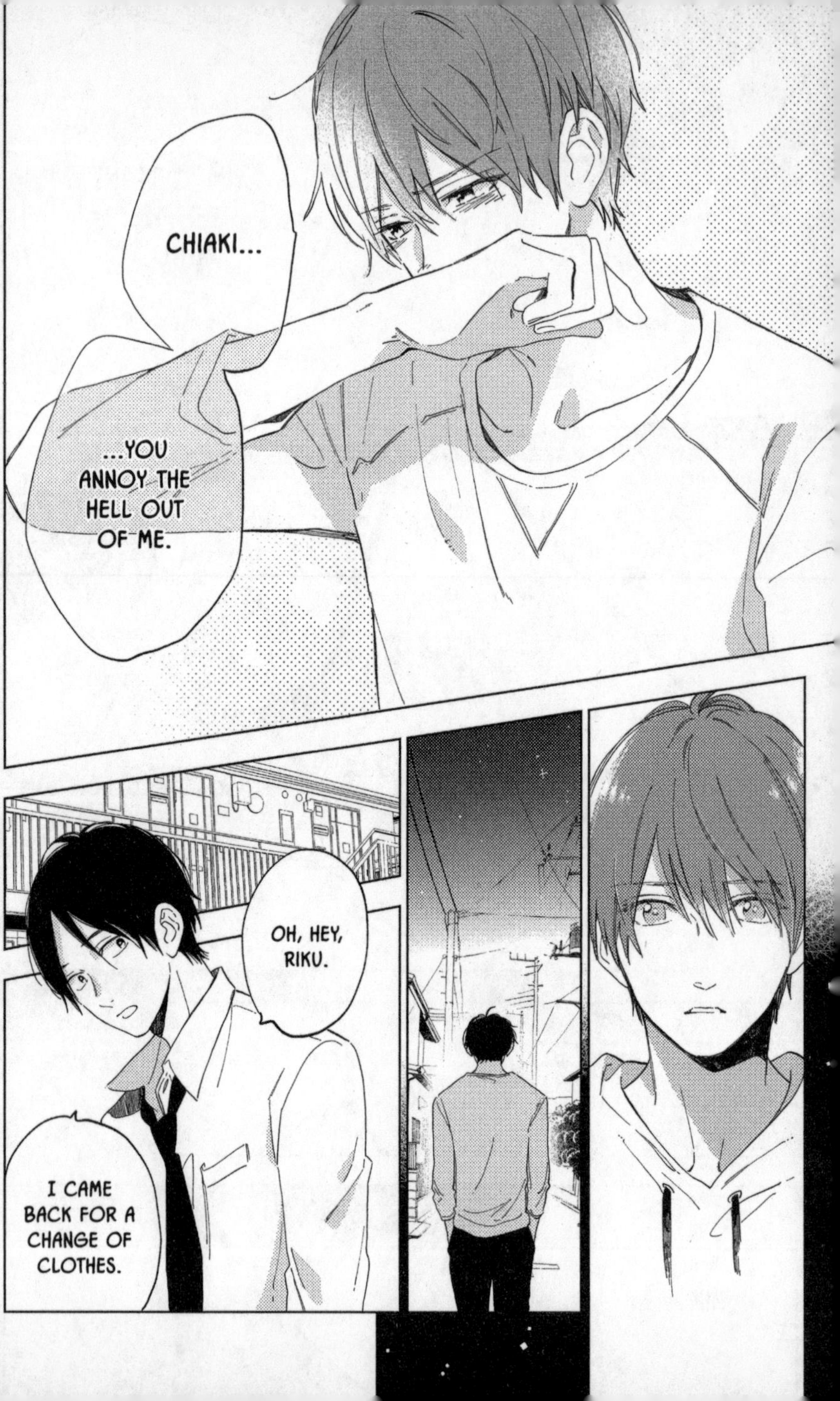
CHIAKI...
...YOU ANNOY THE HELL OUT OF ME.
OH, HEY, RIKU.
I CAME BACK FOR A CHANGE OF CLOTHES.

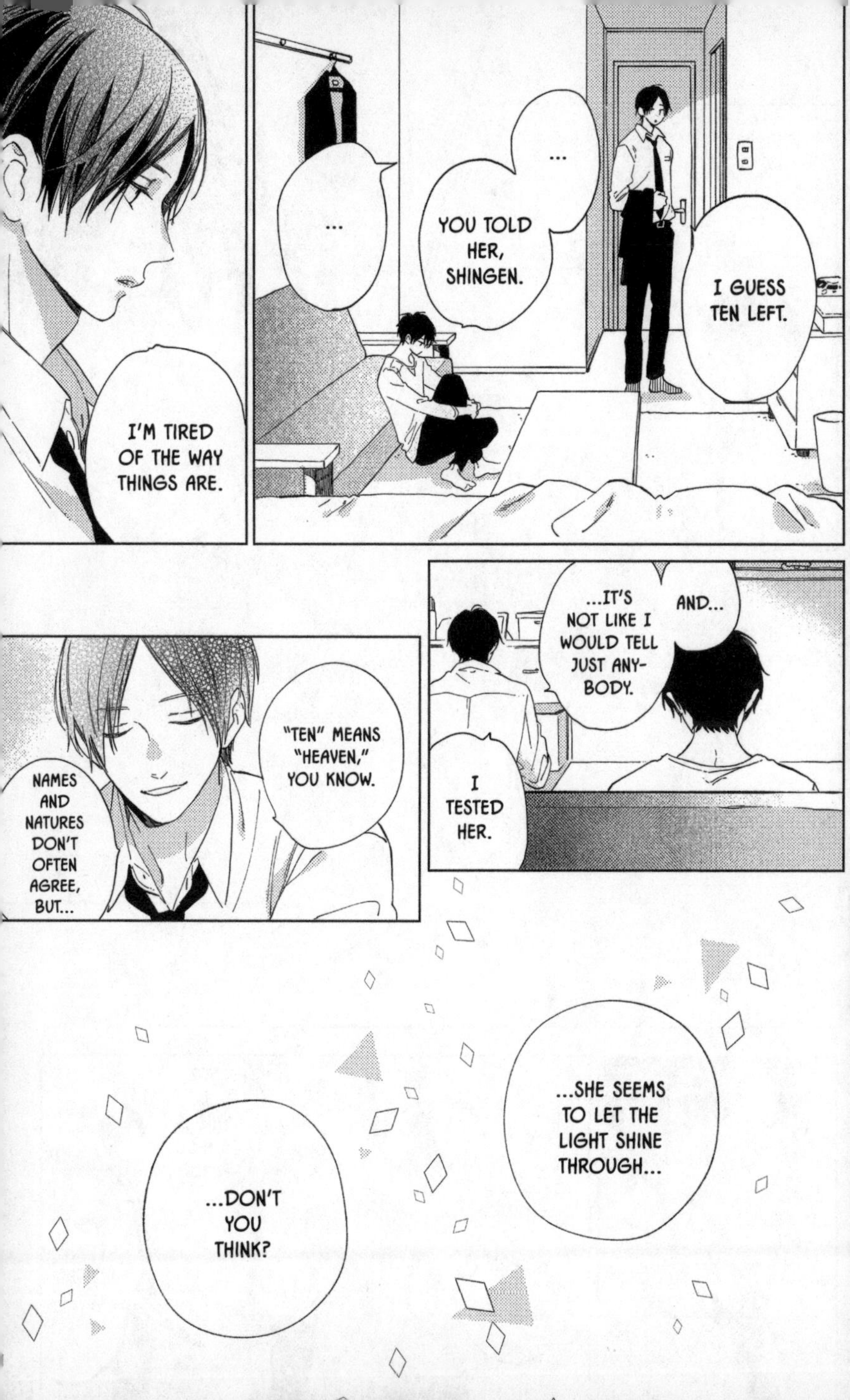
I GUESS TEN LEFT.
...
YOU TOLD HER, SHINGEN.
...
I'M TIRED OF THE WAY THINGS ARE.
AND...
...IT'S NOT LIKE I WOULD TELL JUST ANY-BODY.
I TESTED HER.
"TEN" MEANS "HEAVEN," YOU KNOW.
NAMES AND NATURES DON'T OFTEN AGREE, BUT...
...SHE SEEMS TO LET THE LIGHT SHINE THROUGH...
...DON'T YOU THINK?

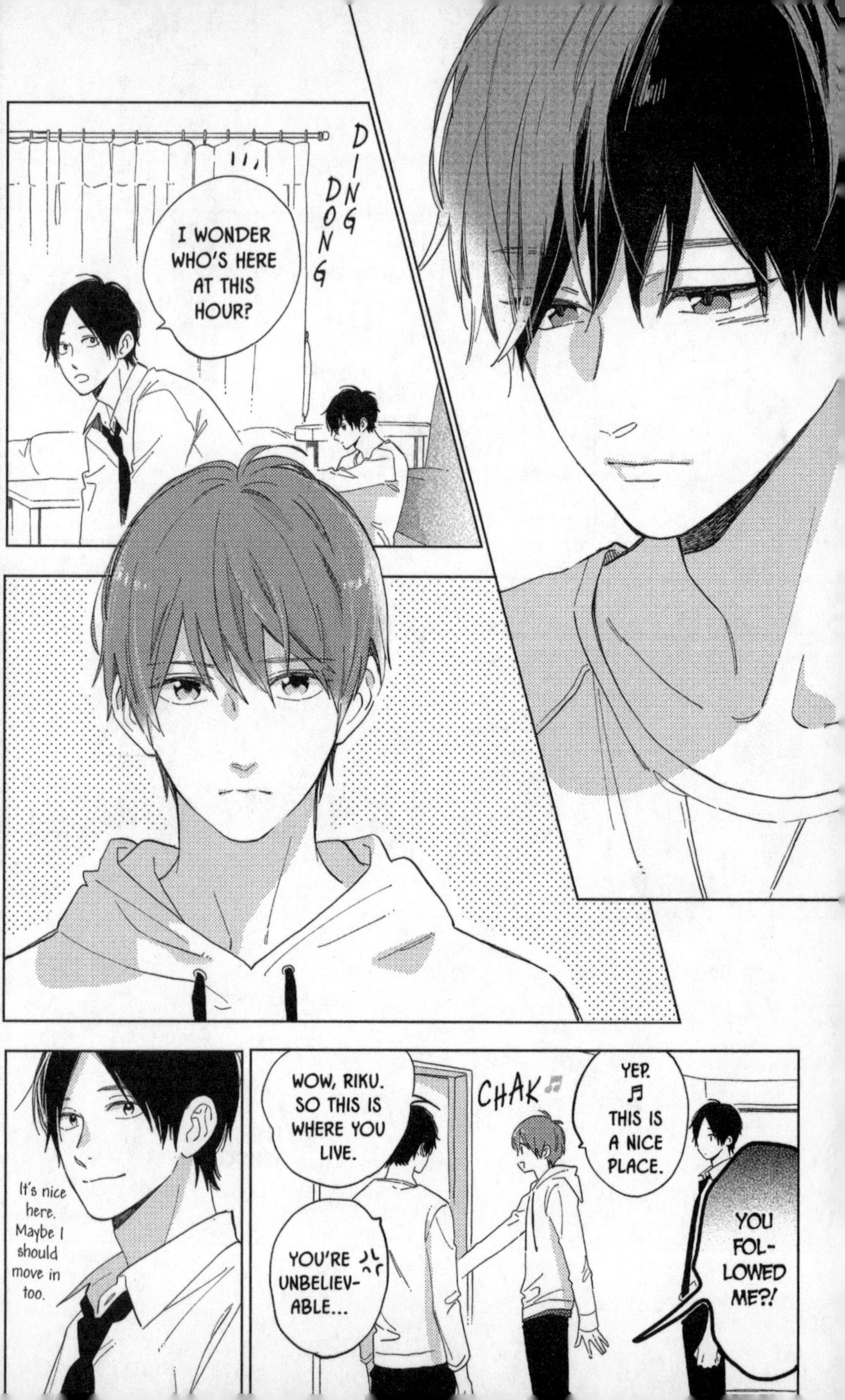
DING DONG
I WONDER WHO'S HERE AT THIS HOUR?
YEP. ♬ THIS IS A NICE PLACE.
CHAK
WOW, RIKU. SO THIS IS WHERE YOU LIVE.
YOU FOL-LOWED ME?!
YOU'RE UNBELIEV-ABLE...
It's nice here. Maybe I should move in too.

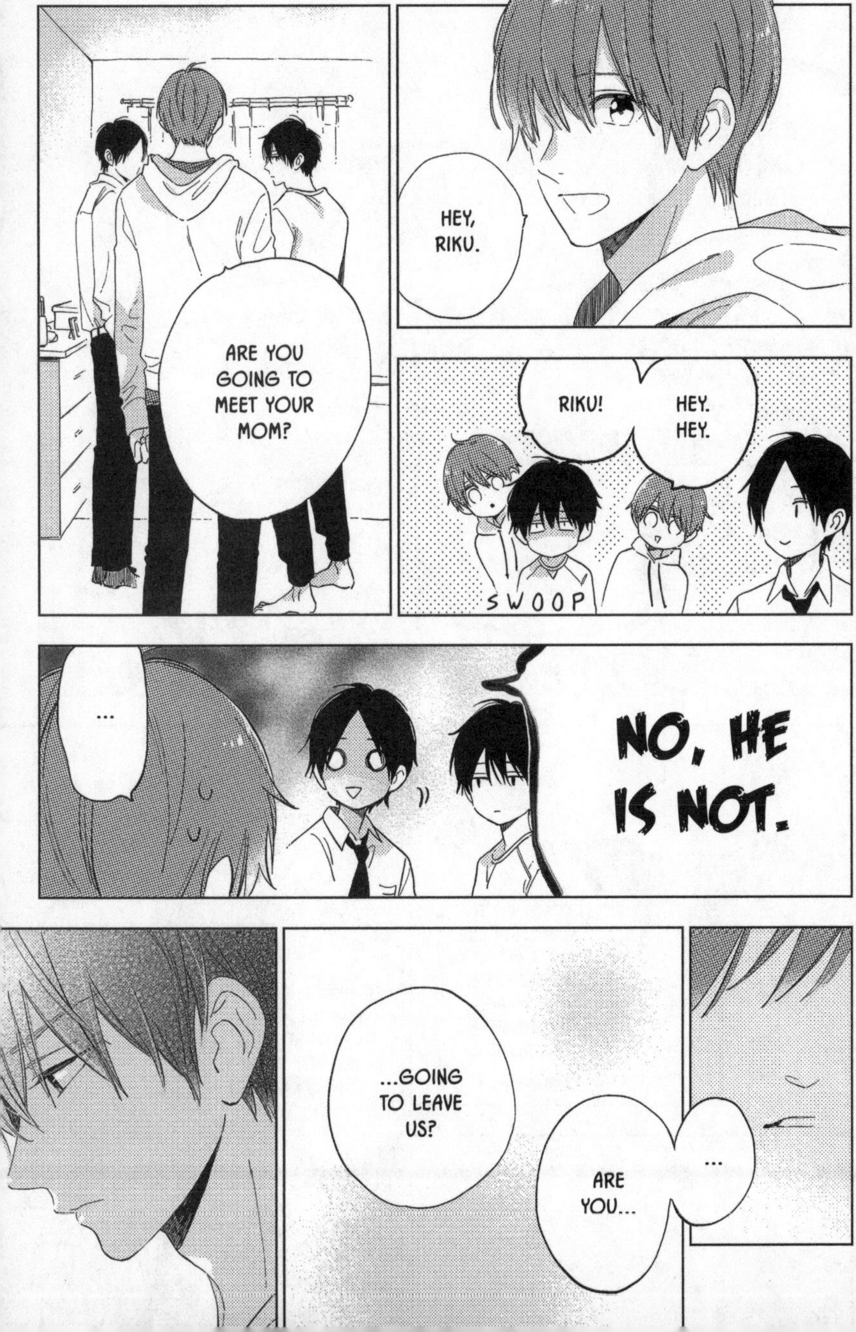
HEY, RIKU.
HEY. HEY.
RIKU!
SWOOP
ARE YOU GOING TO MEET YOUR MOM?
NO, HE IS NOT.
...
...
ARE YOU...
...GOING TO LEAVE US?

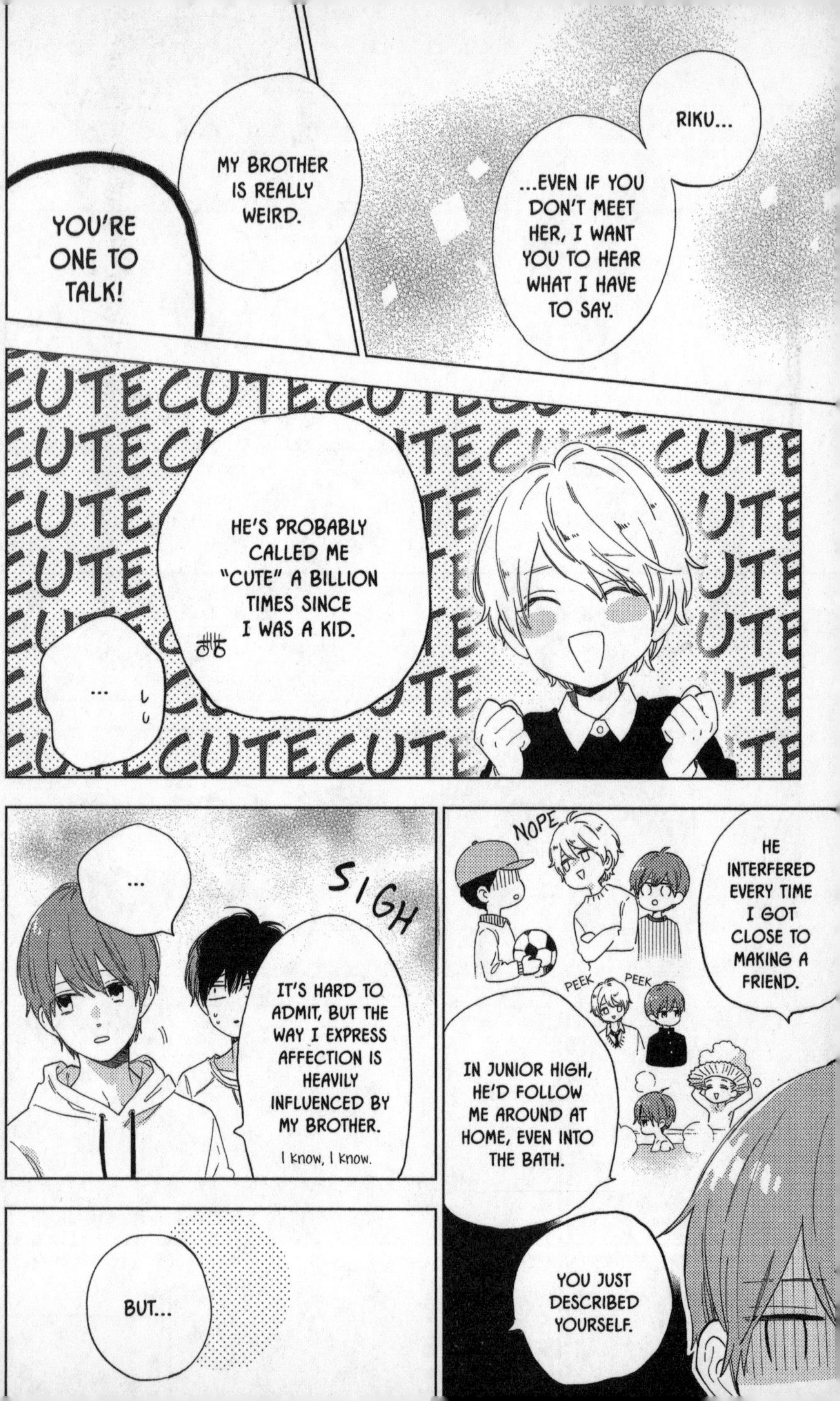
RIKU...
...EVEN IF YOU DON'T MEET HER, I WANT YOU TO HEAR WHAT I HAVE TO SAY.
MY BROTHER IS REALLY WEIRD.
YOU'RE ONE TO TALK!
HE'S PROBABLY CALLED ME "CUTE" A BILLION TIMES SINCE I WAS A KID.
...
HE INTERFERED EVERY TIME I GOT CLOSE TO MAKING A FRIEND.
NOPE
PEEK
PEEK
IN JUNIOR HIGH, HE'D FOLLOW ME AROUND AT HOME, EVEN INTO THE BATH.
YOU JUST DESCRIBED YOURSELF.
SIGH
...
IT'S HARD TO ADMIT, BUT THE WAY I EXPRESS AFFECTION IS HEAVILY INFLUENCED BY MY BROTHER.
I know, I know.
BUT...

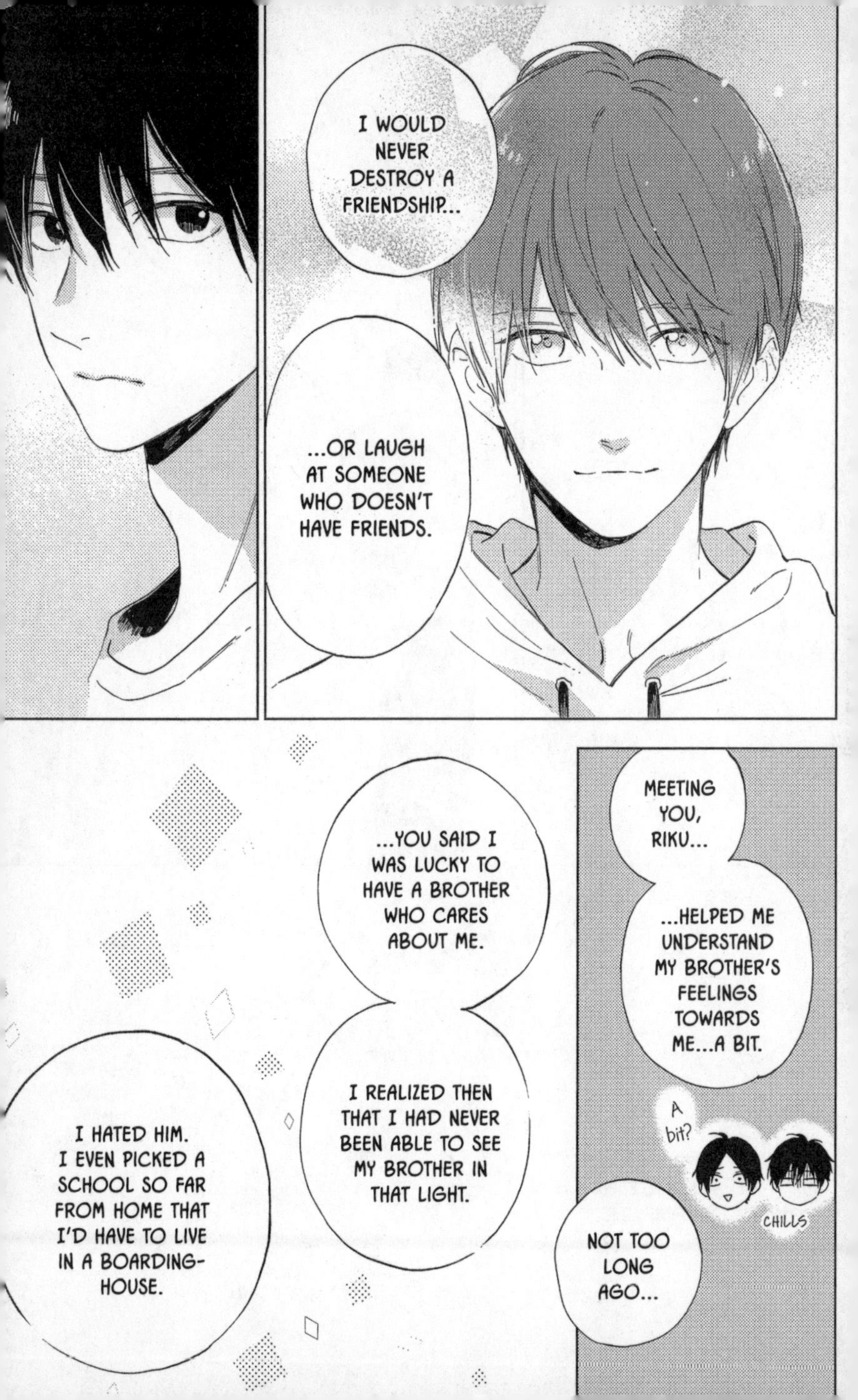
I WOULD NEVER DESTROY A FRIENDSHIP...
...OR LAUGH AT SOMEONE WHO DOESN'T HAVE FRIENDS.
MEETING YOU, RIKU...
...HELPED ME UNDERSTAND MY BROTHER'S FEELINGS TOWARDS ME...A BIT.
A bit?
CHILLS
NOT TOO LONG AGO...
...YOU SAID I WAS LUCKY TO HAVE A BROTHER WHO CARES ABOUT ME.
I REALIZED THEN THAT I HAD NEVER BEEN ABLE TO SEE MY BROTHER IN THAT LIGHT.
I HATED HIM. I EVEN PICKED A SCHOOL SO FAR FROM HOME THAT I'D HAVE TO LIVE IN A BOARDING-HOUSE.

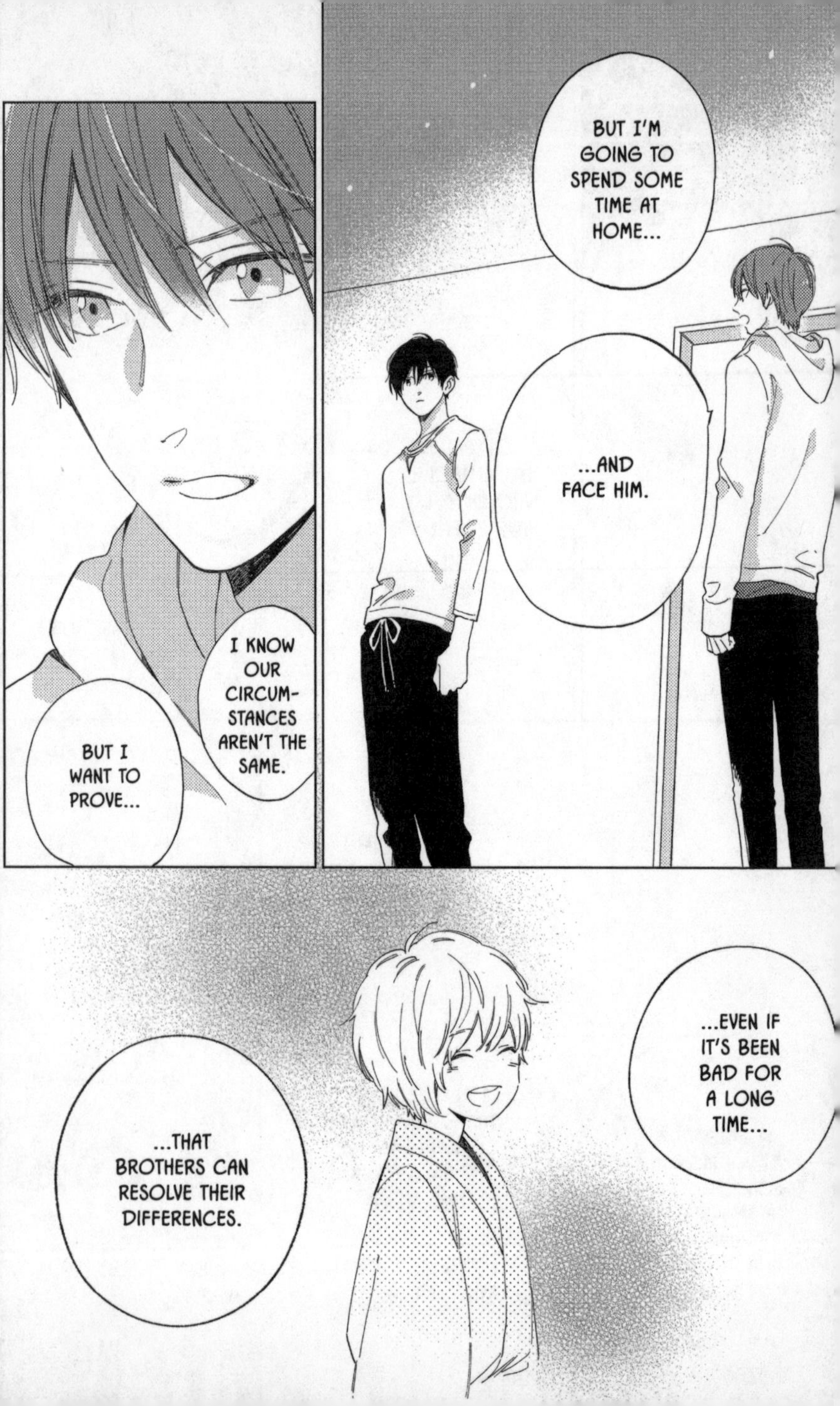
BUT I'M GOING TO SPEND SOME TIME AT HOME...
...AND FACE HIM.
I KNOW OUR CIRCUM-STANCES AREN'T THE SAME.
BUT I WANT TO PROVE...
...EVEN IF IT'S BEEN BAD FOR A LONG TIME...
...THAT BROTHERS CAN RESOLVE THEIR DIFFERENCES.

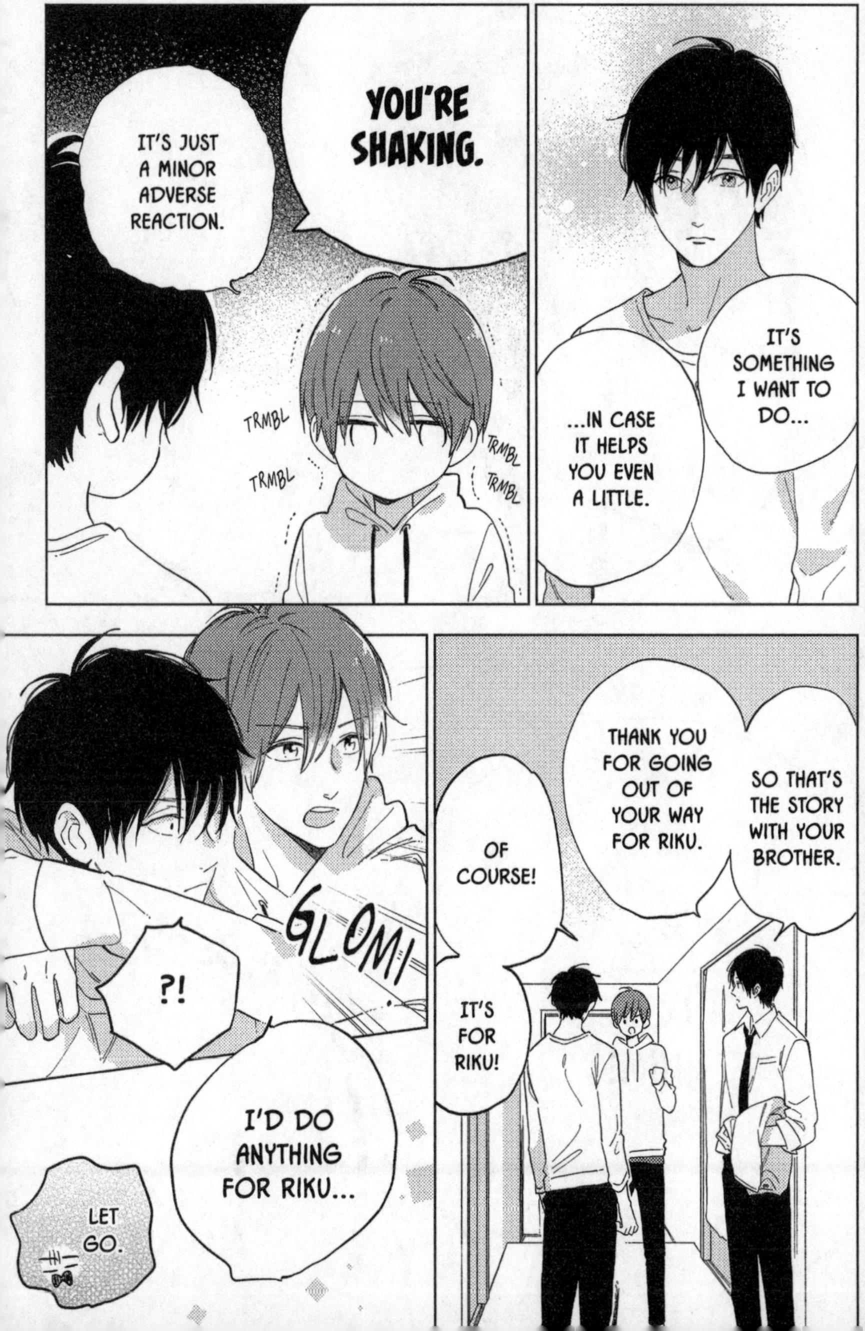
IT'S SOMETHING I WANT TO DO...
...IN CASE IT HELPS YOU EVEN A LITTLE.
YOU'RE SHAKING.
TRMBL TRMBL TRMBL TRMBL
IT'S JUST A MINOR ADVERSE REACTION.
SO THAT'S THE STORY WITH YOUR BROTHER.
THANK YOU FOR GOING OUT OF YOUR WAY FOR RIKU.
OF COURSE!
IT'S FOR RIKU!
GLOMP
?!
I'D DO ANYTHING FOR RIKU...
LET GO.

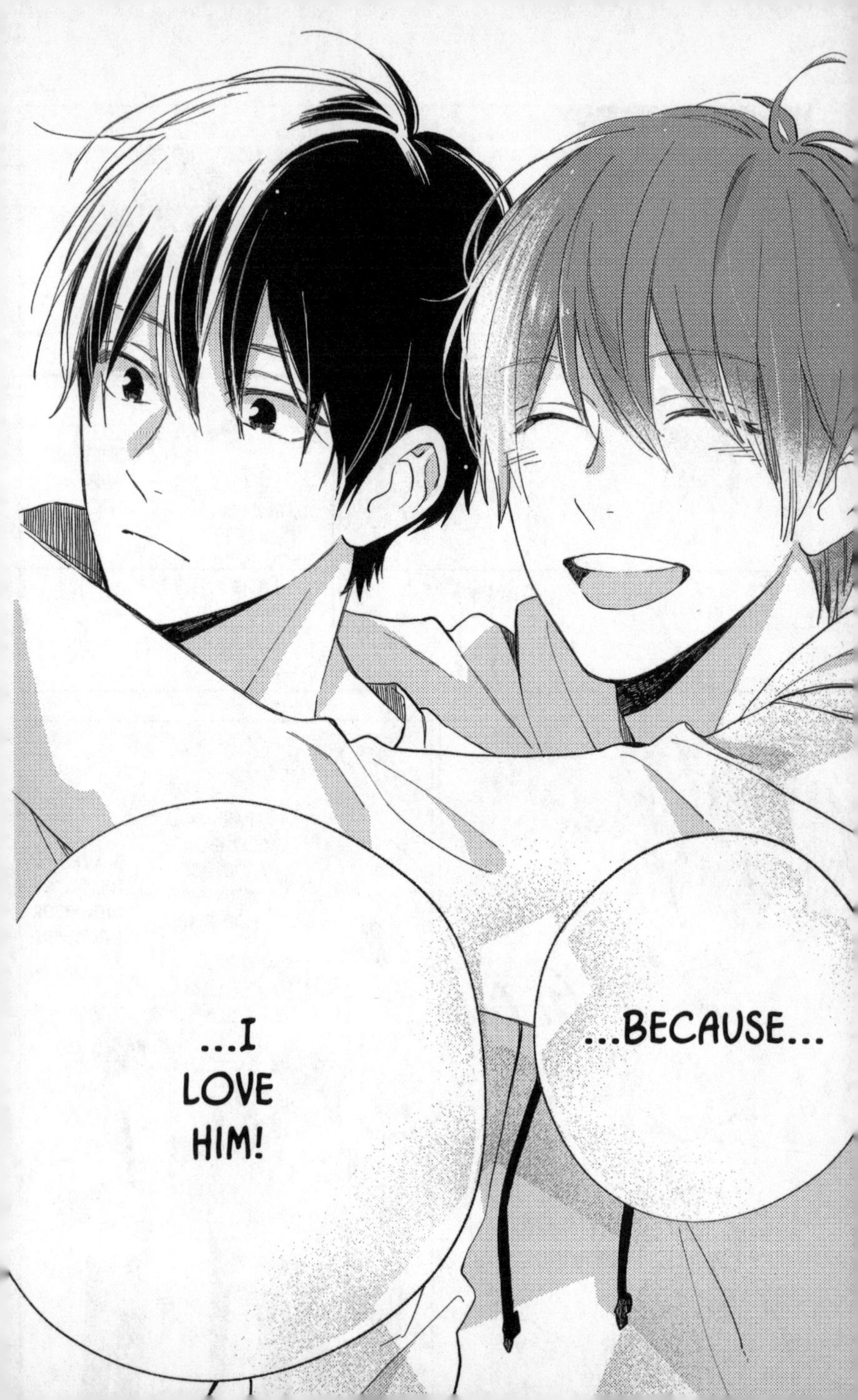
...BECAUSE...
...I LOVE HIM!

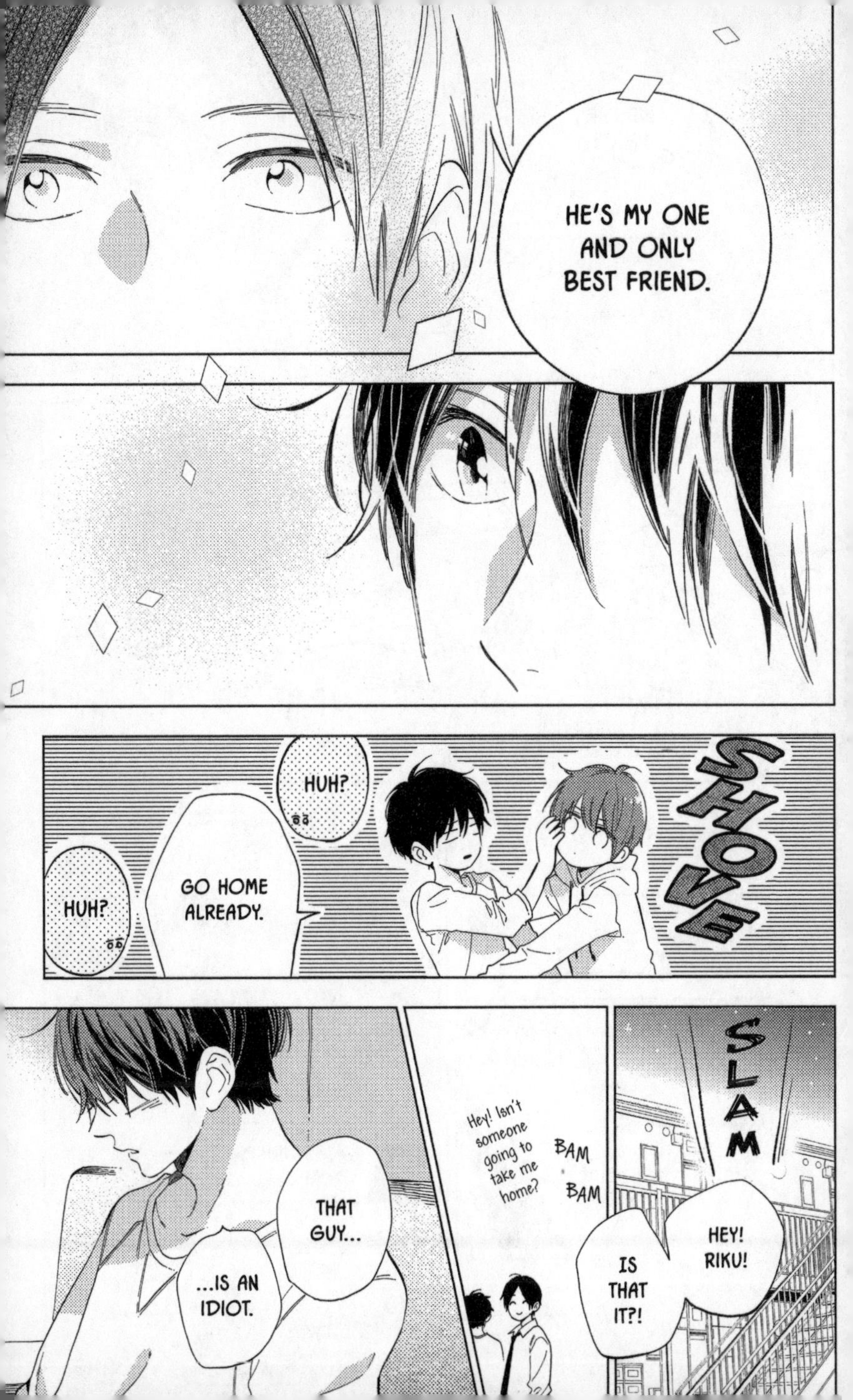
HE'S MY ONE AND ONLY BEST FRIEND.
SHOVE
GO HOME ALREADY.
HUH?
HUH?
SLAM
HEY! RIKU!
IS THAT IT?!
BAM
BAM
Hey! Isn't someone going to take me home?
THAT GUY...
...IS AN IDIOT.

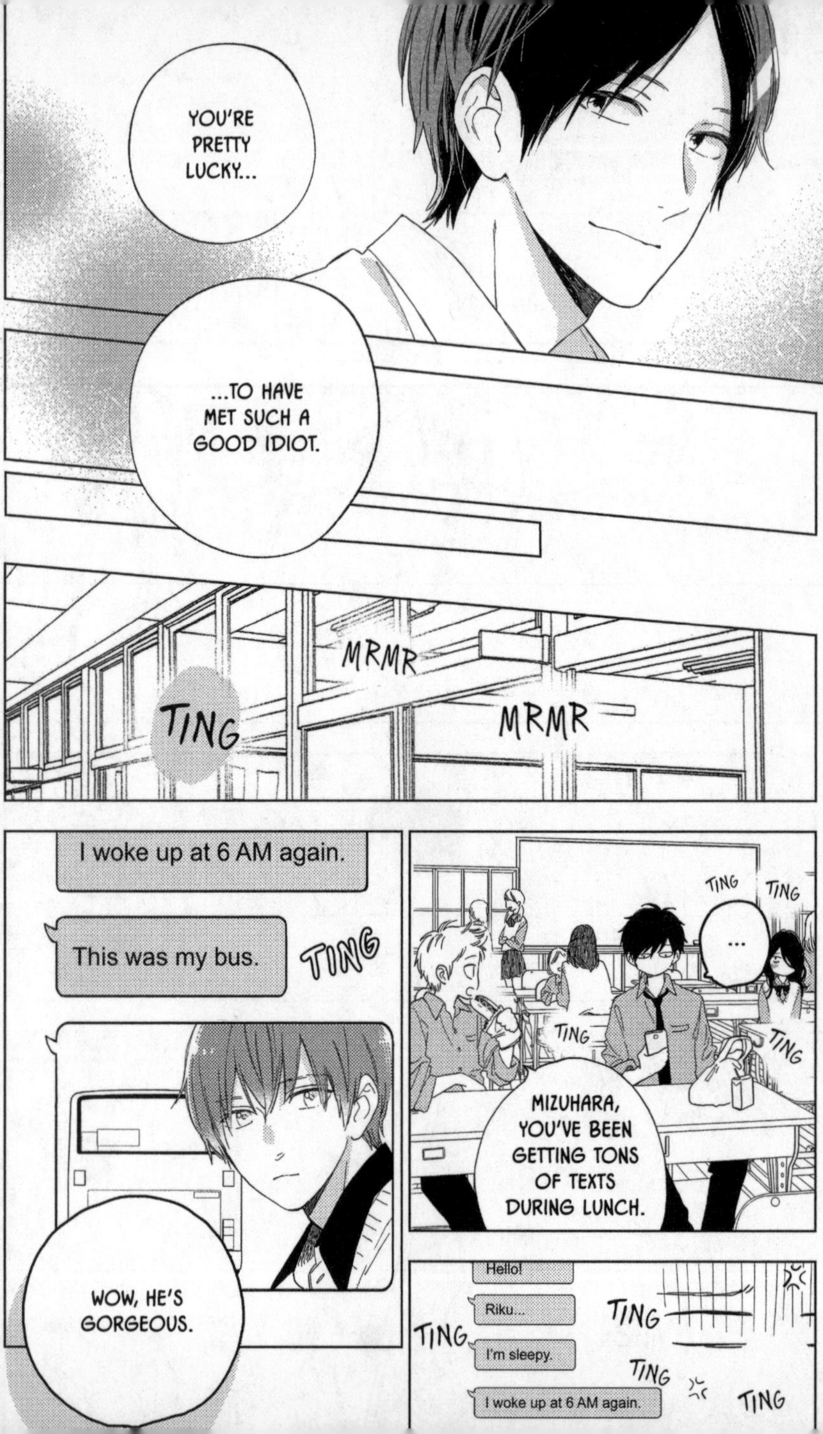
YOU'RE PRETTY LUCKY...
...TO HAVE MET SUCH A GOOD IDIOT.
MRMR
MRMR
TING
TING
TING
...
TING
TING
MIZUHARA, YOU'VE BEEN GETTING TONS OF TEXTS DURING LUNCH.
Hello!
Riku...
I'm sleepy.
I woke up at 6 AM again.
TING
TING
TING
TING
I woke up at 6 AM again.
This was my bus.
TING
WOW, HE'S GORGEOUS.

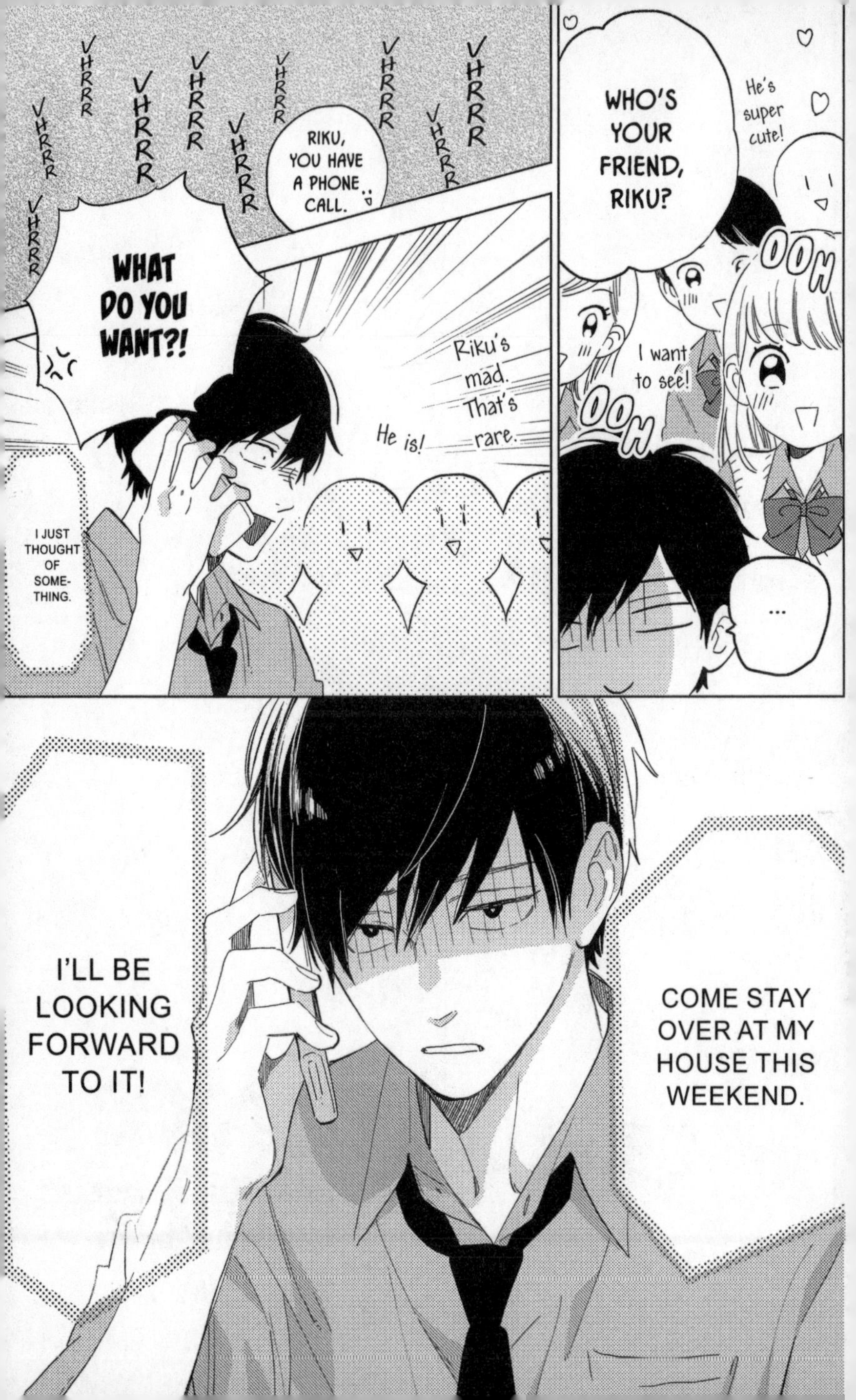
WHO'S YOUR FRIEND, RIKU?
He's super cute!
OOH
I want to see!
OOH
...
VHRRR
VHRRR
VHRRR
VHRRR
VHRRR
VHRRR
VHRRR
VHRRR
VHRRR
VHRRR
RIKU, YOU HAVE A PHONE CALL.
WHAT DO YOU WANT?!
Riku's mad. That's rare.
He is!
I JUST THOUGHT OF SOMETHING.
COME STAY OVER AT MY HOUSE THIS WEEKEND.
I'LL BE LOOKING FORWARD TO IT!

SHORTCAKE CAKE
CAKE

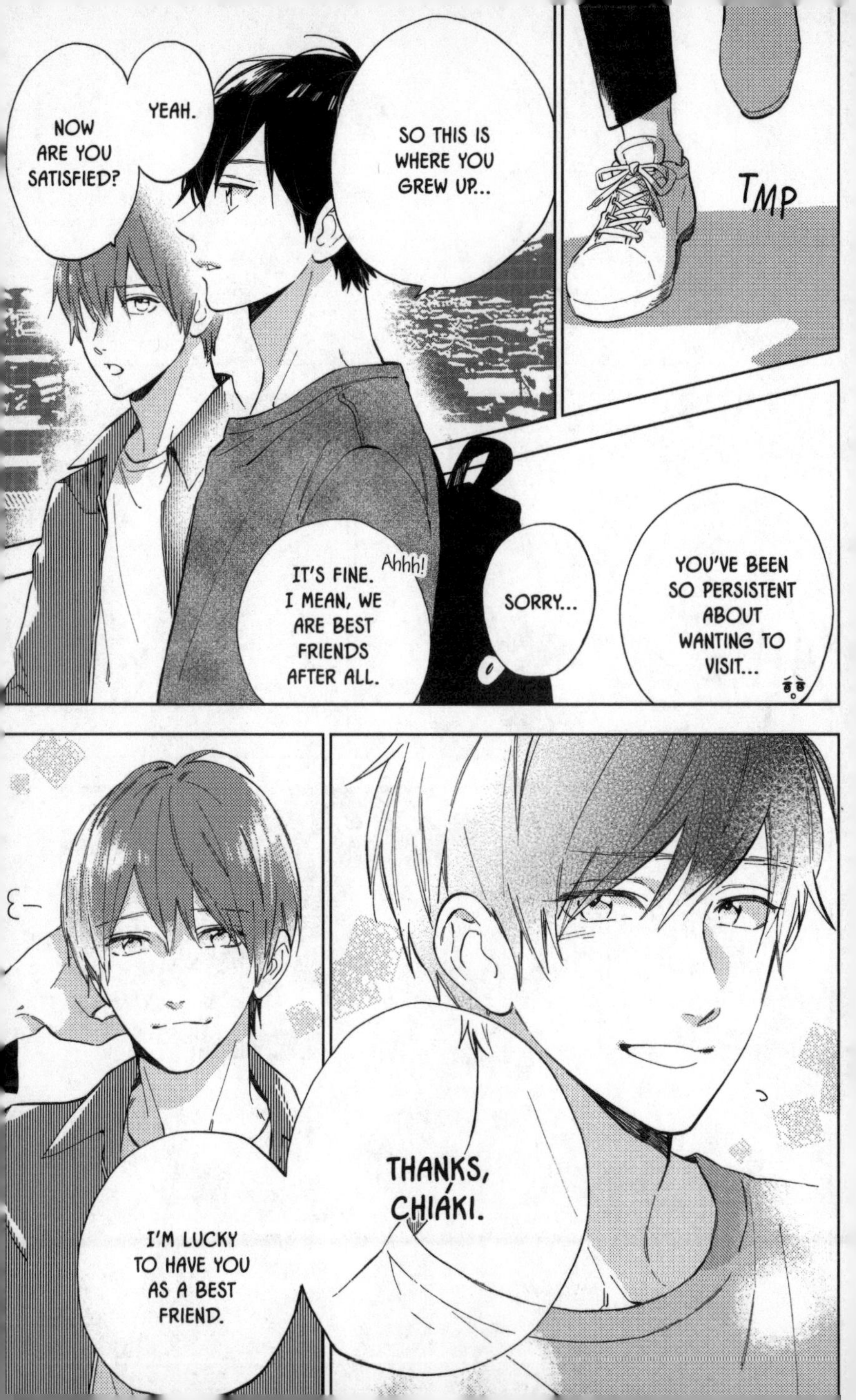
TMP
SO THIS IS WHERE YOU GREW UP...
YEAH.
NOW ARE YOU SATISFIED?
YOU'VE BEEN SO PERSISTENT ABOUT WANTING TO VISIT...
SORRY...
Ahhh!
IT'S FINE. I MEAN, WE ARE BEST FRIENDS AFTER ALL.
THANKS, CHIAKI.
I'M LUCKY TO HAVE YOU AS A BEST FRIEND.

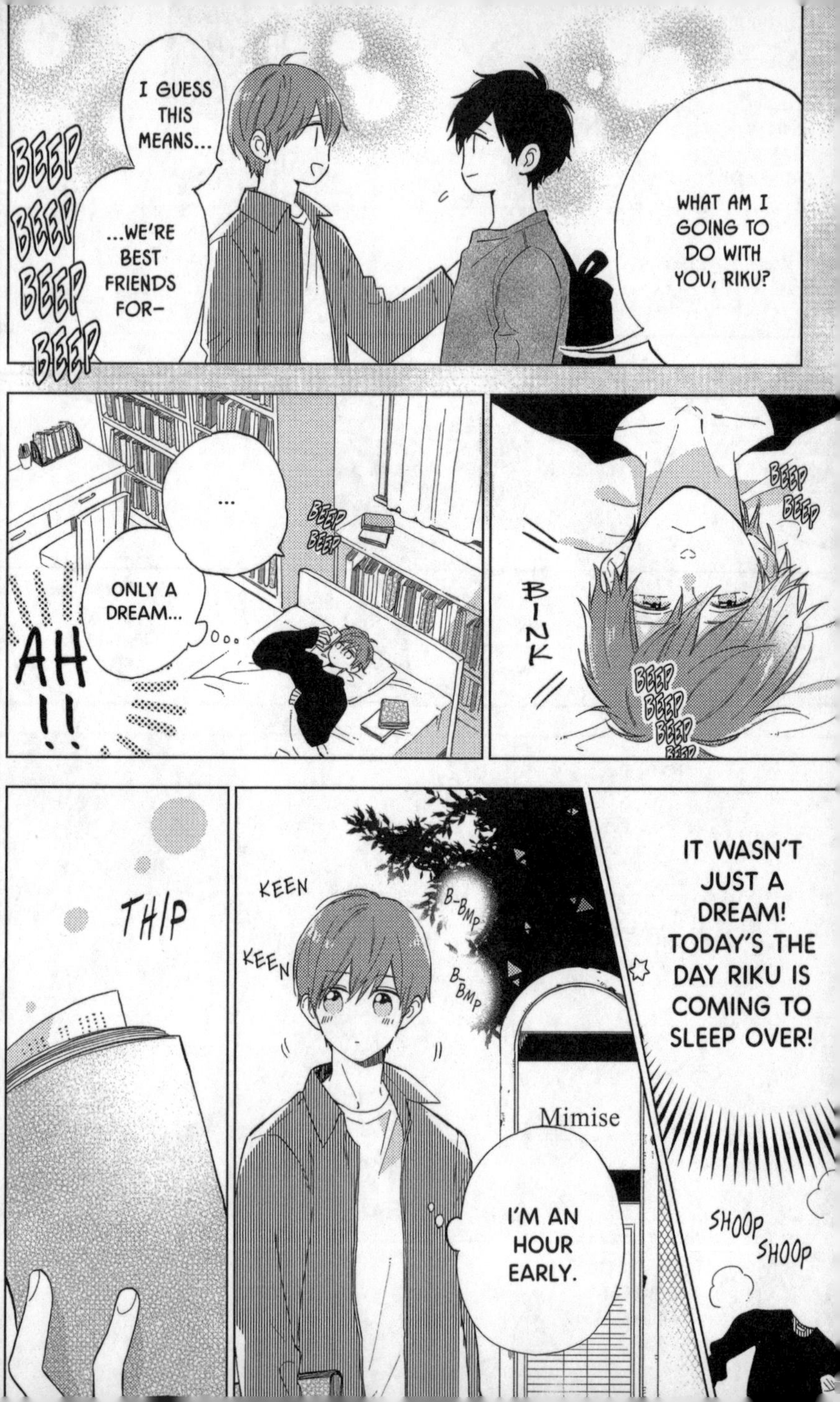
WHAT AM I GOING TO DO WITH YOU, RIKU?
I GUESS THIS MEANS...
...WE'RE BEST FRIENDS FOR–
BEEP BEEP BEEP BEEP
BEEP BEEP
BINK
BEEP BEEP BEEP
BEEP BEEP
...
ONLY A DREAM...
AH!!
IT WASN'T JUST A DREAM! TODAY'S THE DAY RIKU IS COMING TO SLEEP OVER!
SHOOP SHOOP
KEEN KEEN
B-BMP B-BMP
Mimise
I'M AN HOUR EARLY.
THIP

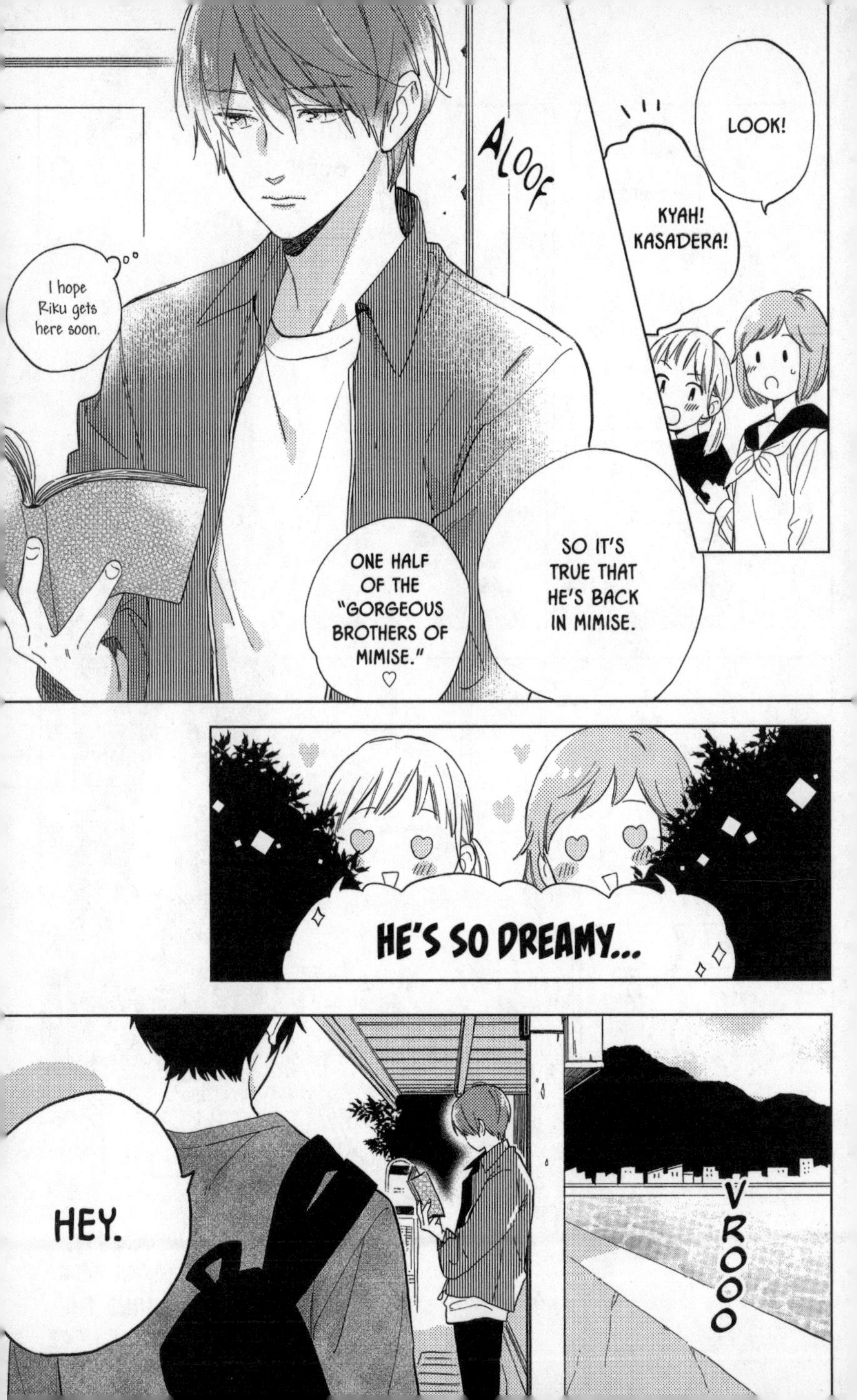
LOOK!
KYAH! KASADERA!
ALOOF
I hope Riku gets here soon.
SO IT'S TRUE THAT HE'S BACK IN MIMISE.
ONE HALF OF THE "GORGEOUS BROTHERS OF MIMISE." ♡
HE'S SO DREAMY...
VROOO
HEY.

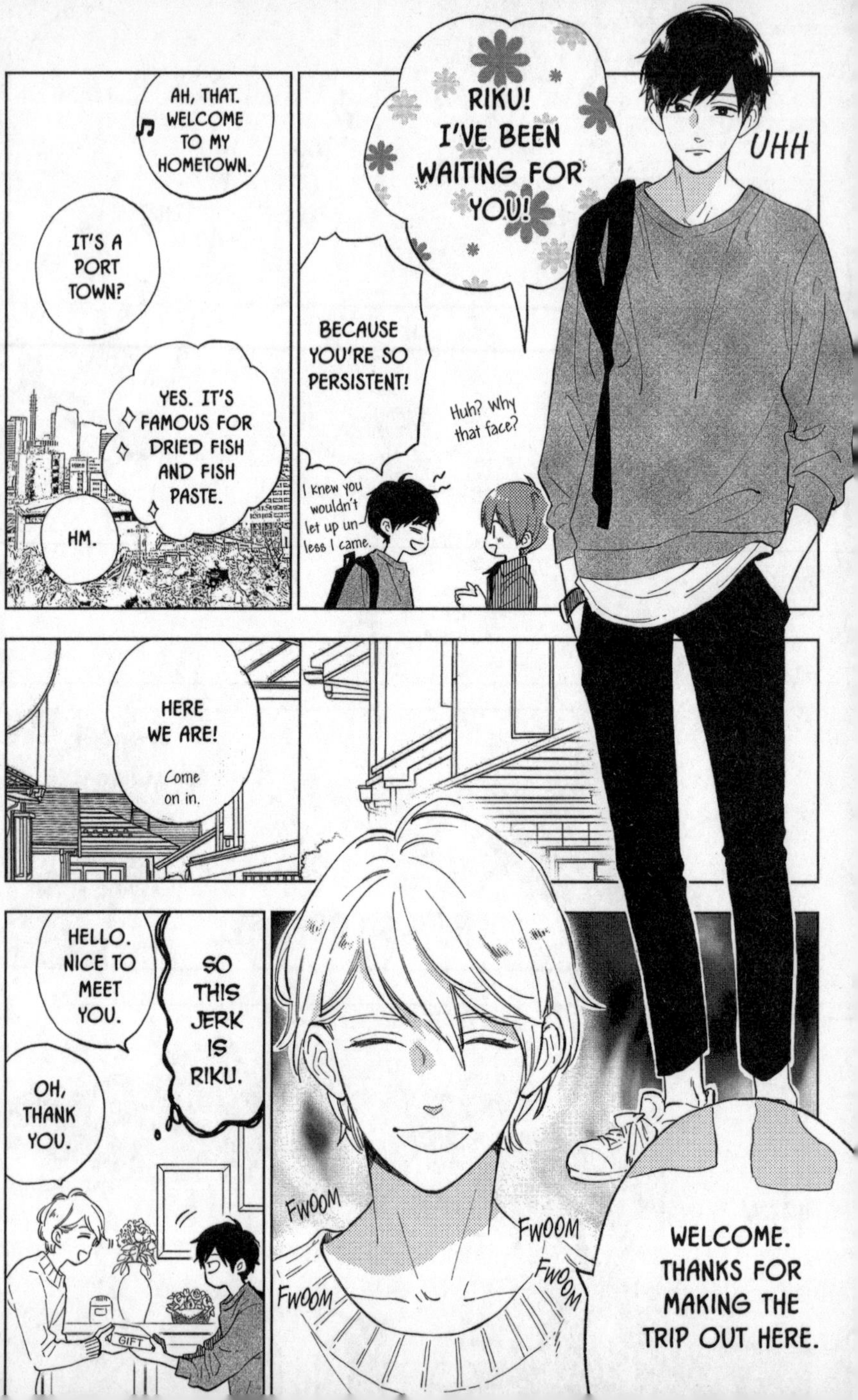
RIKU! I'VE BEEN WAITING FOR YOU!
UHH
BECAUSE YOU'RE SO PERSISTENT!
Huh? Why that face?
I knew you wouldn't let up unless I came.
AH, THAT. WELCOME TO MY HOMETOWN.
IT'S A PORT TOWN?
YES. IT'S FAMOUS FOR DRIED FISH AND FISH PASTE.
HM.
HERE WE ARE!
Come on in.
FWOOM
FWOOM
FWOOM
FWOOM
WELCOME. THANKS FOR MAKING THE TRIP OUT HERE.
HELLO. NICE TO MEET YOU.
SO THIS JERK IS RIKU.
OH, THANK YOU.
GIFT

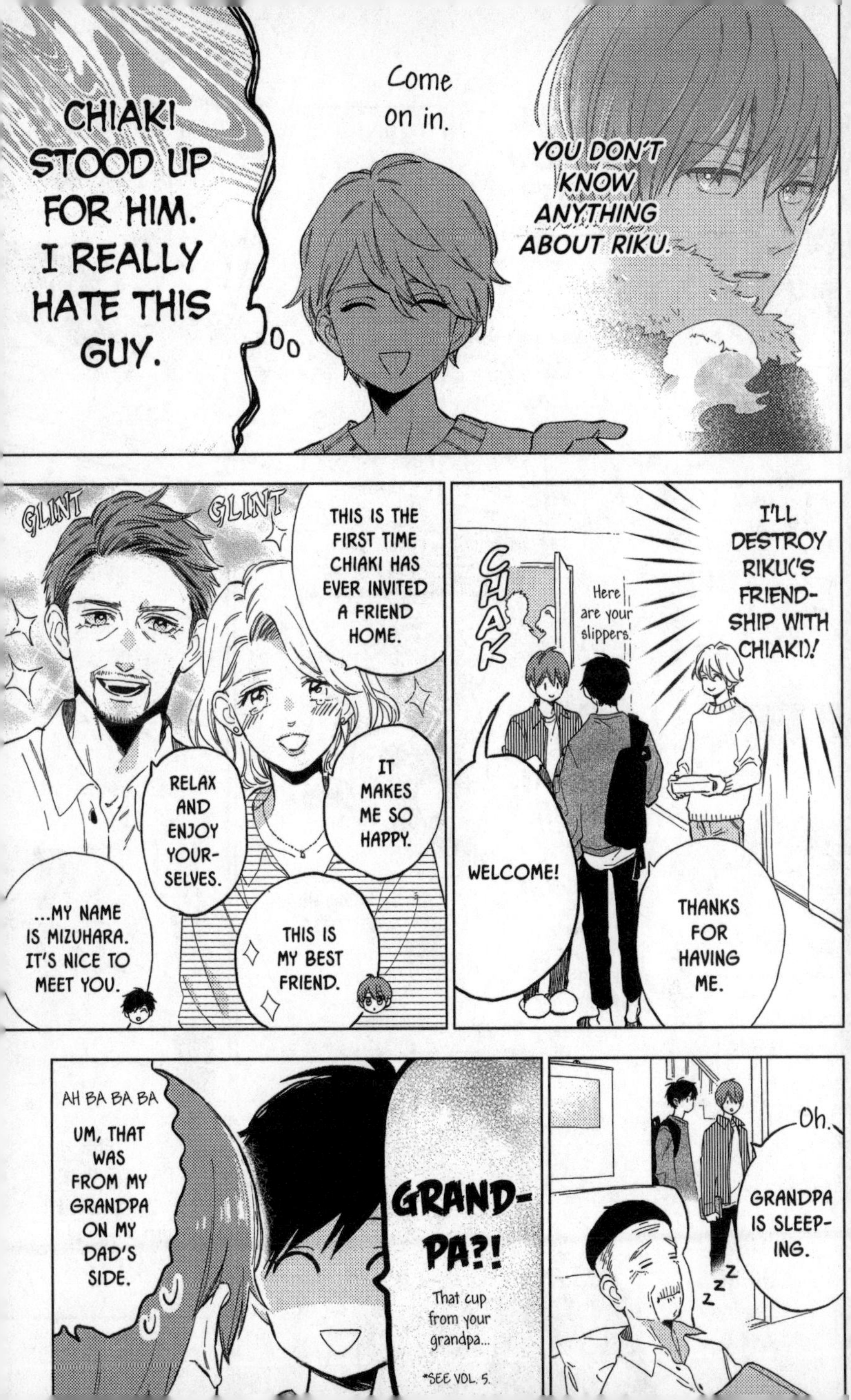
YOU DON'T KNOW ANYTHING ABOUT RIKU.
Come on in.
CHIAKI STOOD UP FOR HIM. I REALLY HATE THIS GUY.
I'LL DESTROY RIKU('S FRIENDSHIP WITH CHIAKI)!
CHAK
Here are your slippers.
THANKS FOR HAVING ME.
WELCOME!
GLINT
GLINT
THIS IS THE FIRST TIME CHIAKI HAS EVER INVITED A FRIEND HOME.
IT MAKES ME SO HAPPY.
RELAX AND ENJOY YOUR-SELVES.
THIS IS MY BEST FRIEND.
...MY NAME IS MIZUHARA. IT'S NICE TO MEET YOU.
Oh.
GRANDPA IS SLEEP-ING.
Z Z Z
GRAND-PA?!
That cup from your grandpa...
*SEE VOL. 5.
AH BA BA BA
UM, THAT WAS FROM MY GRANDPA ON MY DAD'S SIDE.

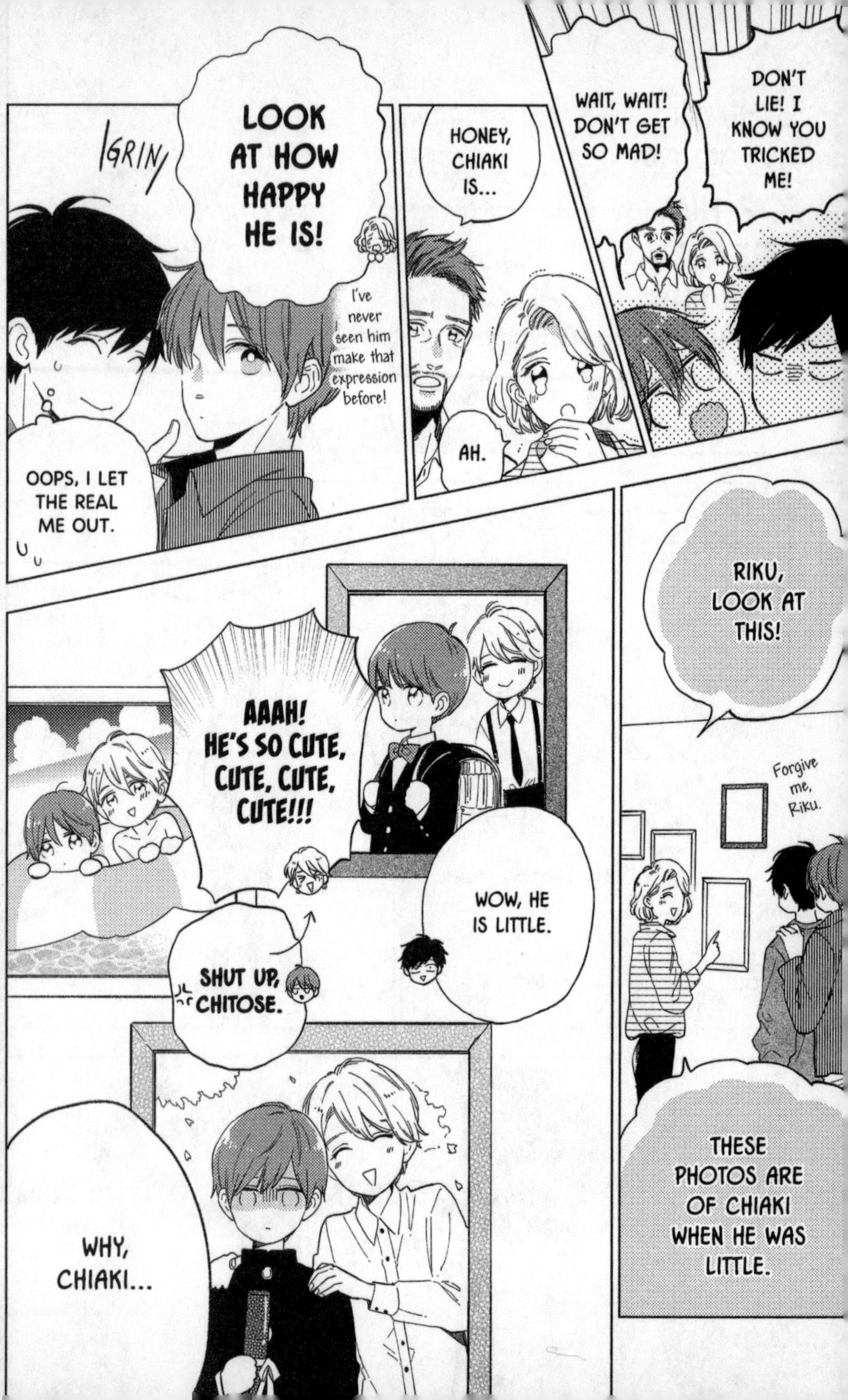
DON'T LIE! I KNOW YOU TRICKED ME!
WAIT, WAIT! DON'T GET SO MAD!
HONEY, CHIAKI IS...
AH.
LOOK AT HOW HAPPY HE IS!
I've never seen him make that expression before!
GRIN
OOPS, I LET THE REAL ME OUT.
RIKU, LOOK AT THIS!
Forgive me, Riku.
THESE PHOTOS ARE OF CHIAKI WHEN HE WAS LITTLE.
AAAH! HE'S SO CUTE, CUTE, CUTE, CUTE!!!
WOW, HE IS LITTLE.
SHUT UP, CHITOSE.
WHY, CHIAKI...

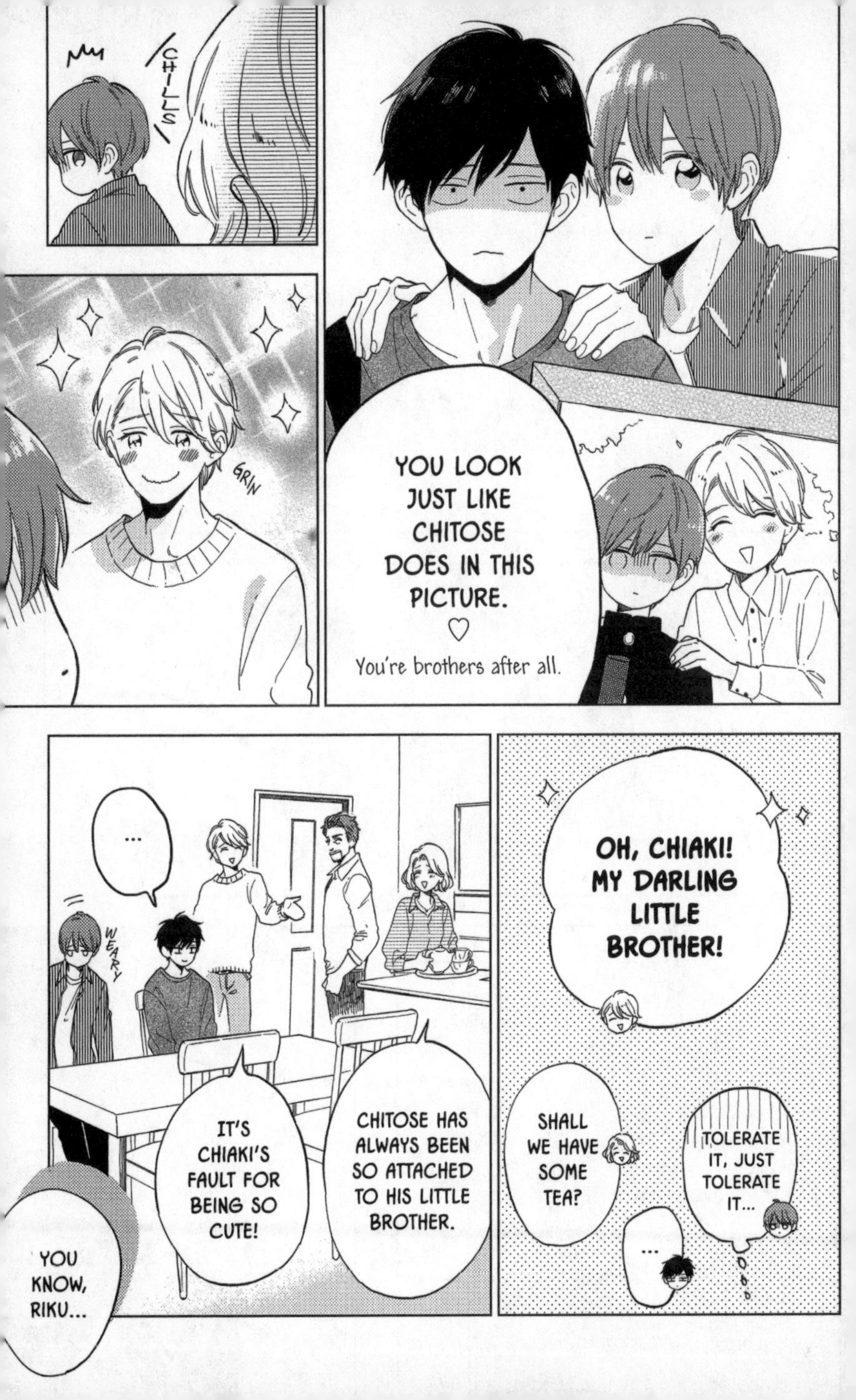

YOU LOOK JUST LIKE CHITOSE DOES IN THIS PICTURE. ♡
You're brothers after all.
NN
CHILLS
GRIN
OH, CHIAKI! MY DARLING LITTLE BROTHER!
TOLERATE IT, JUST TOLERATE IT...
SHALL WE HAVE SOME TEA?
...
...
WEARY
CHITOSE HAS ALWAYS BEEN SO ATTACHED TO HIS LITTLE BROTHER.
IT'S CHIAKI'S FAULT FOR BEING SO CUTE!
YOU KNOW, RIKU...

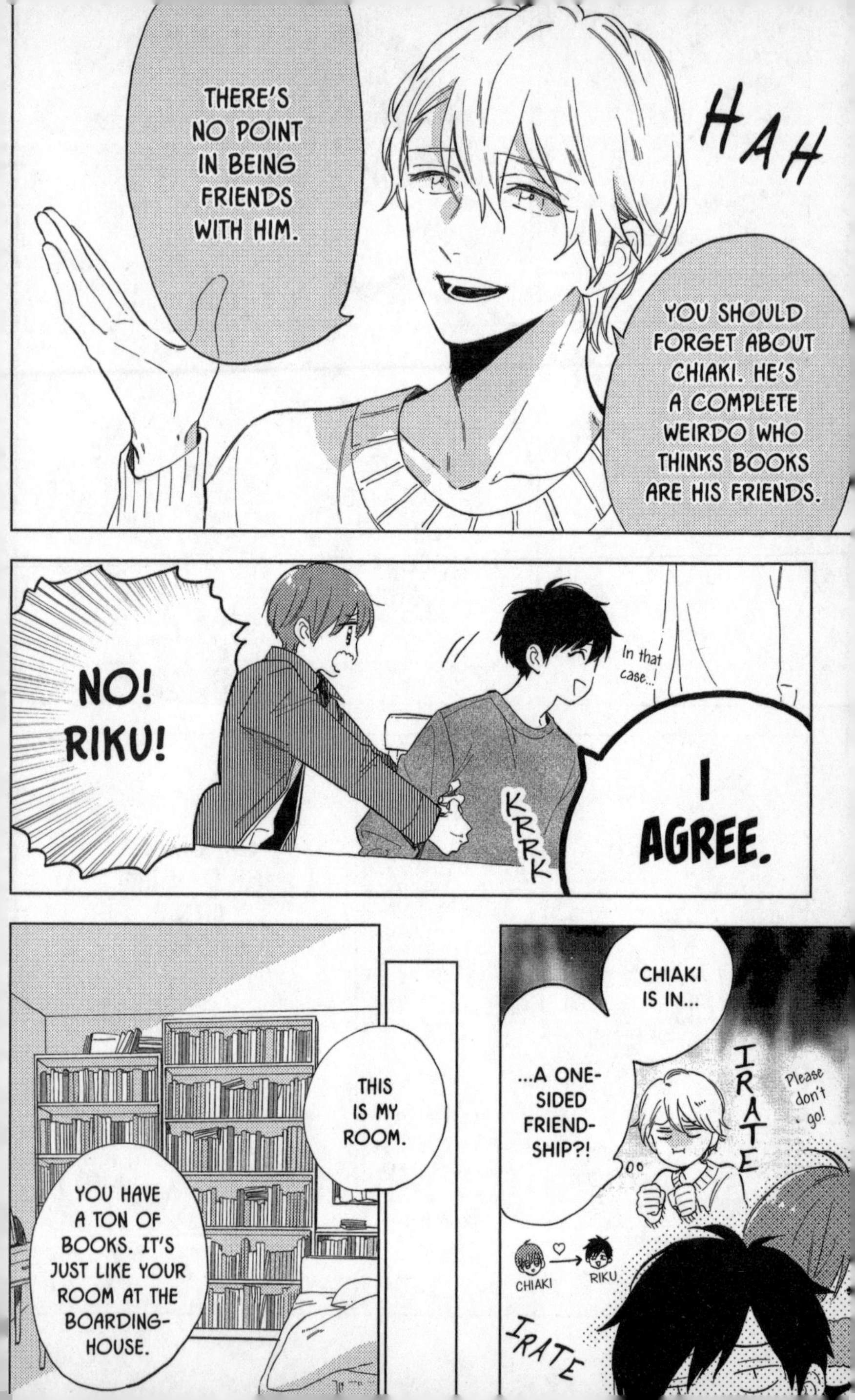
HAH
YOU SHOULD FORGET ABOUT CHIAKI. HE'S A COMPLETE WEIRDO WHO THINKS BOOKS ARE HIS FRIENDS.
THERE'S NO POINT IN BEING FRIENDS WITH HIM.
In that case...!
I AGREE.
KRRK
NO! RIKU!
CHIAKI IS IN...
...A ONE-SIDED FRIENDSHIP?!
IRATE
Please don't go!
CHIAKI
RIKU
IRATE
THIS IS MY ROOM.
YOU HAVE A TON OF BOOKS. IT'S JUST LIKE YOUR ROOM AT THE BOARDINGHOUSE.

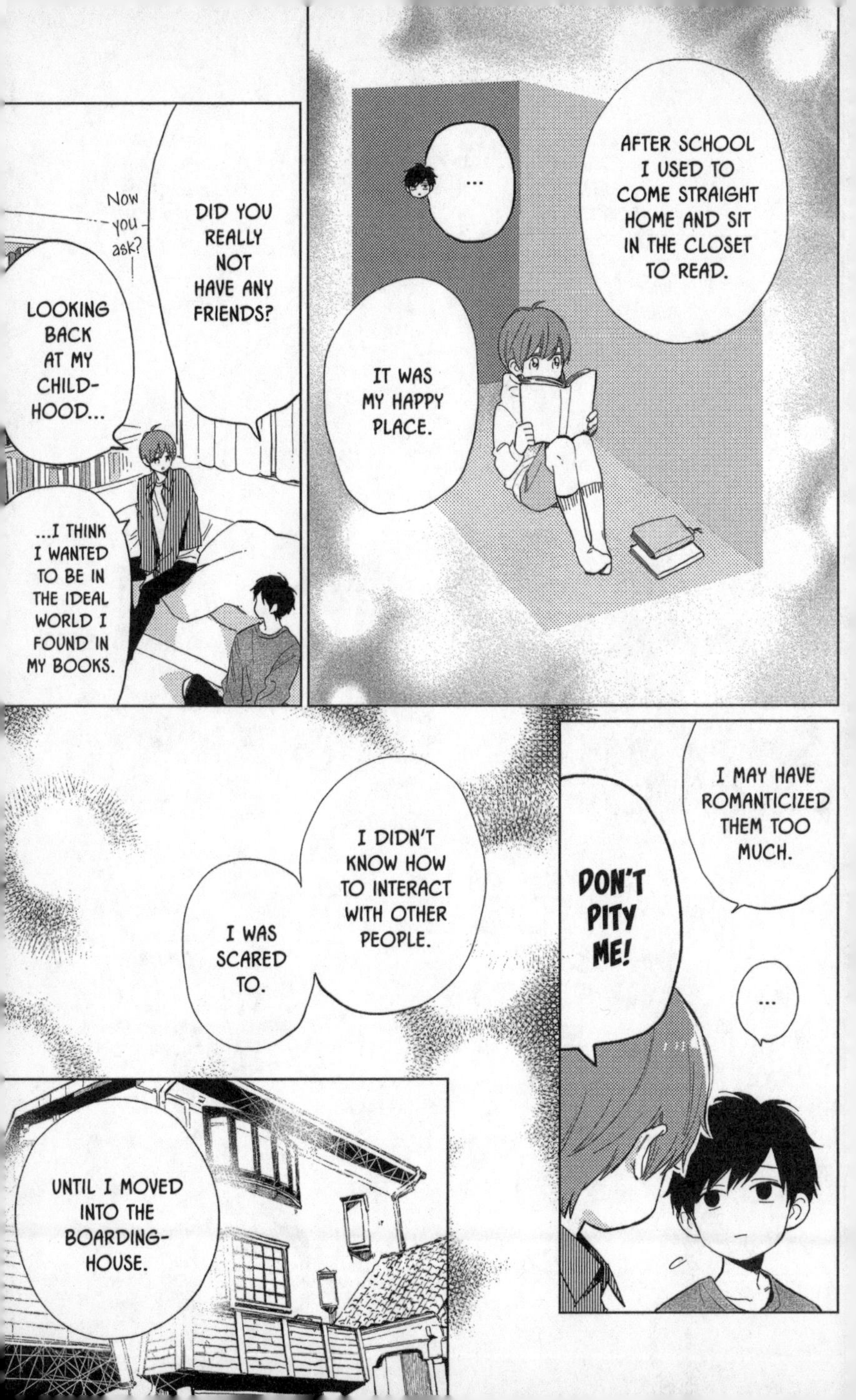
AFTER SCHOOL I USED TO COME STRAIGHT HOME AND SIT IN THE CLOSET TO READ.
...
IT WAS MY HAPPY PLACE.
DID YOU REALLY NOT HAVE ANY FRIENDS?
Now you ask?!
LOOKING BACK AT MY CHILDHOOD...
...I THINK I WANTED TO BE IN THE IDEAL WORLD I FOUND IN MY BOOKS.
I MAY HAVE ROMANTICIZED THEM TOO MUCH.
DON'T PITY ME!
...
I DIDN'T KNOW HOW TO INTERACT WITH OTHER PEOPLE.
I WAS SCARED TO.
UNTIL I MOVED INTO THE BOARDINGHOUSE.

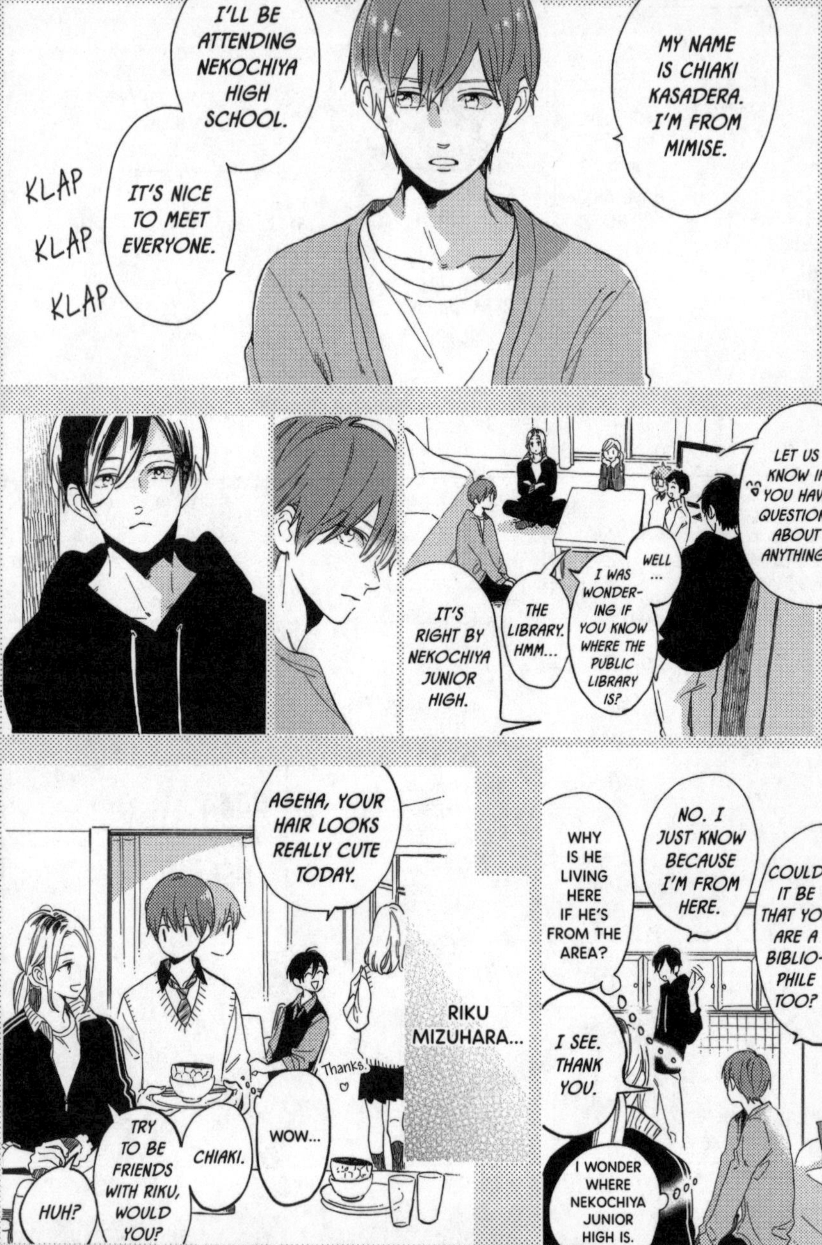
MY NAME IS CHIAKI KASADERA. I'M FROM MIMISE.
I'LL BE ATTENDING NEKOCHIYA HIGH SCHOOL.
IT'S NICE TO MEET EVERYONE.
KLAP
KLAP
KLAP
LET US KNOW IF YOU HAVE QUESTIONS ABOUT ANYTHING.
WELL ...
I WAS WONDERING IF YOU KNOW WHERE THE PUBLIC LIBRARY IS?
THE LIBRARY. HMM...
IT'S RIGHT BY NEKOCHIYA JUNIOR HIGH.
COULD IT BE THAT YOU ARE A BIBLIOPHILE TOO?
NO. I JUST KNOW BECAUSE I'M FROM HERE.
WHY IS HE LIVING HERE IF HE'S FROM THE AREA?
I SEE. THANK YOU.
I WONDER WHERE NEKOCHIYA JUNIOR HIGH IS.
RIKU MIZUHARA...
AGEHA, YOUR HAIR LOOKS REALLY CUTE TODAY.
Thanks.
WOW...
CHIAKI.
TRY TO BE FRIENDS WITH RIKU, WOULD YOU?
HUH?

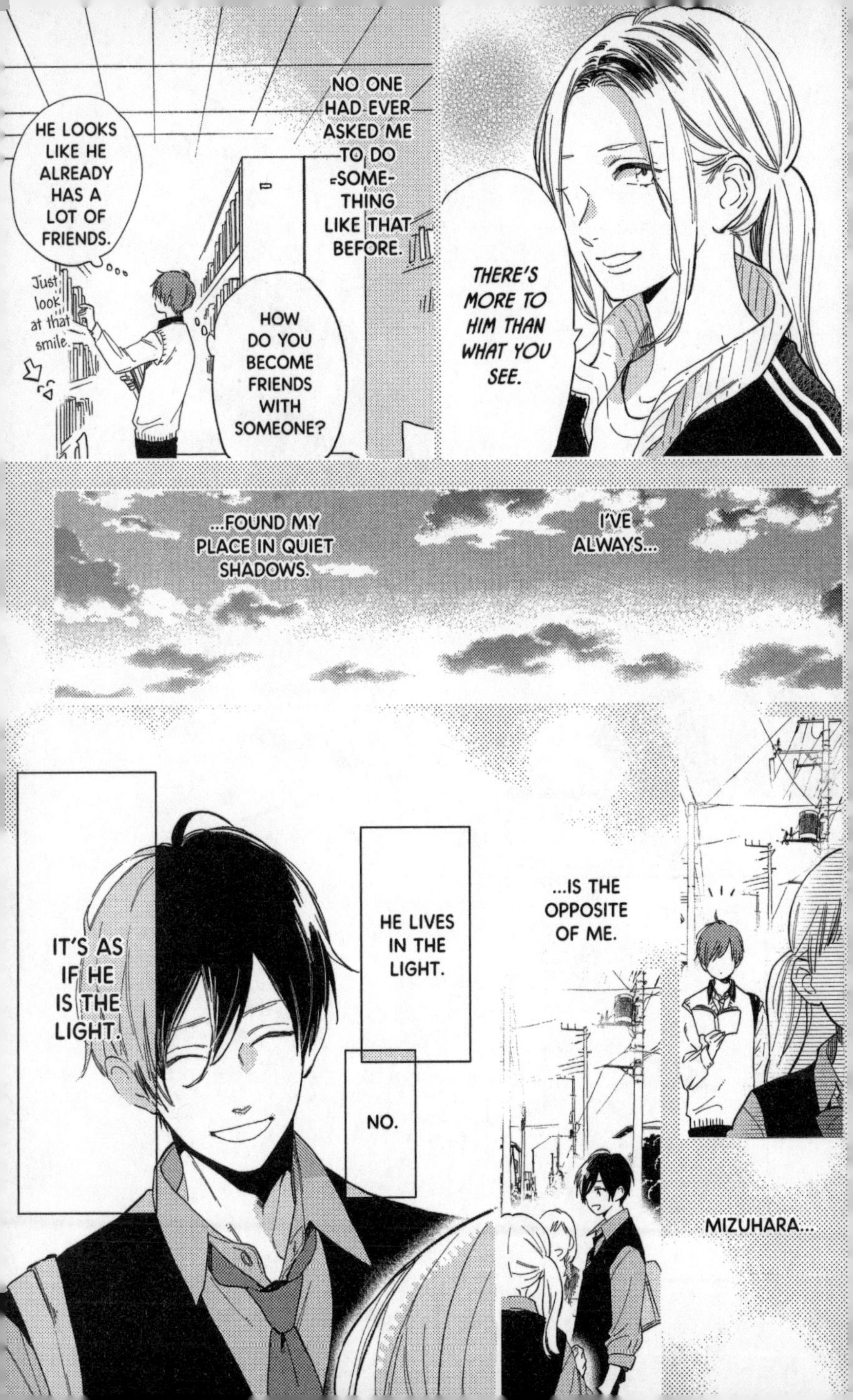
THERE'S MORE TO HIM THAN WHAT YOU SEE.
NO ONE HAD EVER ASKED ME TO DO SOME-THING LIKE THAT BEFORE.
HOW DO YOU BECOME FRIENDS WITH SOMEONE?
HE LOOKS LIKE HE ALREADY HAS A LOT OF FRIENDS.
Just look at that smile.
I'VE ALWAYS...
...FOUND MY PLACE IN QUIET SHADOWS.
MIZUHARA...
...IS THE OPPOSITE OF ME.
HE LIVES IN THE LIGHT.
NO.
IT'S AS IF HE IS THE LIGHT.

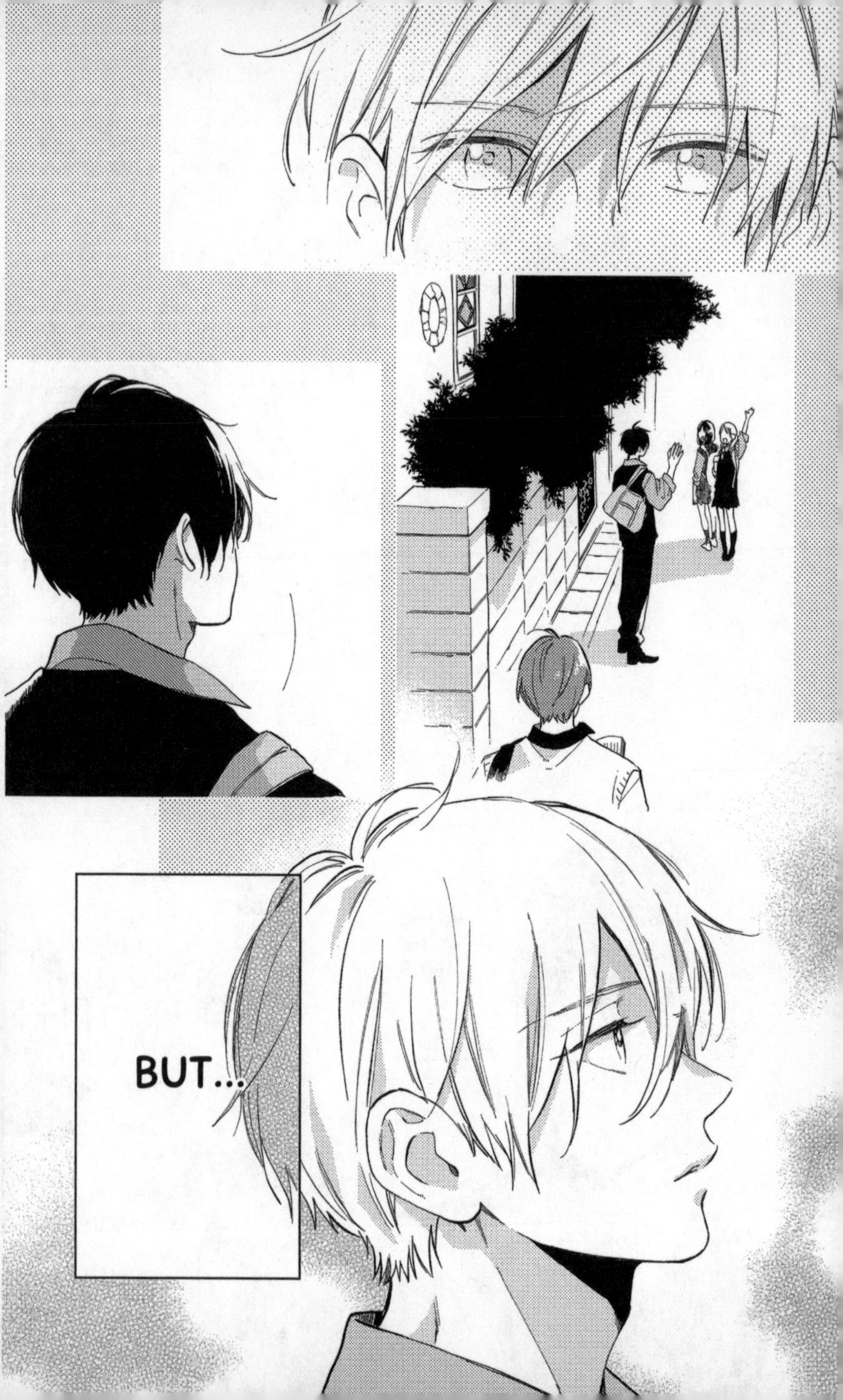
BUT...

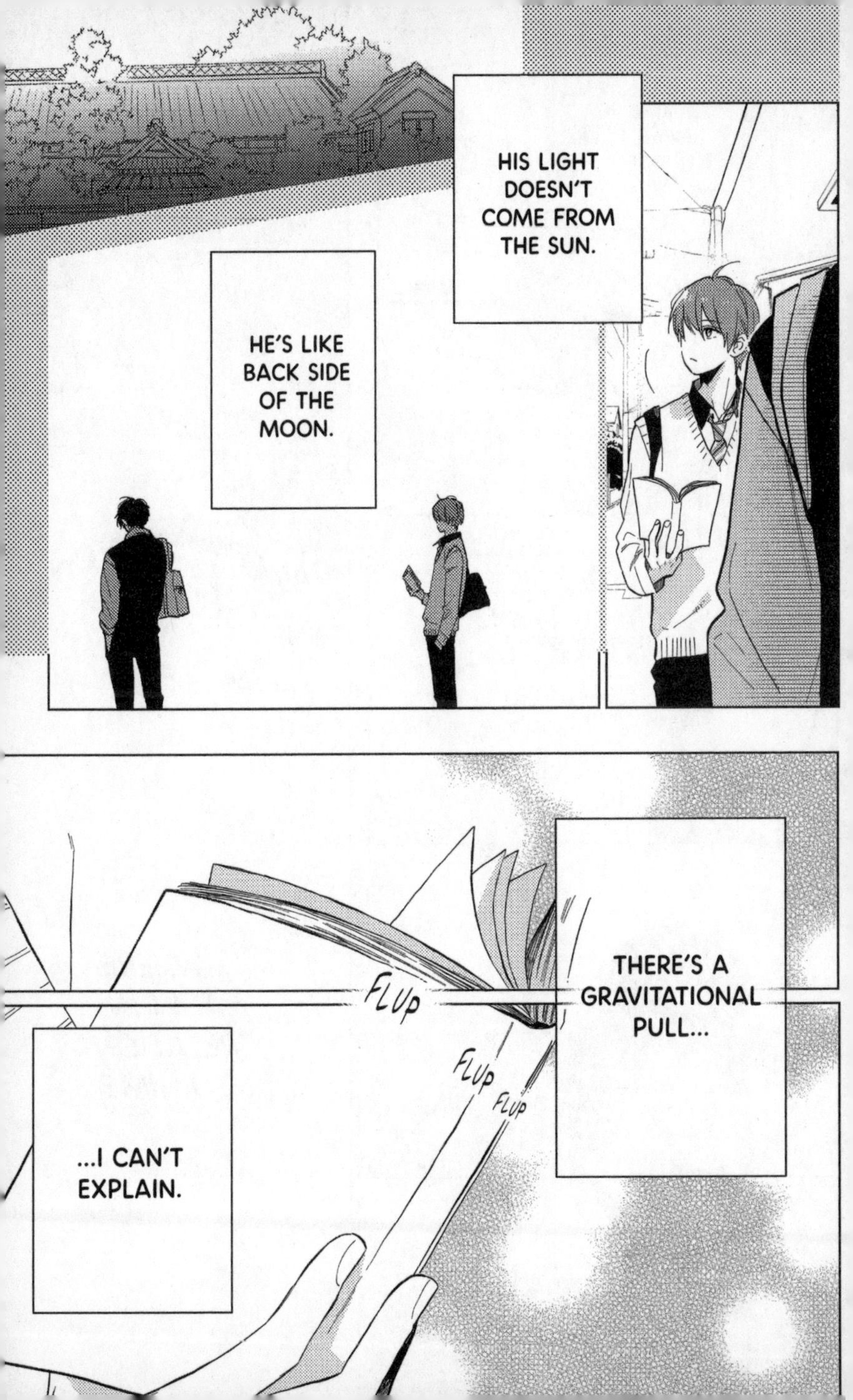
HIS LIGHT DOESN'T COME FROM THE SUN.
HE'S LIKE BACK SIDE OF THE MOON.
THERE'S A GRAVITATIONAL PULL...
FLUP
FLUP
FLUP
...I CAN'T EXPLAIN.

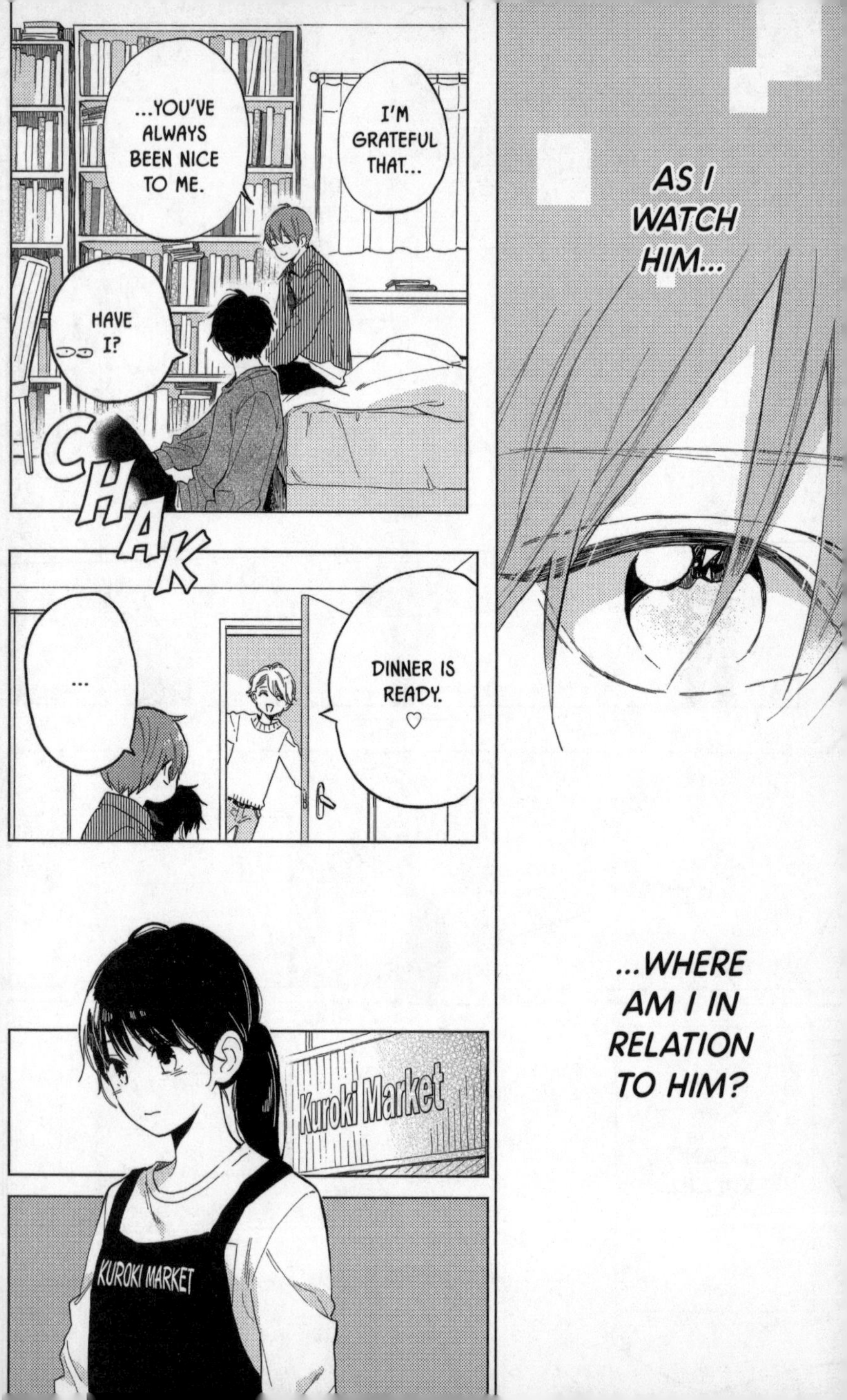
AS I WATCH HIM...
...WHERE AM I IN RELATION TO HIM?
I'M GRATEFUL THAT...
...YOU'VE ALWAYS BEEN NICE TO ME.
HAVE I?
CHAK
DINNER IS READY. ♡
...
Kuroki Market
KUROKI MARKET

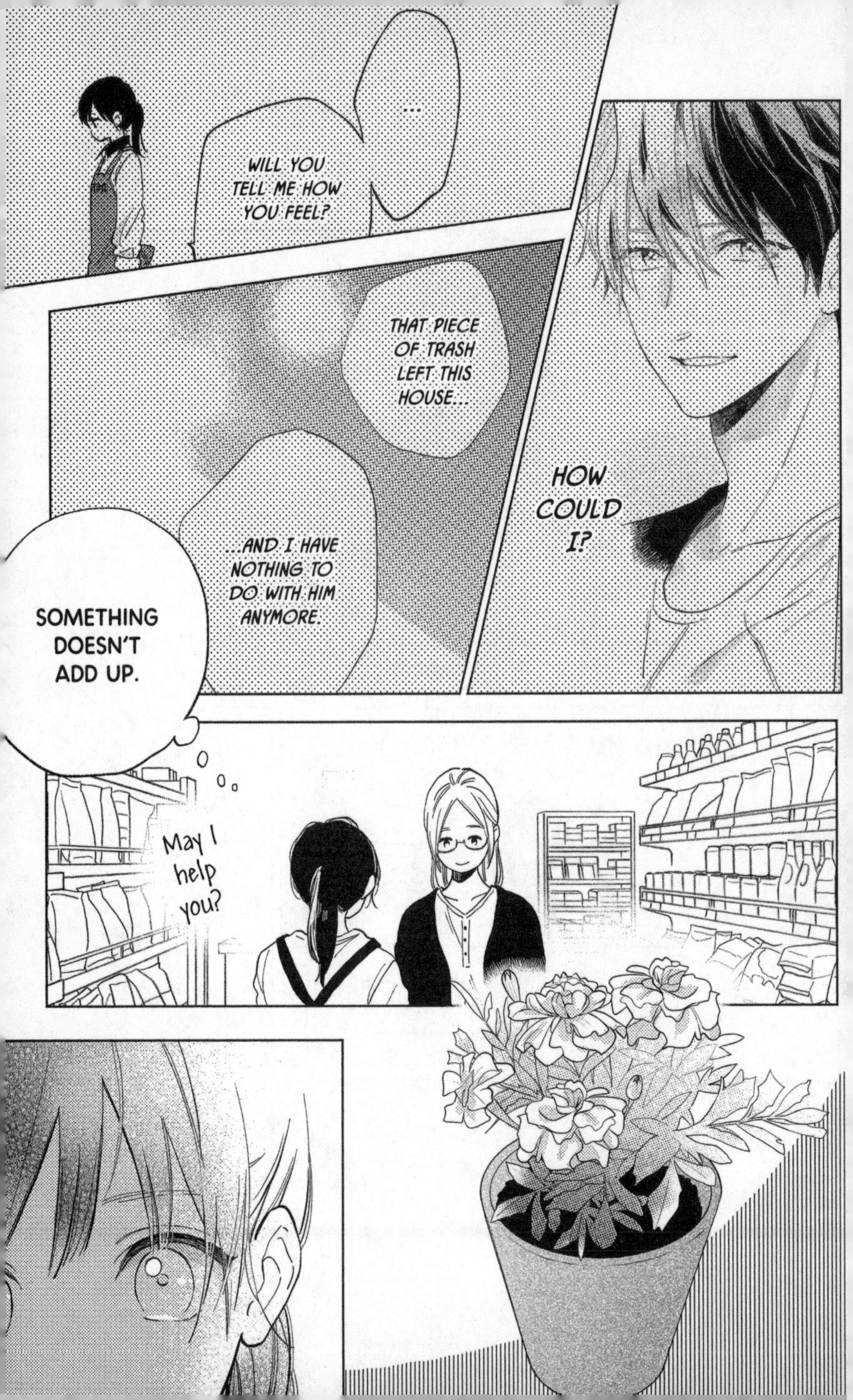
...
WILL YOU TELL ME HOW YOU FEEL?
HOW COULD I?
THAT PIECE OF TRASH LEFT THIS HOUSE...
...AND I HAVE NOTHING TO DO WITH HIM ANYMORE.
SOMETHING DOESN'T ADD UP.
May I help you?

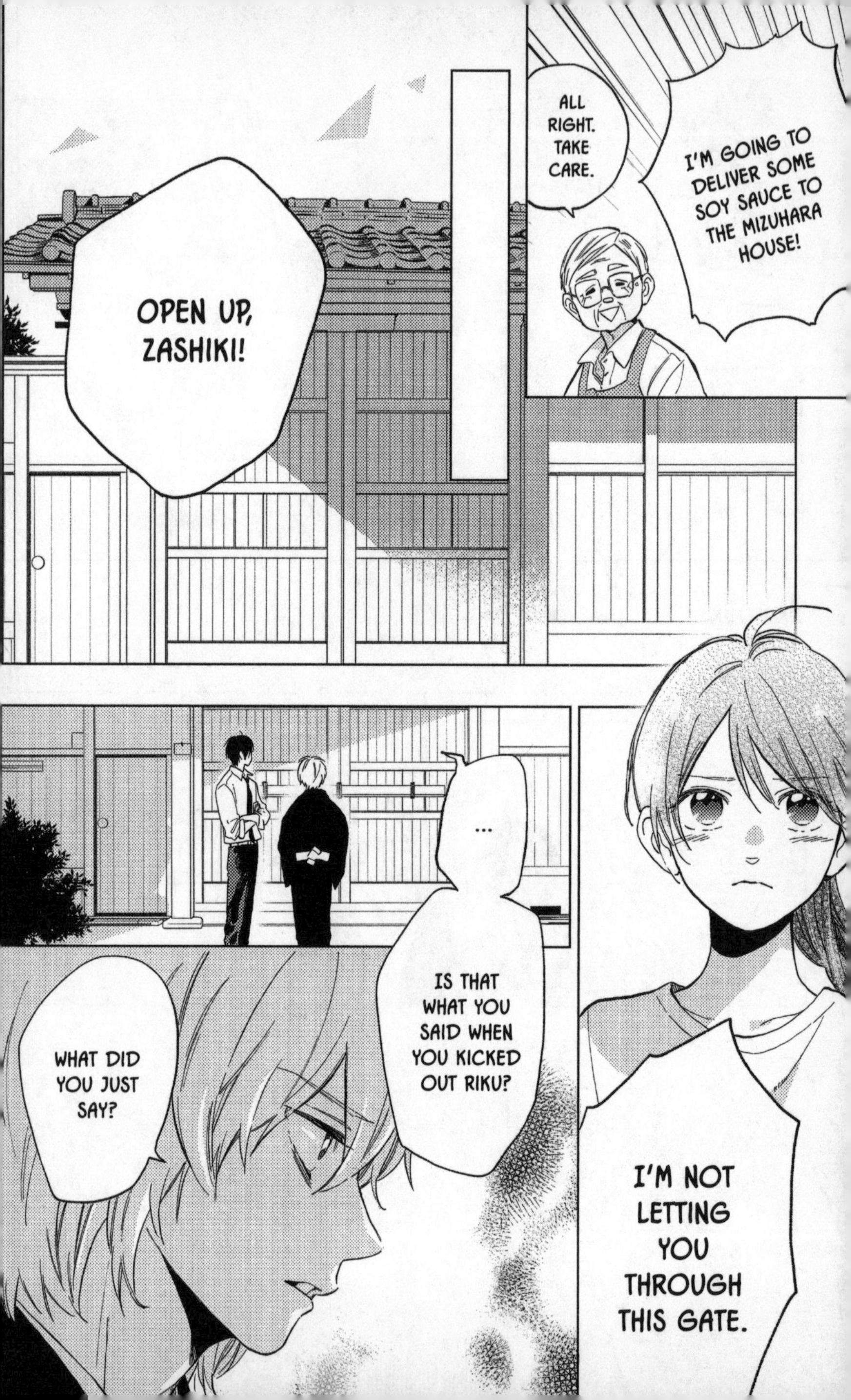
I'M GOING TO DELIVER SOME SOY SAUCE TO THE MIZUHARA HOUSE!
ALL RIGHT. TAKE CARE.
OPEN UP, ZASHIKI!
I'M NOT LETTING YOU THROUGH THIS GATE.
...
IS THAT WHAT YOU SAID WHEN YOU KICKED OUT RIKU?
WHAT DID YOU JUST SAY?

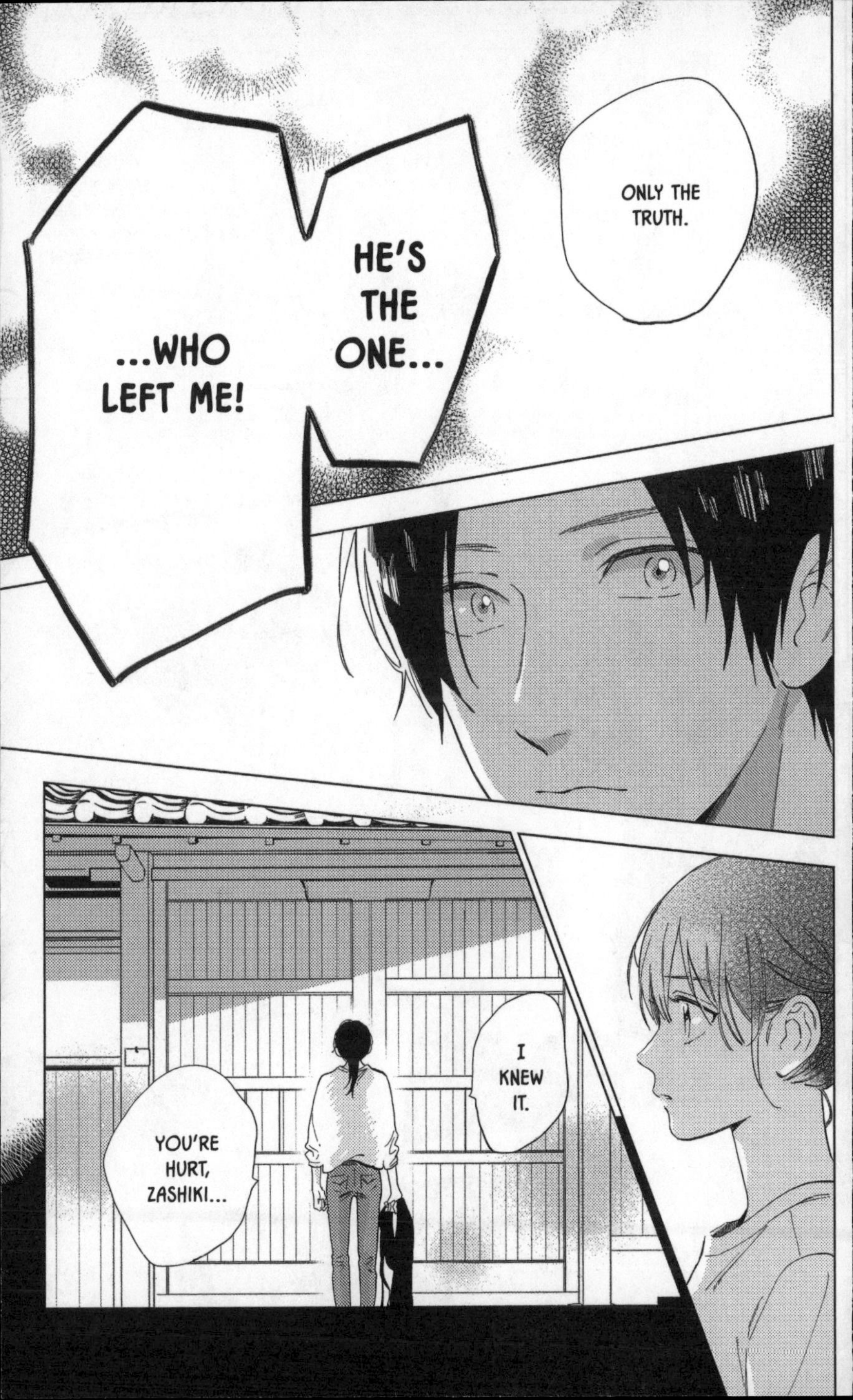
ONLY THE TRUTH.
HE'S THE ONE...
...WHO LEFT ME!
I KNEW IT.
YOU'RE HURT, ZASHIKI...

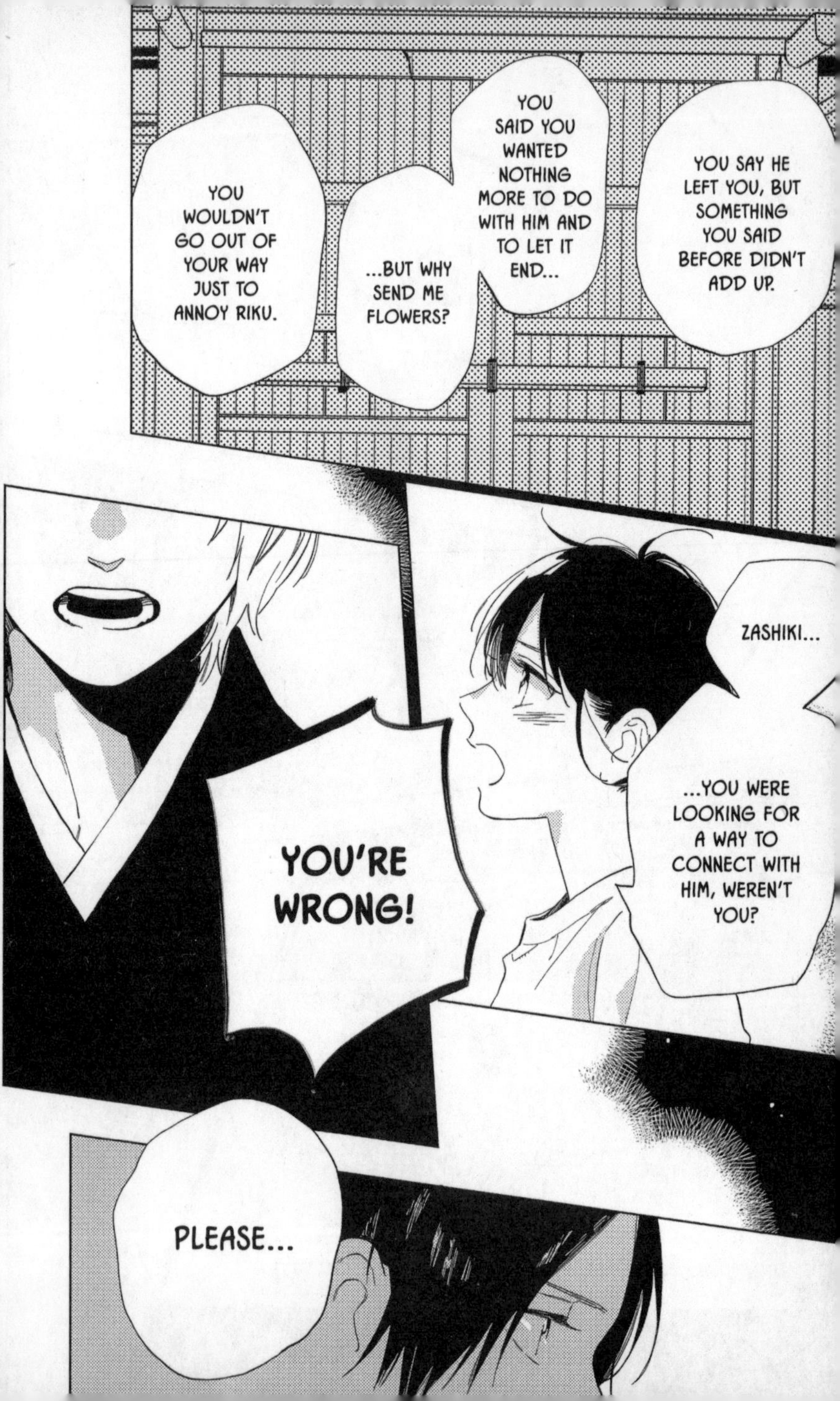
YOU SAY HE LEFT YOU, BUT SOMETHING YOU SAID BEFORE DIDN'T ADD UP.
YOU SAID YOU WANTED NOTHING MORE TO DO WITH HIM AND TO LET IT END...
...BUT WHY SEND ME FLOWERS?
YOU WOULDN'T GO OUT OF YOUR WAY JUST TO ANNOY RIKU.
ZASHIKI...
...YOU WERE LOOKING FOR A WAY TO CONNECT WITH HIM, WEREN'T YOU?
YOU'RE WRONG!
PLEASE...

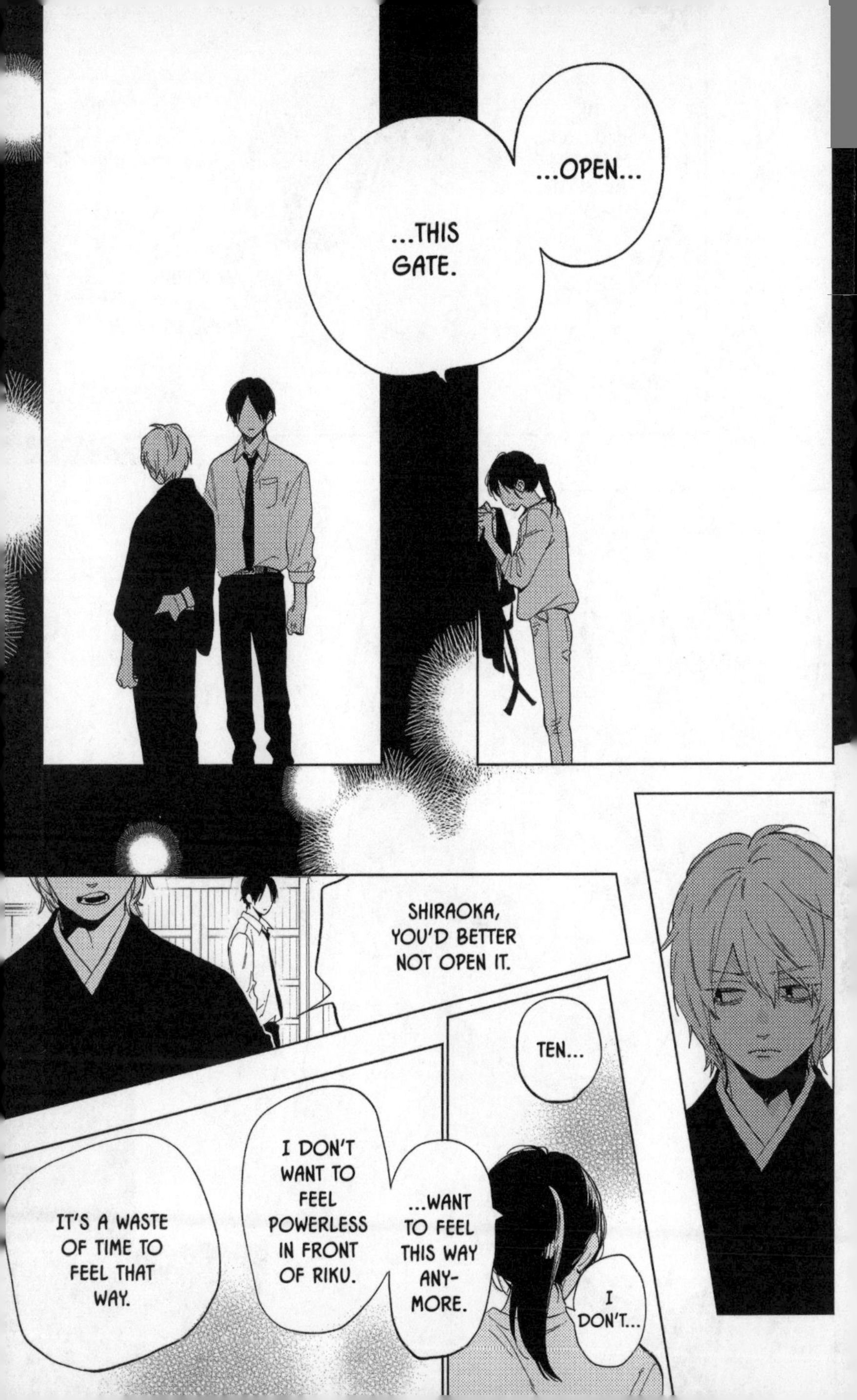
...OPEN...
...THIS GATE.
SHIRAOKA, YOU'D BETTER NOT OPEN IT.
TEN...
I DON'T...
...WANT TO FEEL THIS WAY ANY-MORE.
I DON'T WANT TO FEEL POWERLESS IN FRONT OF RIKU.
IT'S A WASTE OF TIME TO FEEL THAT WAY.

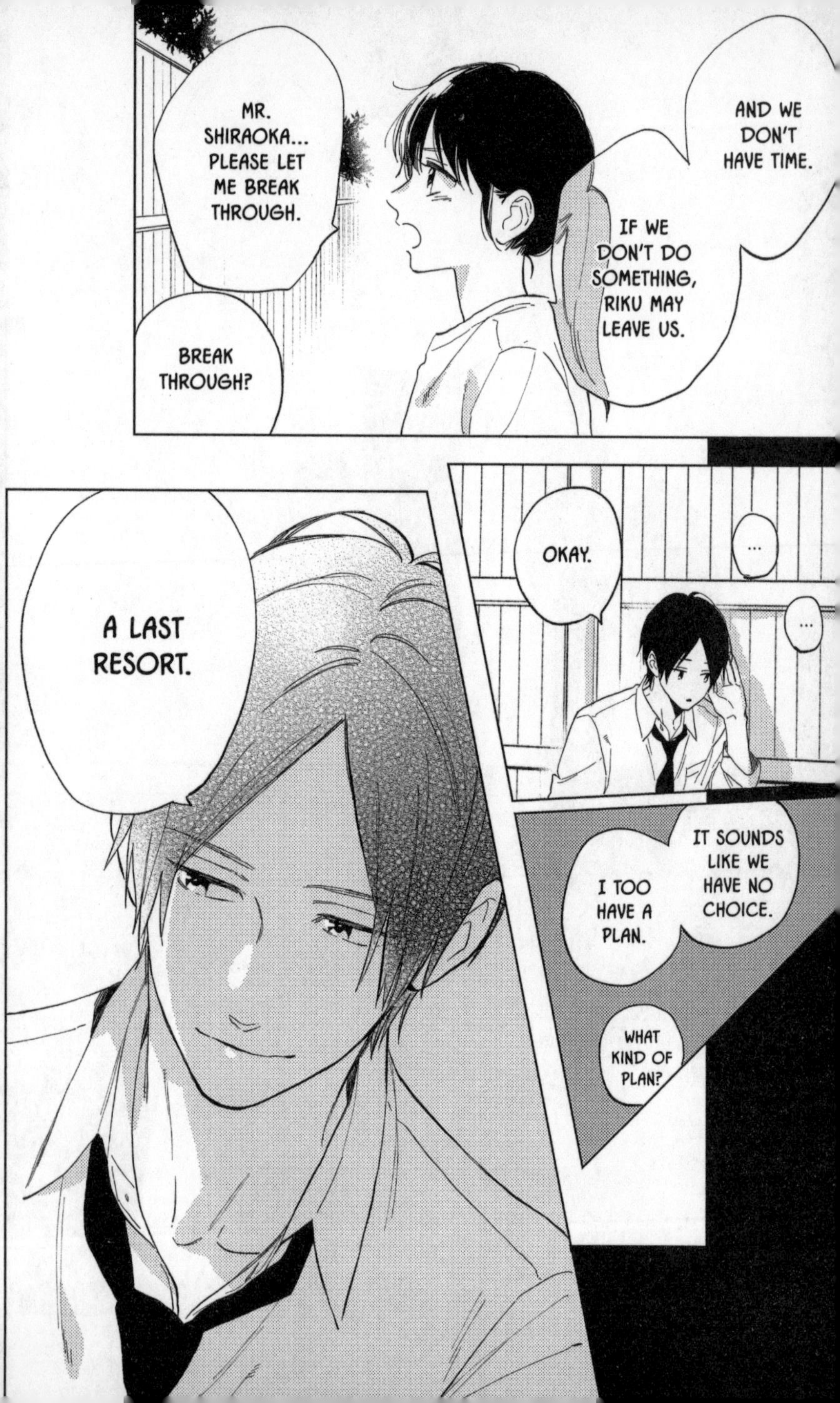
AND WE DON'T HAVE TIME.
IF WE DON'T DO SOMETHING, RIKU MAY LEAVE US.
MR. SHIRAOKA... PLEASE LET ME BREAK THROUGH.
BREAK THROUGH?
...
...
OKAY.
IT SOUNDS LIKE WE HAVE NO CHOICE.
I TOO HAVE A PLAN.
WHAT KIND OF PLAN?
A LAST RESORT.

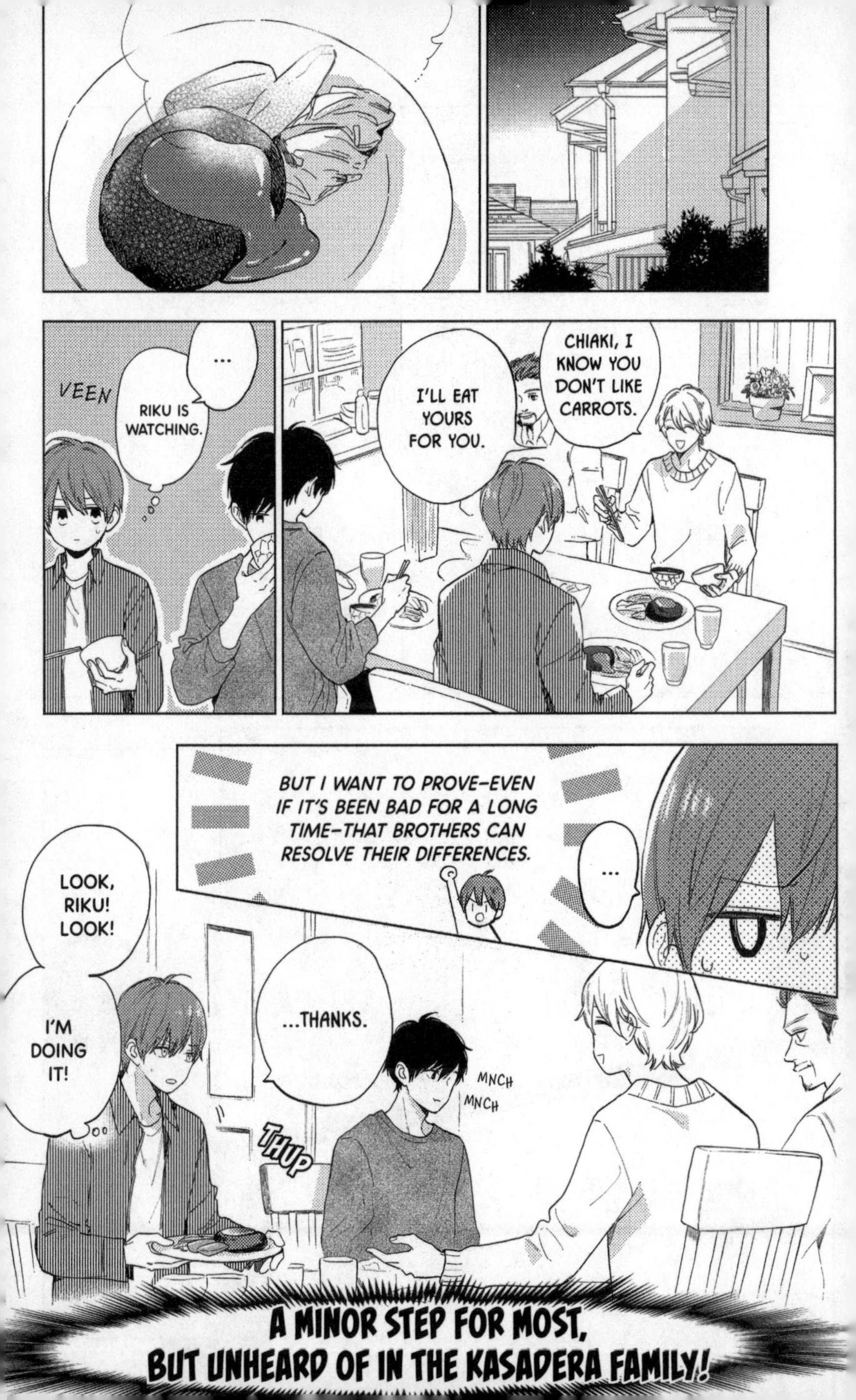
CHIAKI, I KNOW YOU DON'T LIKE CARROTS.
I'LL EAT YOURS FOR YOU.
...
RIKU IS WATCHING.
VEEN
BUT I WANT TO PROVE–EVEN IF IT'S BEEN BAD FOR A LONG TIME–THAT BROTHERS CAN RESOLVE THEIR DIFFERENCES.
...
...THANKS.
MNCH
MNCH
LOOK, RIKU! LOOK!
I'M DOING IT!
THUP
A MINOR STEP FOR MOST, BUT UNHEARD OF IN THE KASADERA FAMILY!

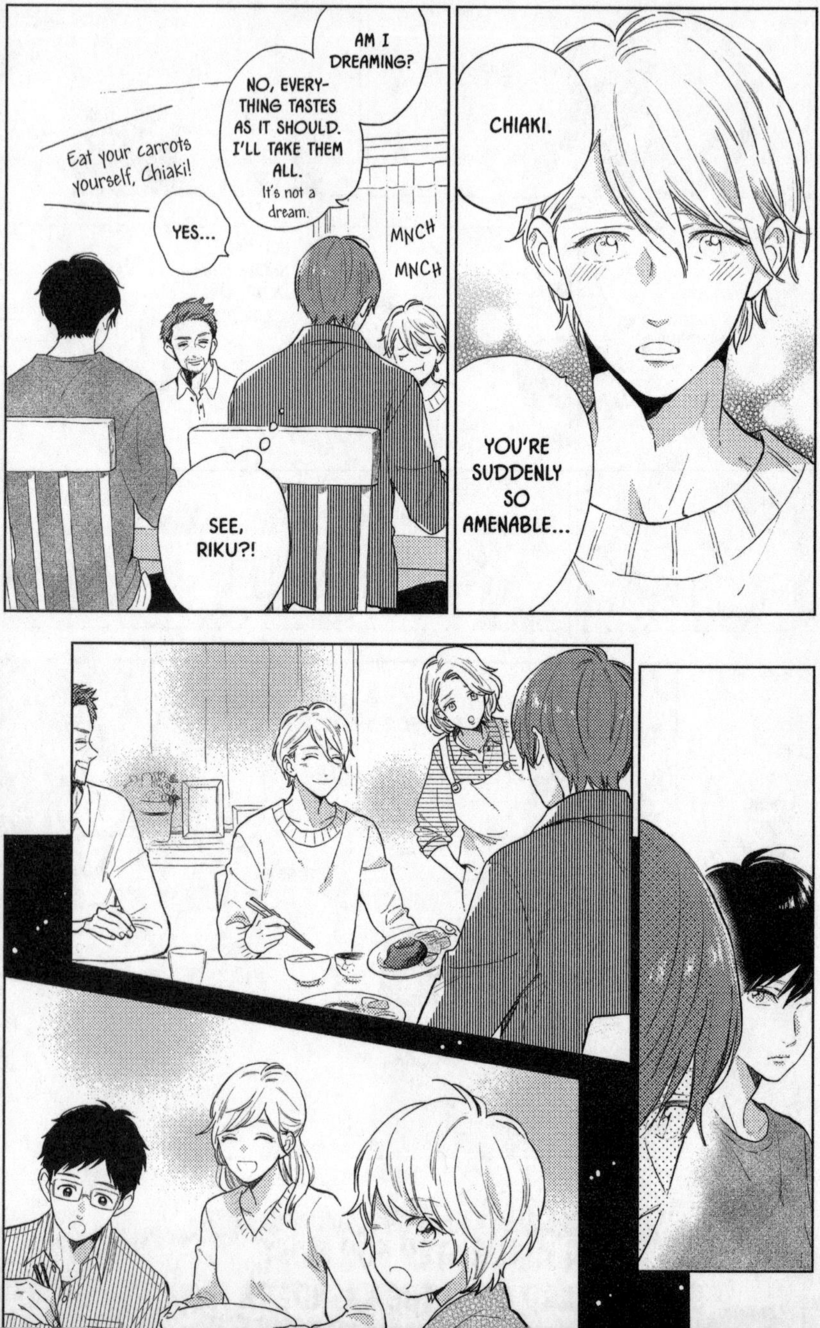
CHIAKI.
YOU'RE SUDDENLY SO AMENABLE...
AM I DREAMING?
NO, EVERY-THING TASTES AS IT SHOULD. I'LL TAKE THEM ALL.
It's not a dream.
MNCH MNCH
Eat your carrots yourself, Chiaki!
YES...
SEE, RIKU?!

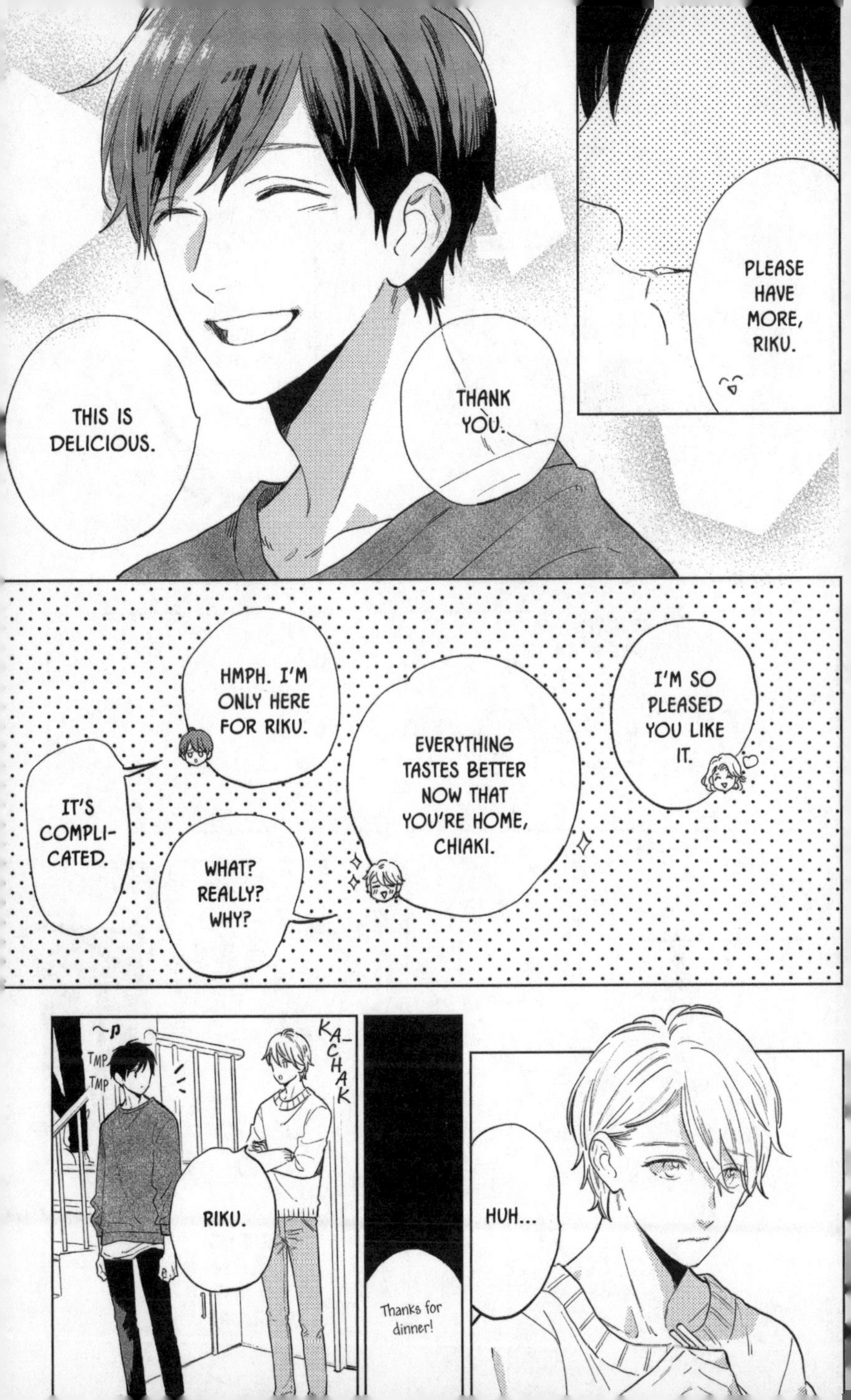
PLEASE HAVE MORE, RIKU.
THANK YOU.
THIS IS DELICIOUS.
I'M SO PLEASED YOU LIKE IT.
EVERYTHING TASTES BETTER NOW THAT YOU'RE HOME, CHIAKI.
HMPH. I'M ONLY HERE FOR RIKU.
WHAT? REALLY? WHY?
IT'S COMPLICATED.
HUH...
Thanks for dinner!
KACHAK
RIKU.
TMP TMP

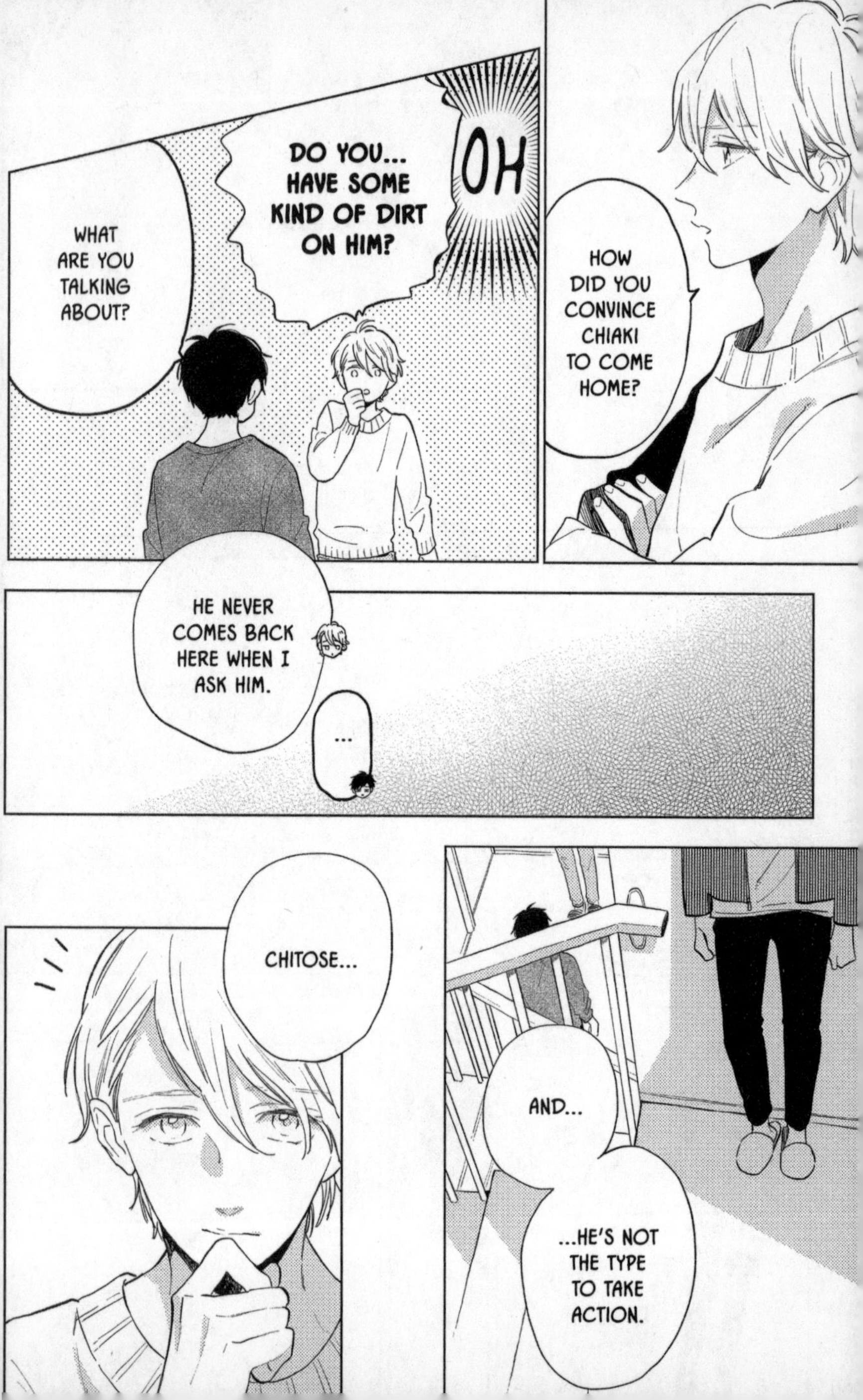
HOW DID YOU CONVINCE CHIAKI TO COME HOME?
OH
DO YOU... HAVE SOME KIND OF DIRT ON HIM?
WHAT ARE YOU TALKING ABOUT?
HE NEVER COMES BACK HERE WHEN I ASK HIM.
...
AND...
...HE'S NOT THE TYPE TO TAKE ACTION.
CHITOSE...

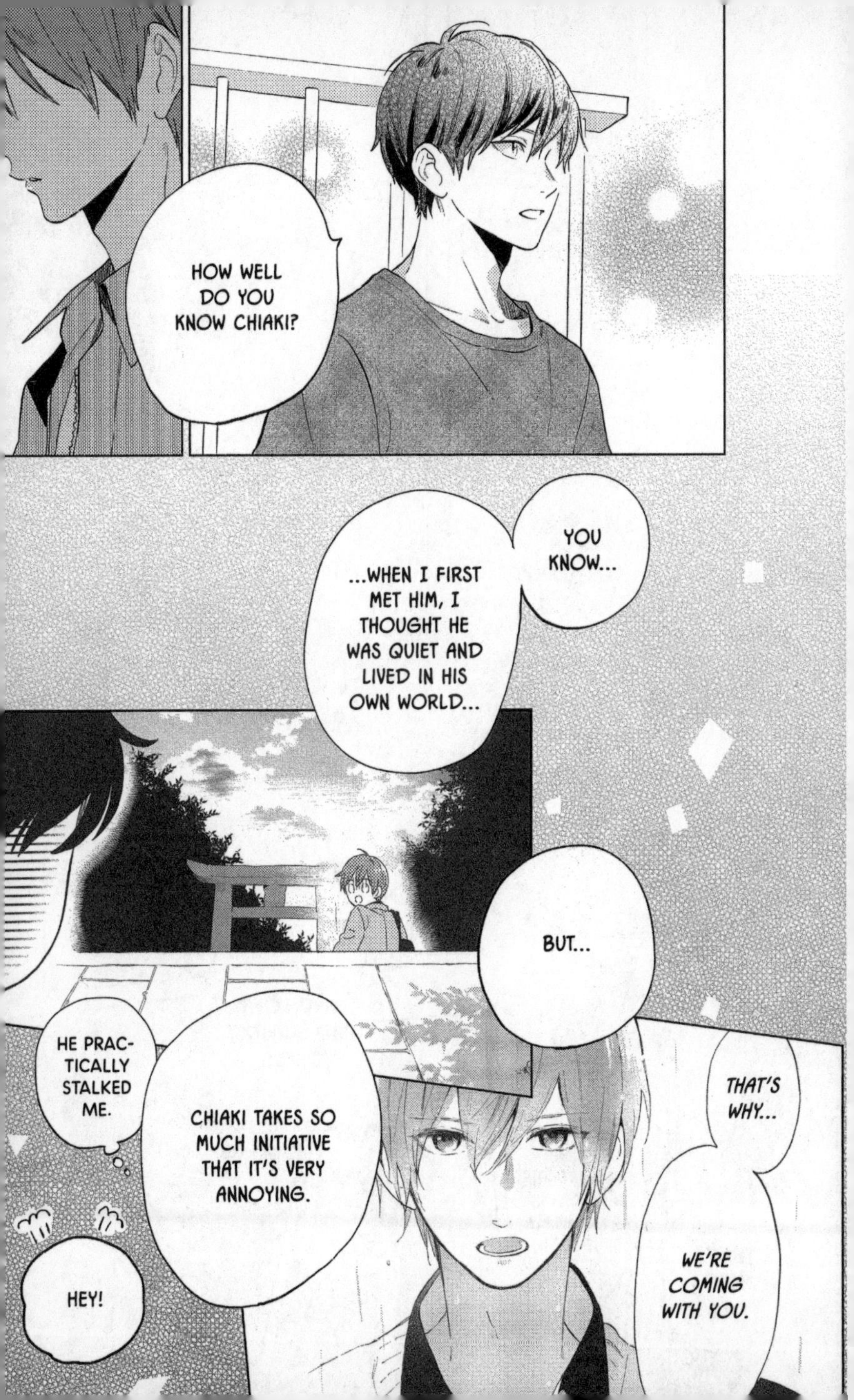
HOW WELL DO YOU KNOW CHIAKI?
YOU KNOW...
...WHEN I FIRST MET HIM, I THOUGHT HE WAS QUIET AND LIVED IN HIS OWN WORLD...
BUT...
CHIAKI TAKES SO MUCH INITIATIVE THAT IT'S VERY ANNOYING.
HE PRAC-TICALLY STALKED ME.
HEY!
THAT'S WHY...
WE'RE COMING WITH YOU.

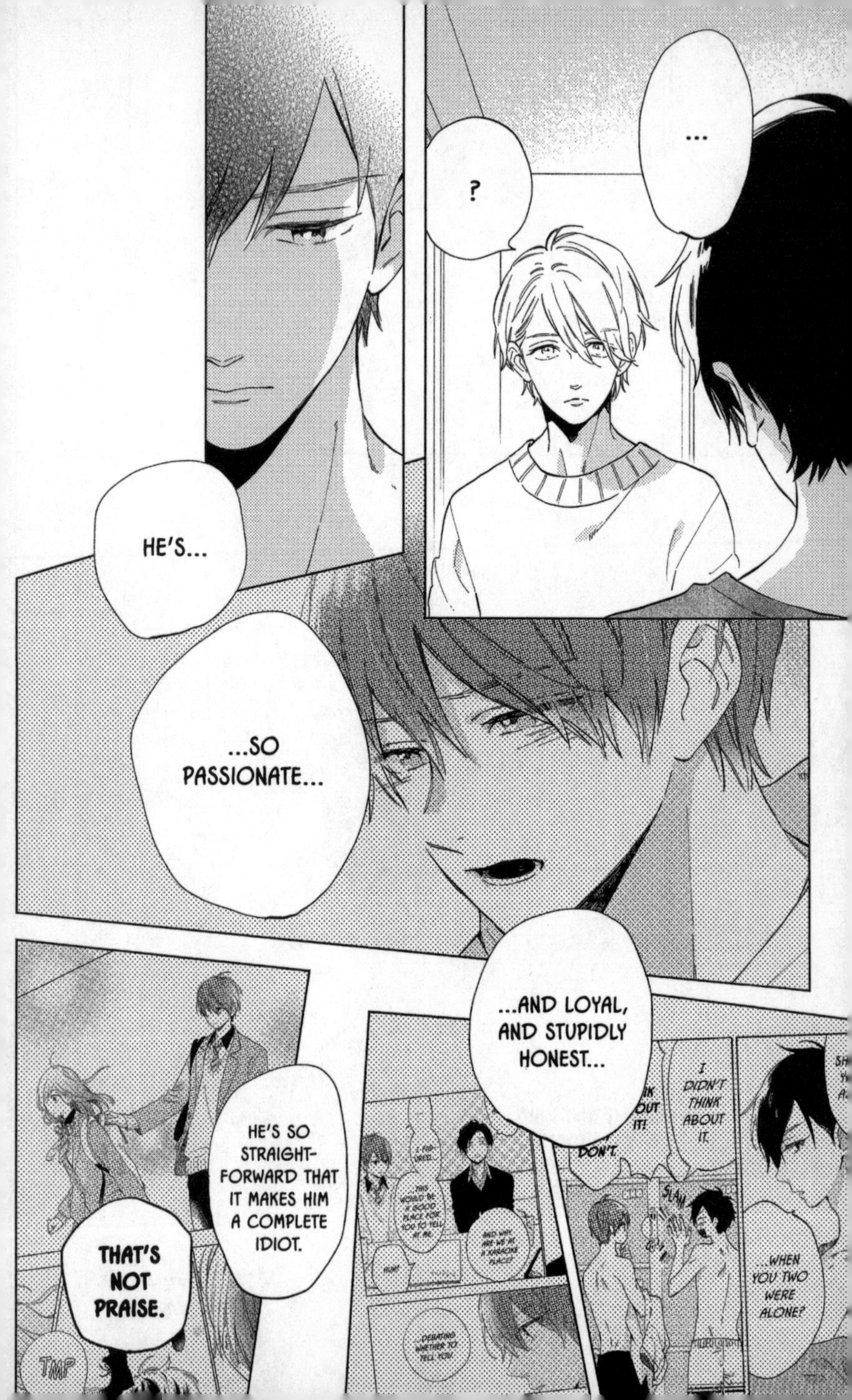
...
?
HE'S...
...SO PASSIONATE...
...AND LOYAL, AND STUPIDLY HONEST...
...WHEN YOU TWO WERE ALONE?
I DIDN'T THINK ABOUT IT.
DON'T.
SLAM
I FIGURED...
...THIS WOULD BE A GOOD PLACE FOR YOU TO YELL AT ME.
AND WHY ARE WE AT A KARAOKE PLACE?
...DEBATING WHETHER TO TELL YOU.
HE'S SO STRAIGHT-FORWARD THAT IT MAKES HIM A COMPLETE IDIOT.
THAT'S NOT PRAISE.
TMP

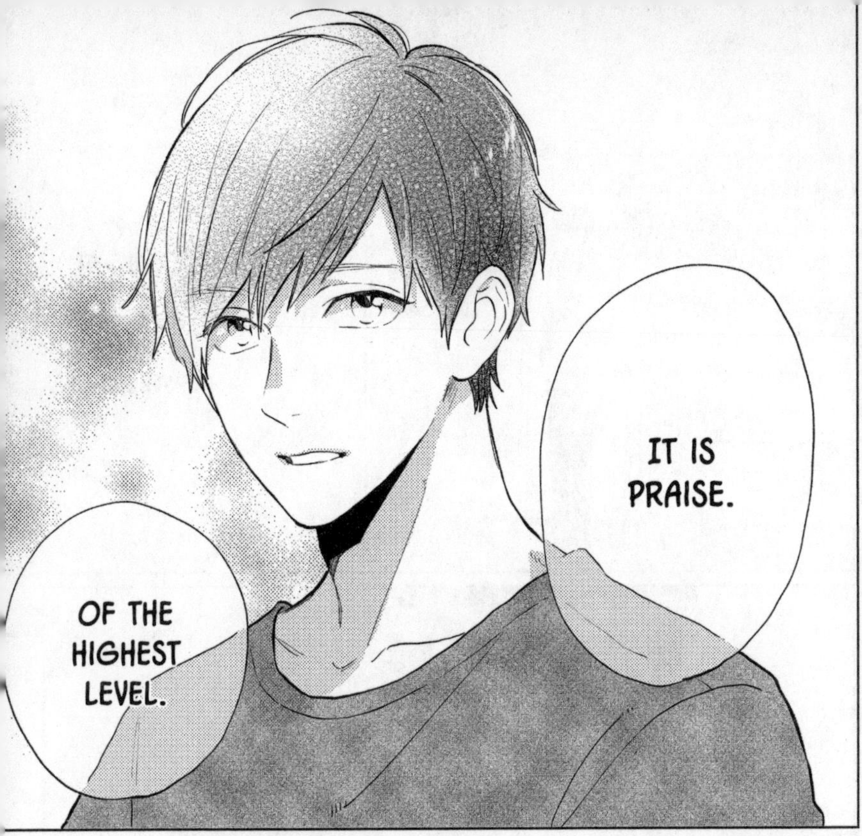
IT IS PRAISE.
OF THE HIGHEST LEVEL.
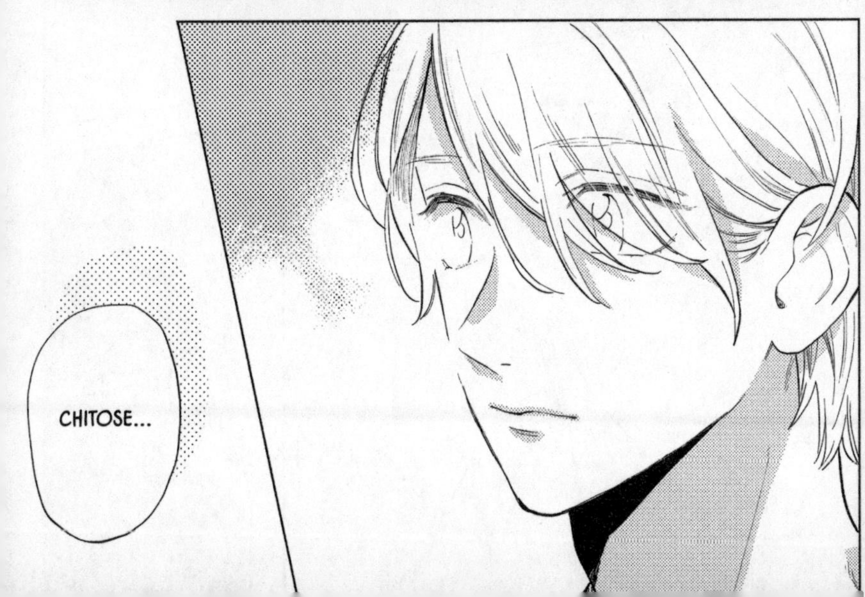
CHITOSE...

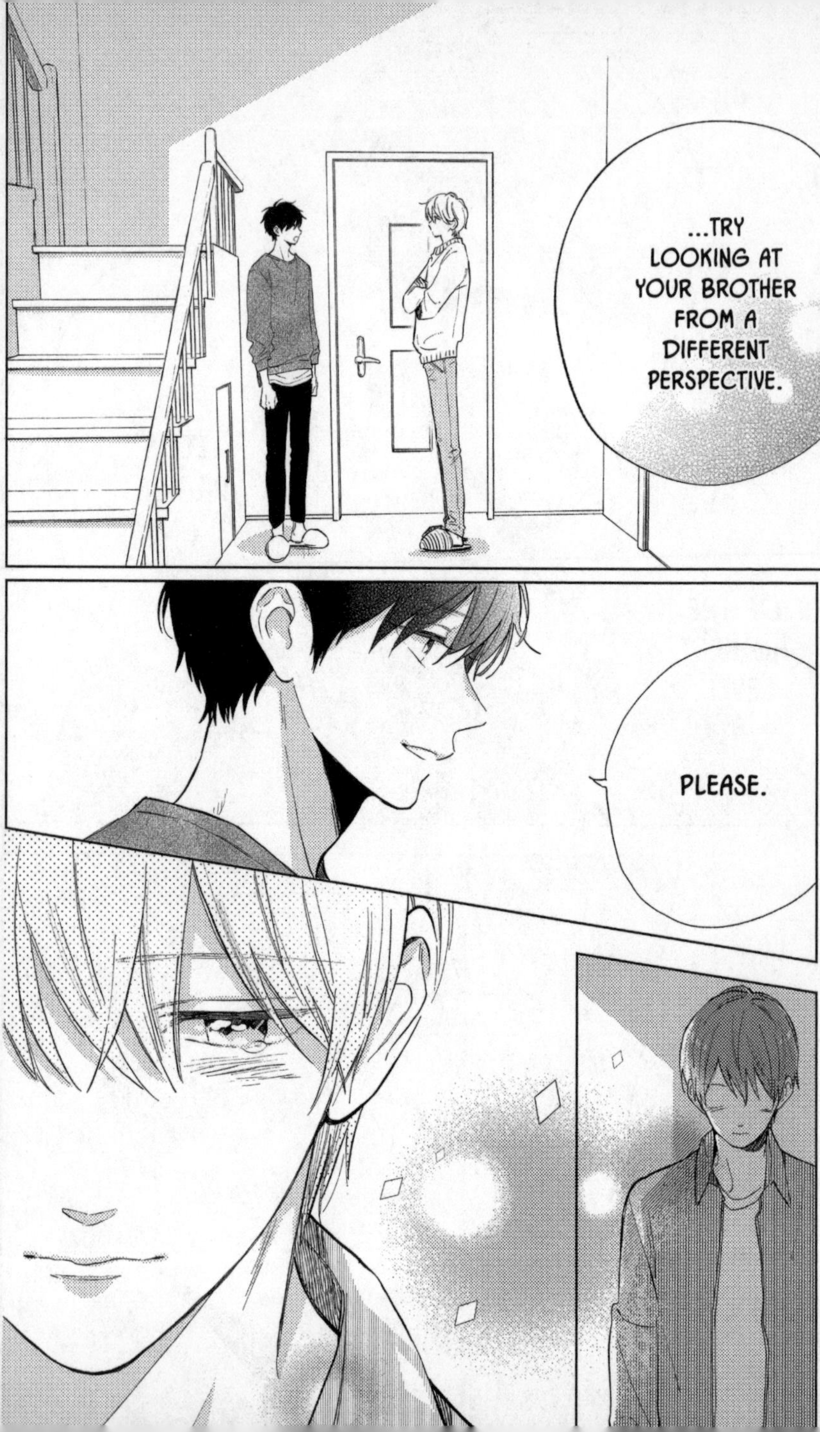
...TRY LOOKING AT YOUR BROTHER FROM A DIFFERENT PERSPECTIVE.
PLEASE.

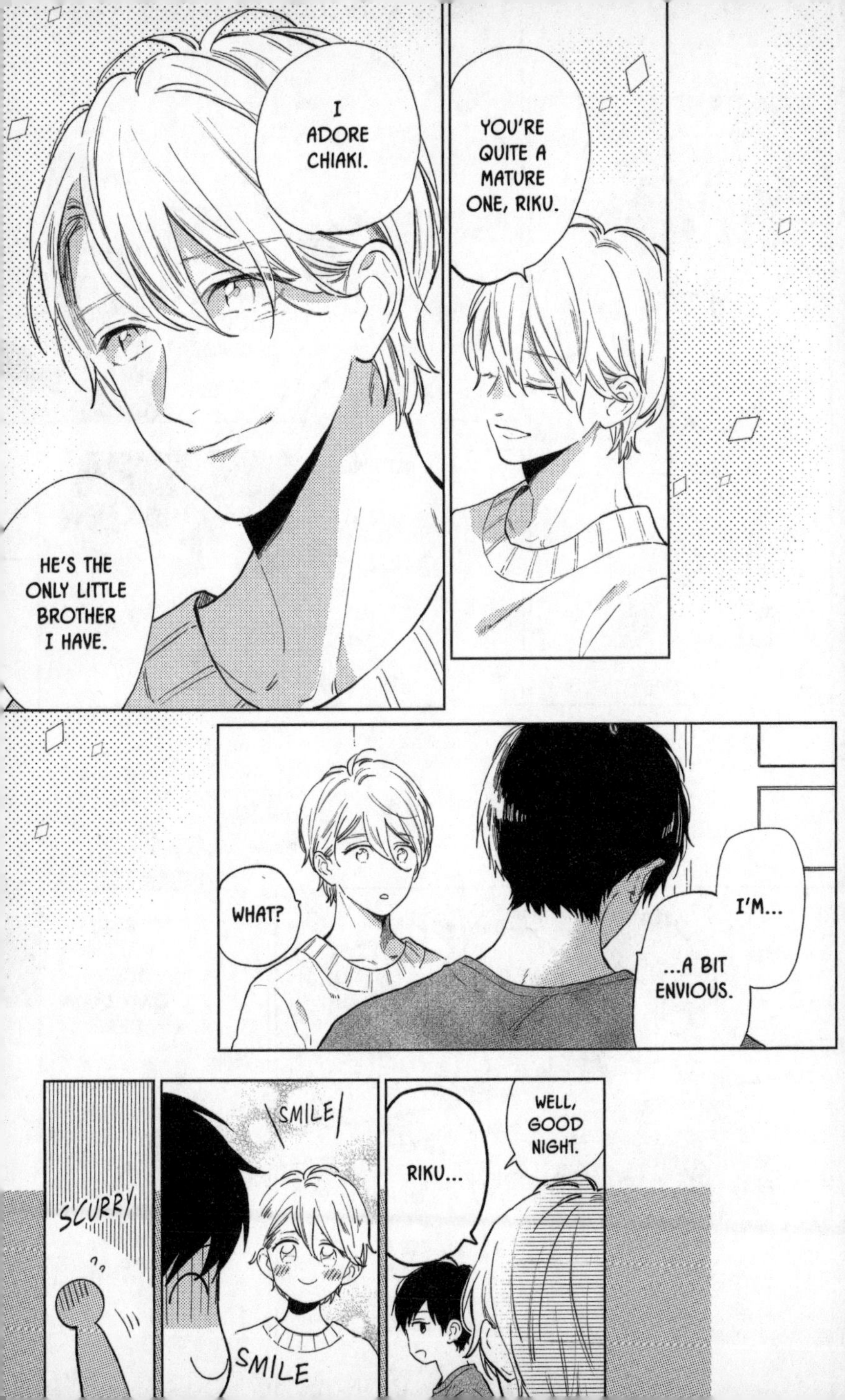
YOU'RE QUITE A MATURE ONE, RIKU.
I ADORE CHIAKI.
HE'S THE ONLY LITTLE BROTHER I HAVE.
I'M...
...A BIT ENVIOUS.
WHAT?
WELL, GOOD NIGHT.
RIKU...
SMILE
SMILE
SCURRY

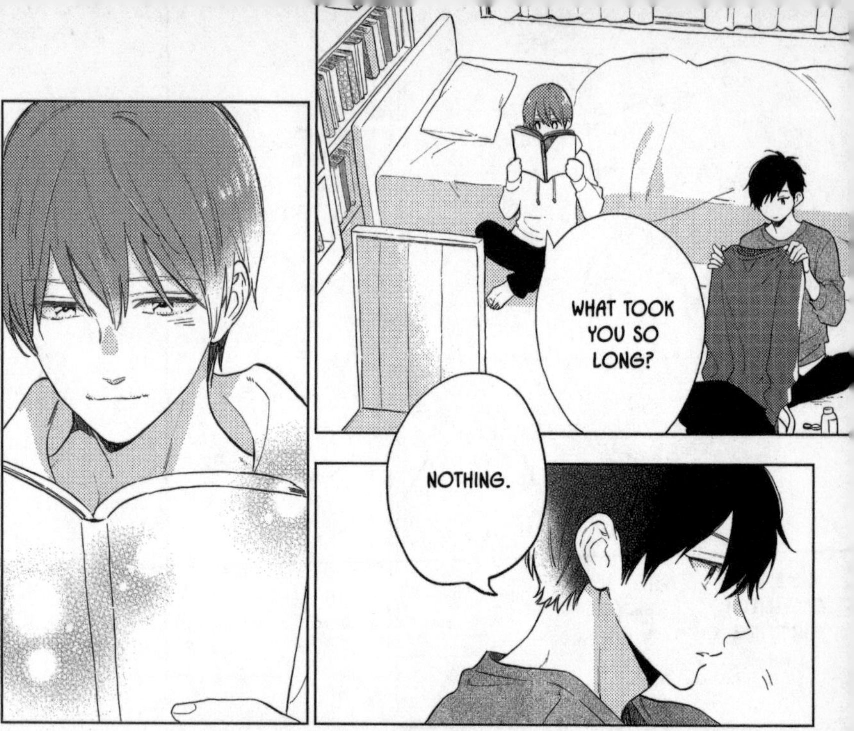
WHAT TOOK YOU SO LONG?
NOTHING.

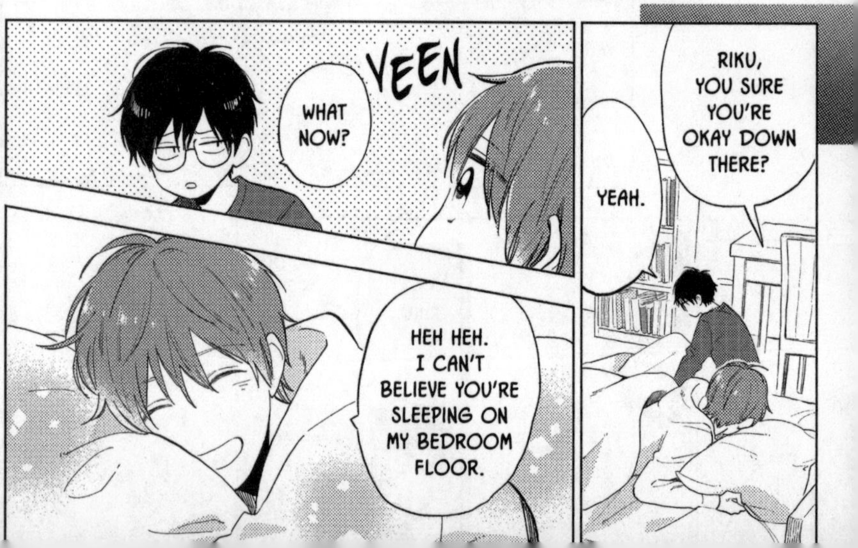
RIKU, YOU SURE YOU'RE OKAY DOWN THERE?
YEAH.
VEEN
WHAT NOW?
HEH HEH. I CAN'T BELIEVE YOU'RE SLEEPING ON MY BEDROOM FLOOR.

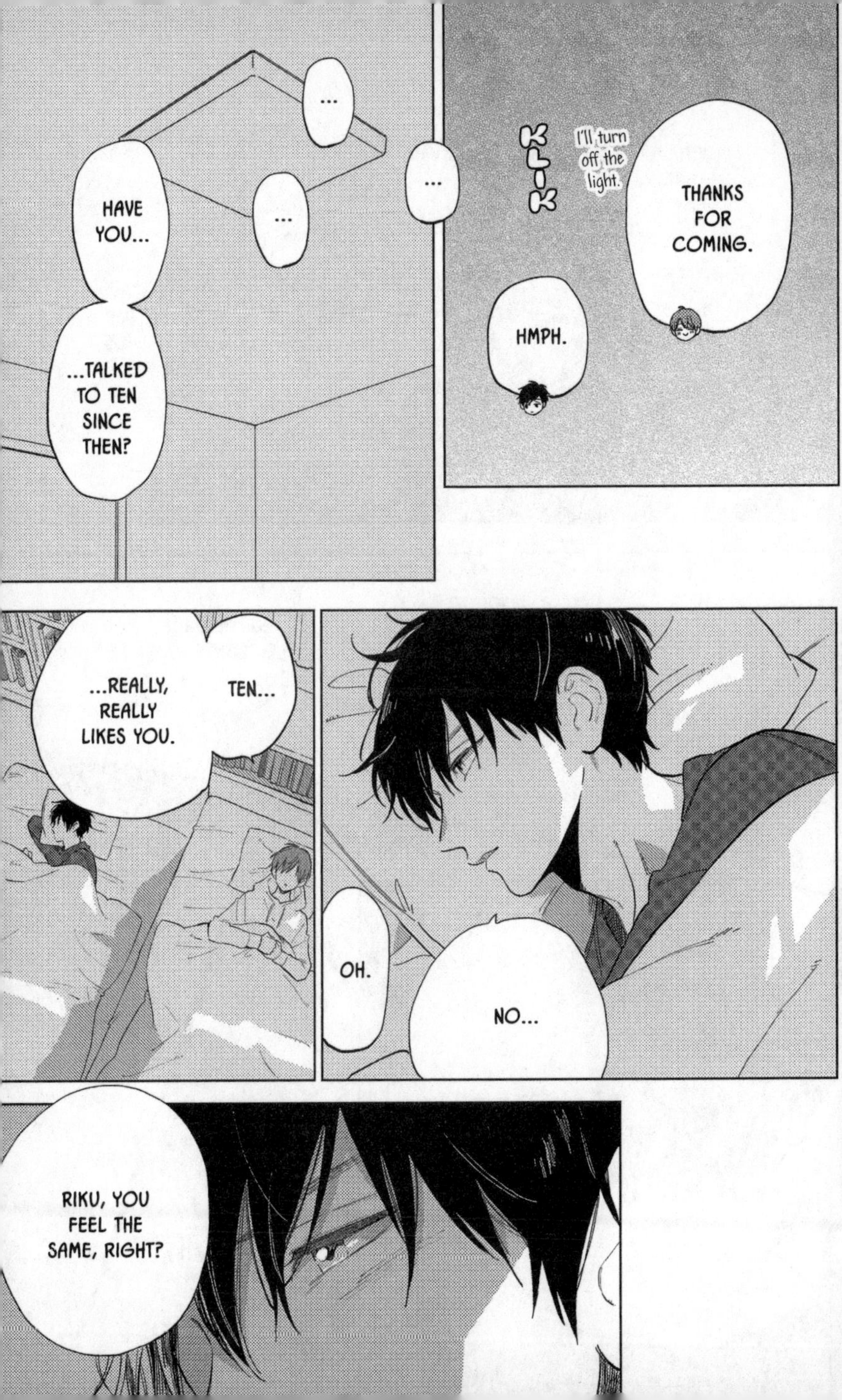
THANKS FOR COMING.
HMPH.
I'll turn off the light.
KLIK
...
...
...
HAVE YOU...
...TALKED TO TEN SINCE THEN?
NO...
OH.
TEN...
...REALLY, REALLY LIKES YOU.
RIKU, YOU FEEL THE SAME, RIGHT?

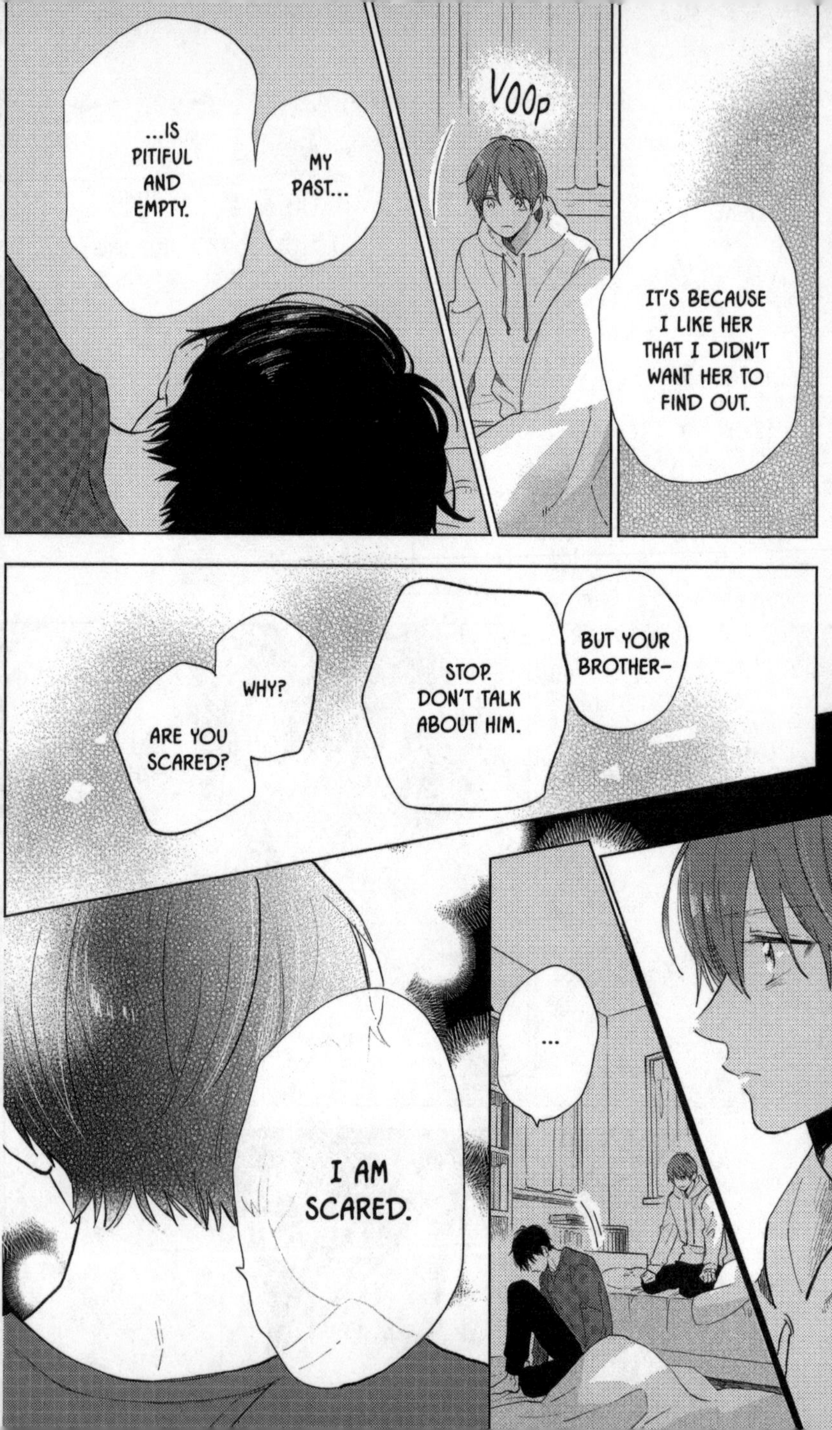
IT'S BECAUSE I LIKE HER THAT I DIDN'T WANT HER TO FIND OUT.
VOOp
MY PAST...
...IS PITIFUL AND EMPTY.
BUT YOUR BROTHER—
STOP. DON'T TALK ABOUT HIM.
WHY?
ARE YOU SCARED?
...
I AM SCARED.

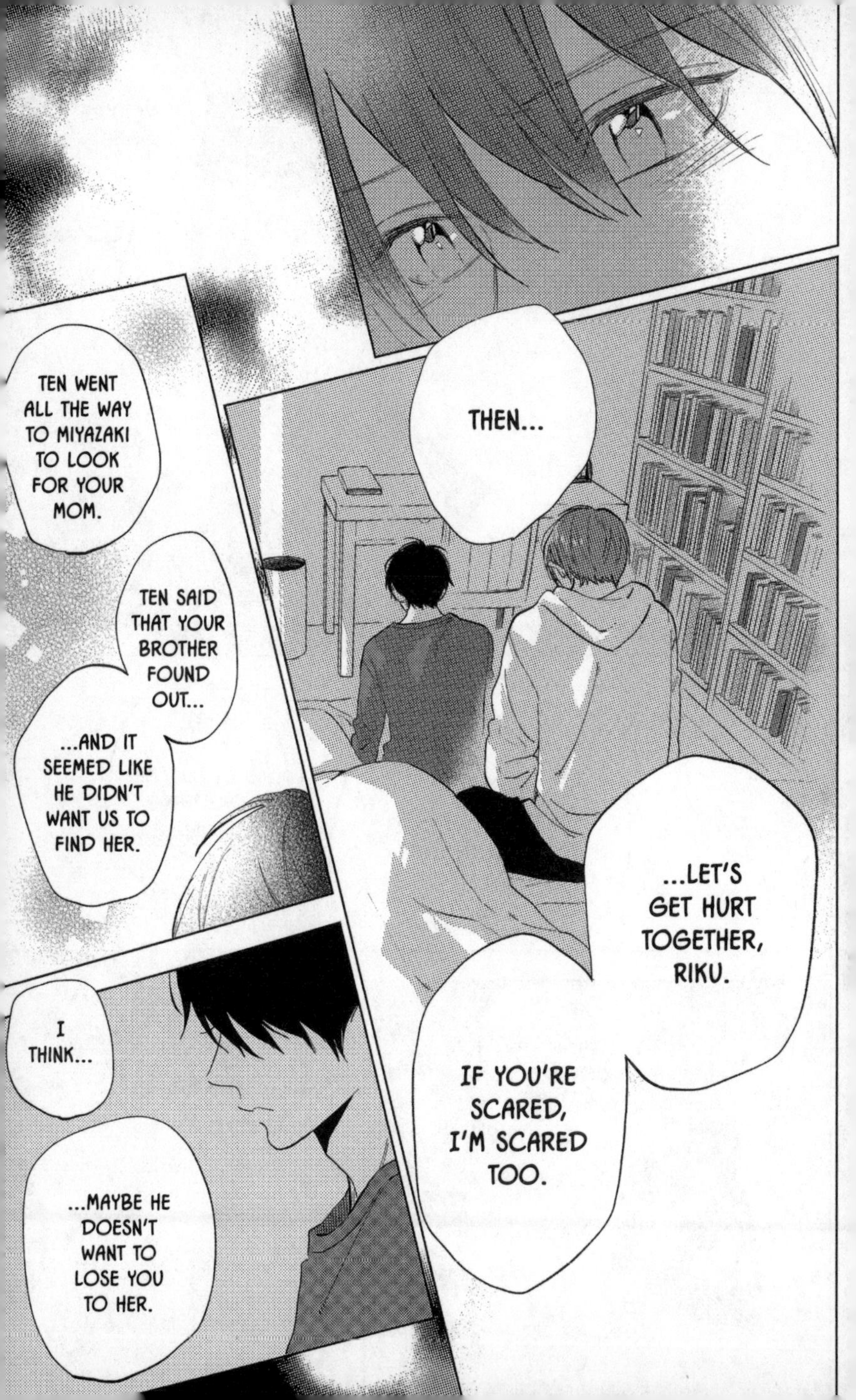
THEN...
...LET'S GET HURT TOGETHER, RIKU.
IF YOU'RE SCARED, I'M SCARED TOO.
TEN WENT ALL THE WAY TO MIYAZAKI TO LOOK FOR YOUR MOM.
TEN SAID THAT YOUR BROTHER FOUND OUT...
...AND IT SEEMED LIKE HE DIDN'T WANT US TO FIND HER.
I THINK...
...MAYBE HE DOESN'T WANT TO LOSE YOU TO HER.

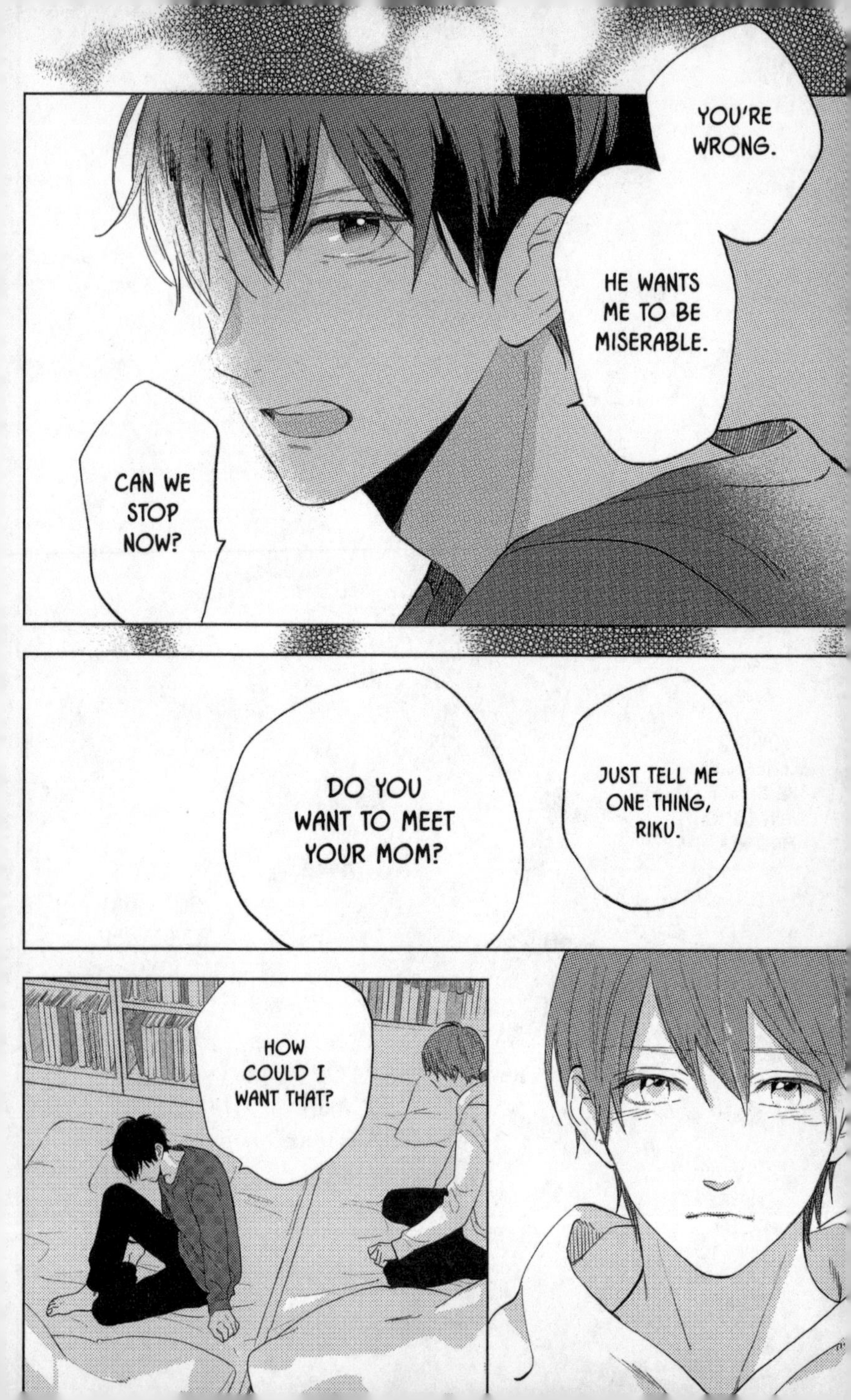
YOU'RE WRONG.
HE WANTS ME TO BE MISERABLE.
CAN WE STOP NOW?
JUST TELL ME ONE THING, RIKU.
DO YOU WANT TO MEET YOUR MOM?
HOW COULD I WANT THAT?

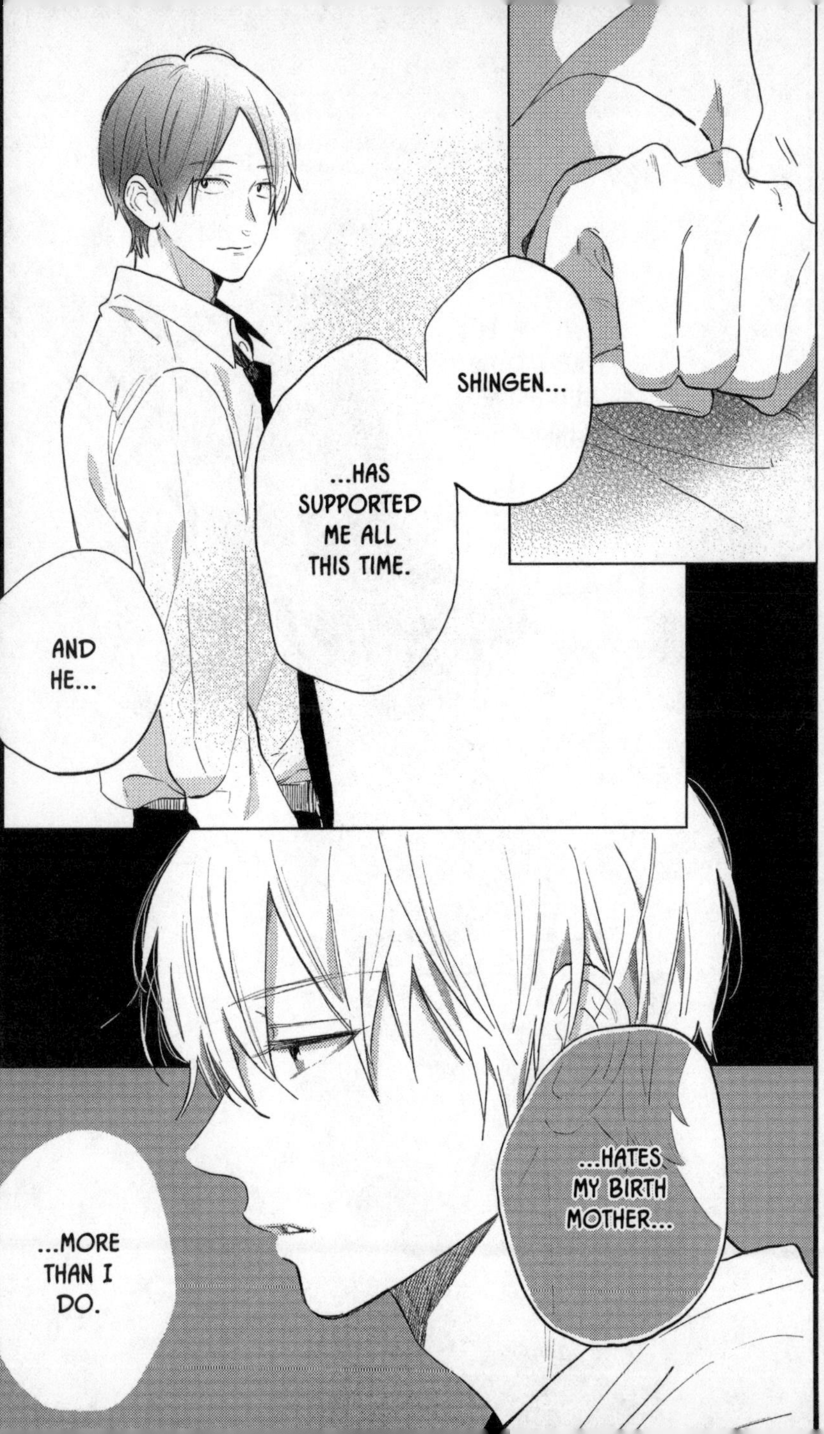
SHINGEN...
...HAS SUPPORTED ME ALL THIS TIME.
AND HE...
...HATES MY BIRTH MOTHER...
...MORE THAN I DO.

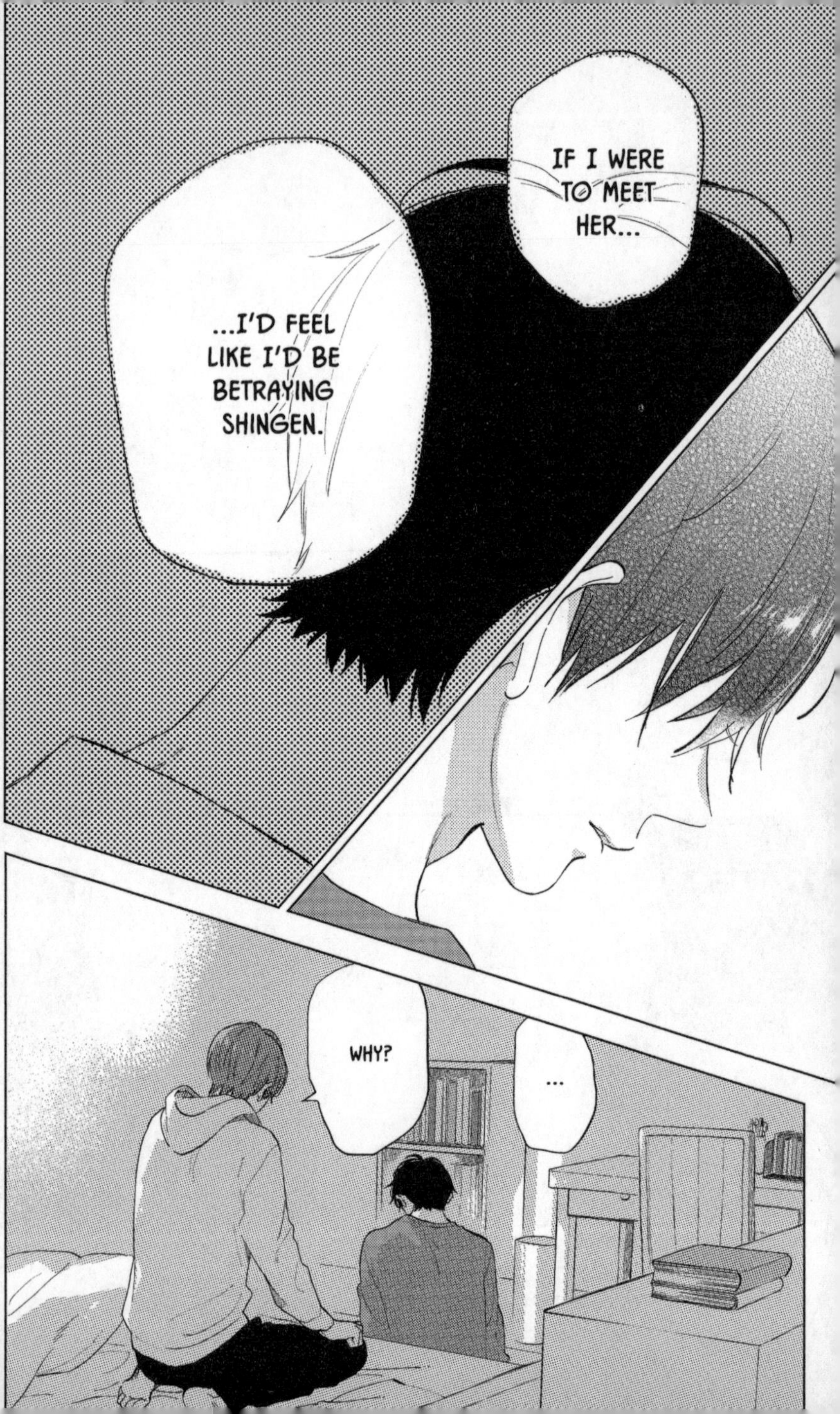
IF I WERE TO MEET HER...
...I'D FEEL LIKE I'D BE BETRAYING SHINGEN.
...
WHY?

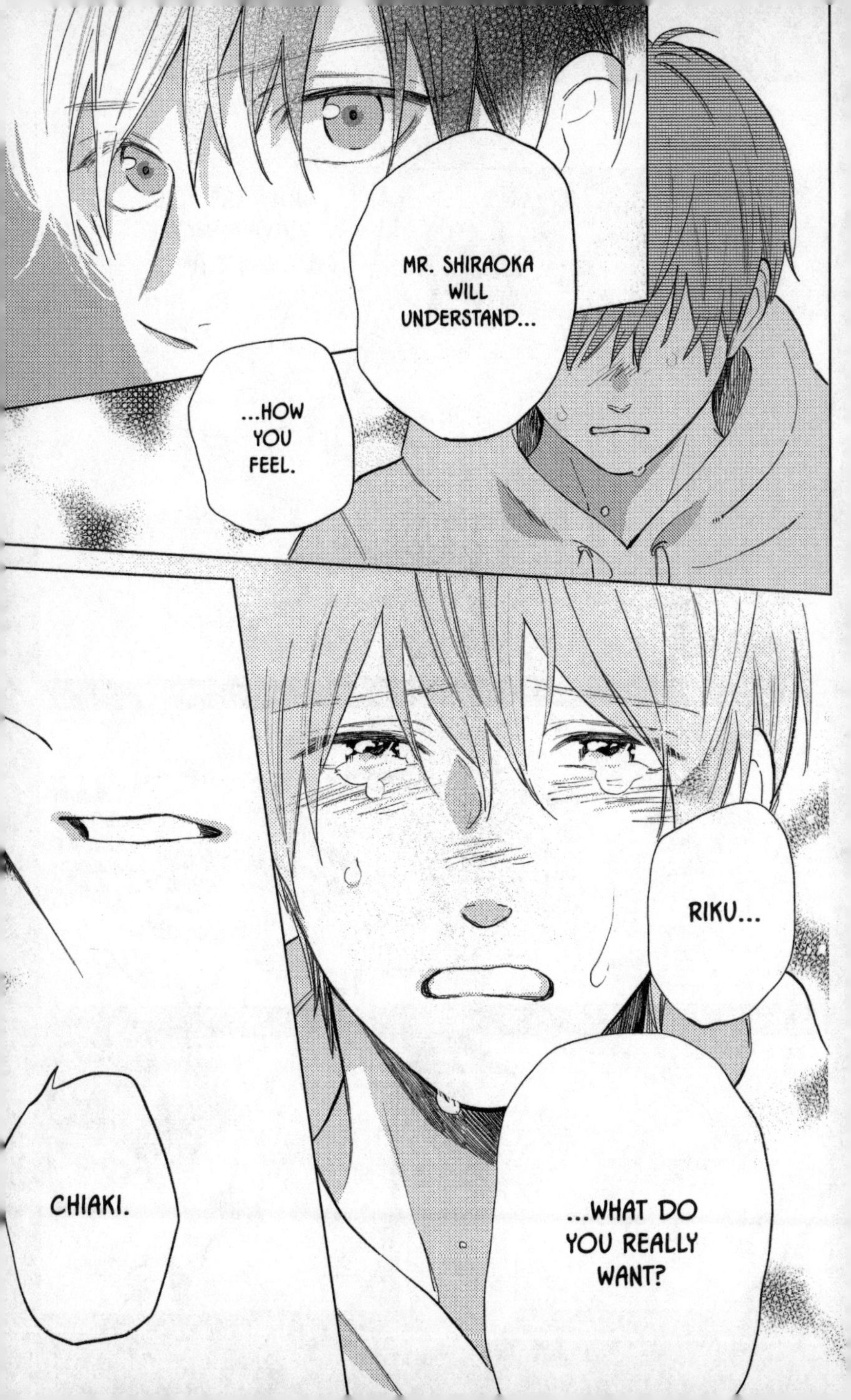
MR. SHIRAOKA WILL UNDERSTAND...
...HOW YOU FEEL.
RIKU...
...WHAT DO YOU REALLY WANT?
CHIAKI.

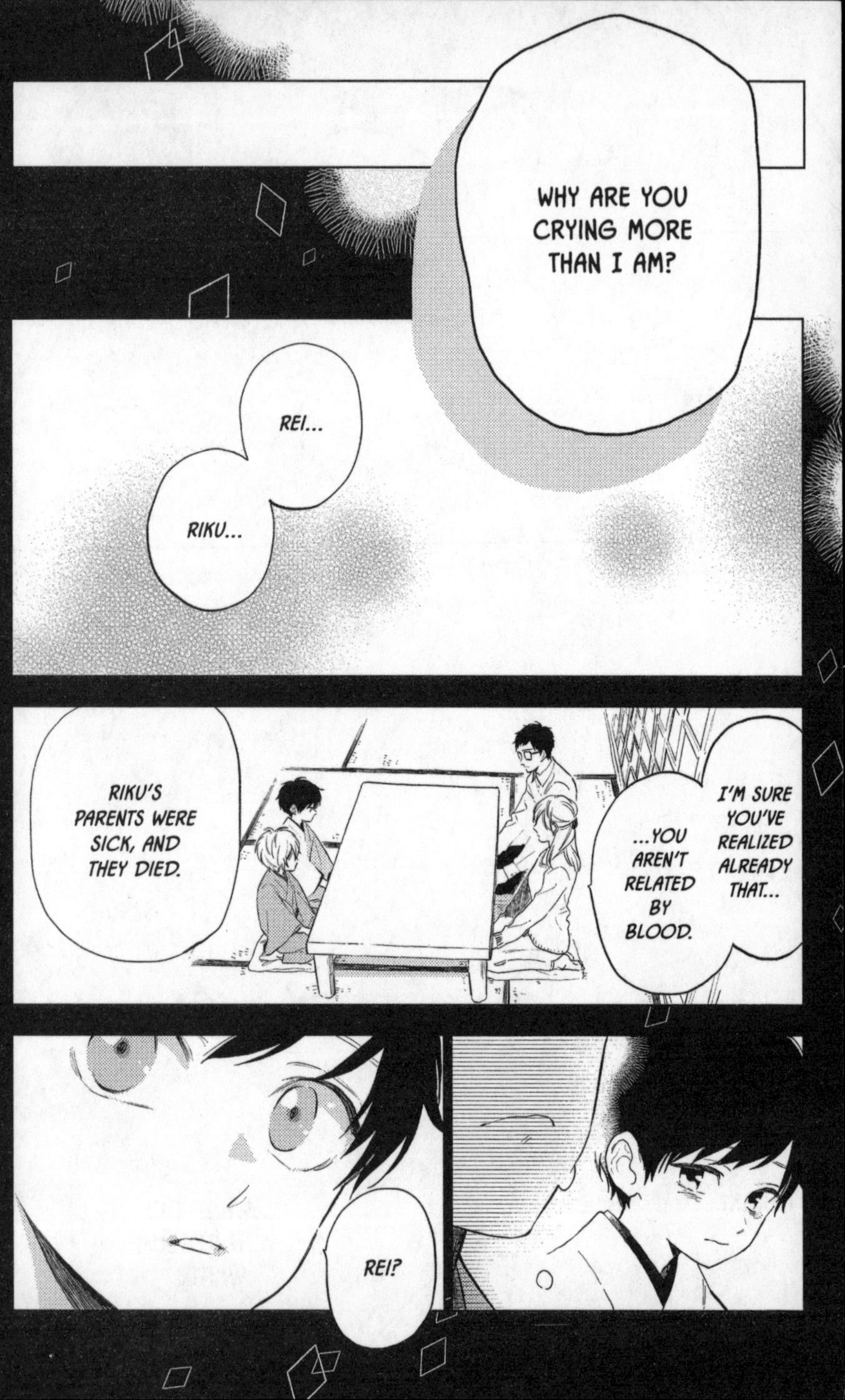
WHY ARE YOU CRYING MORE THAN I AM?
REI...
RIKU...
I'M SURE YOU'VE REALIZED ALREADY THAT...
...YOU AREN'T RELATED BY BLOOD.
RIKU'S PARENTS WERE SICK, AND THEY DIED.
REI?

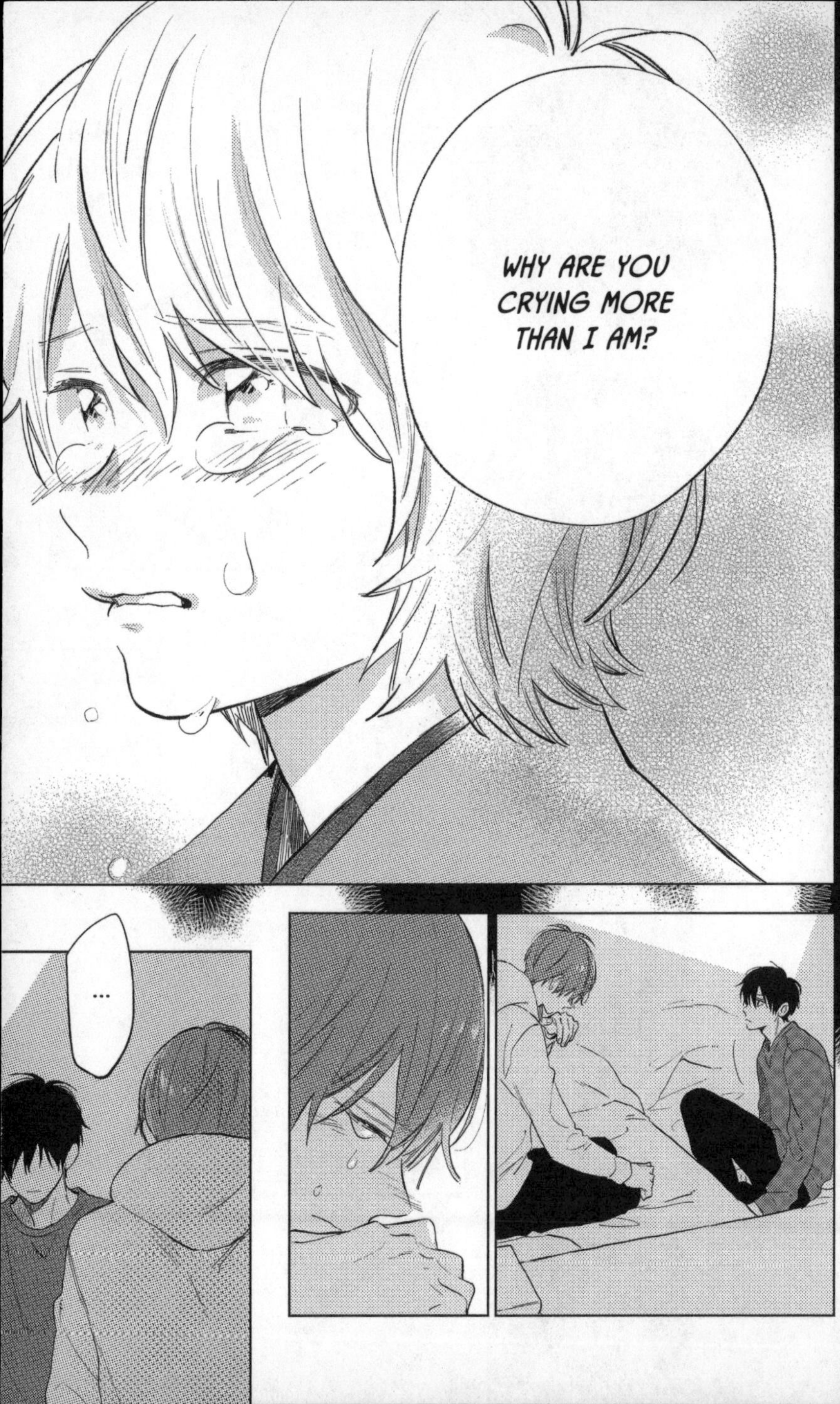
WHY ARE YOU CRYING MORE THAN I AM?
...

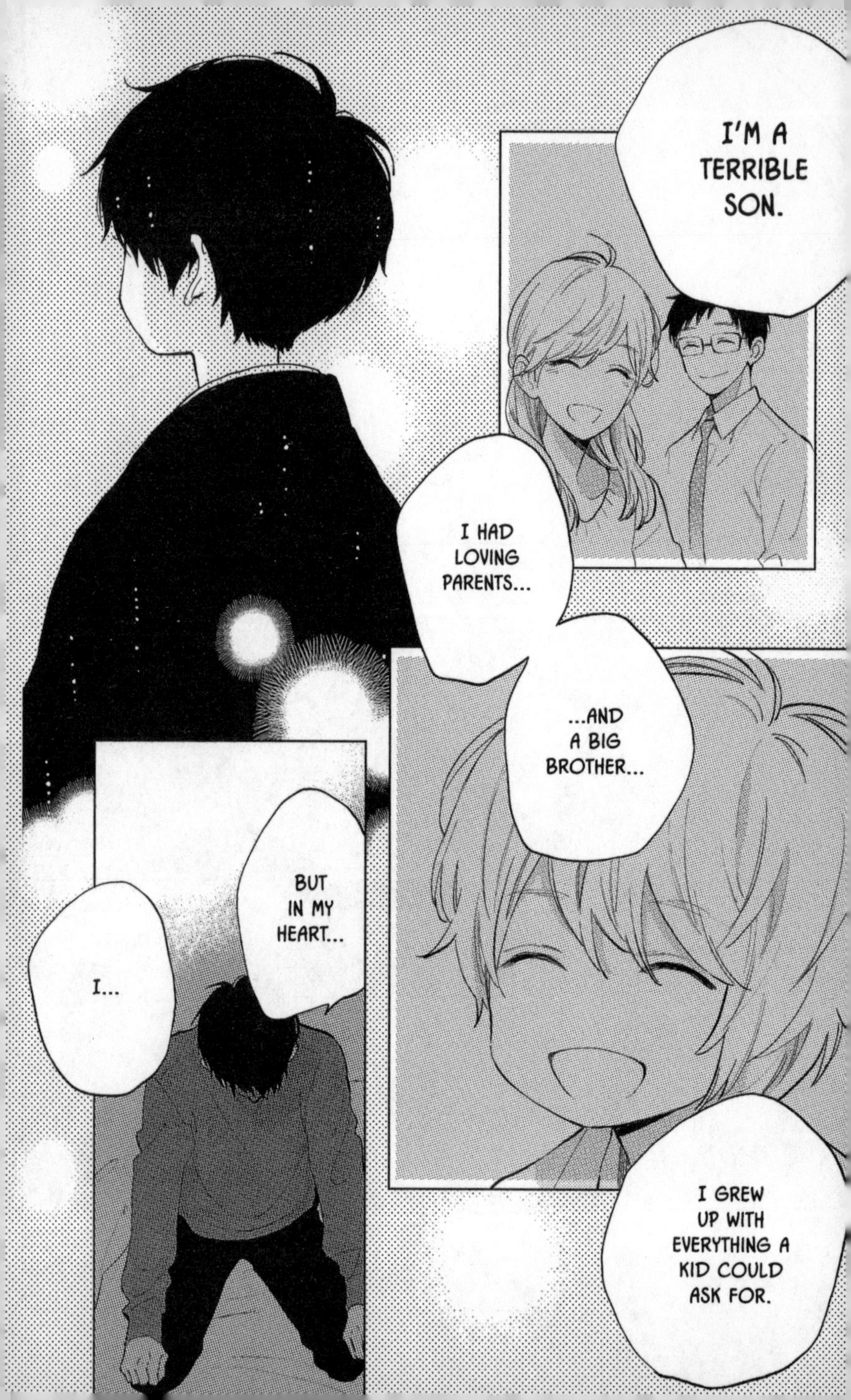
I'M A TERRIBLE SON.
I HAD LOVING PARENTS...
...AND A BIG BROTHER...
I GREW UP WITH EVERYTHING A KID COULD ASK FOR.
BUT IN MY HEART...
I...

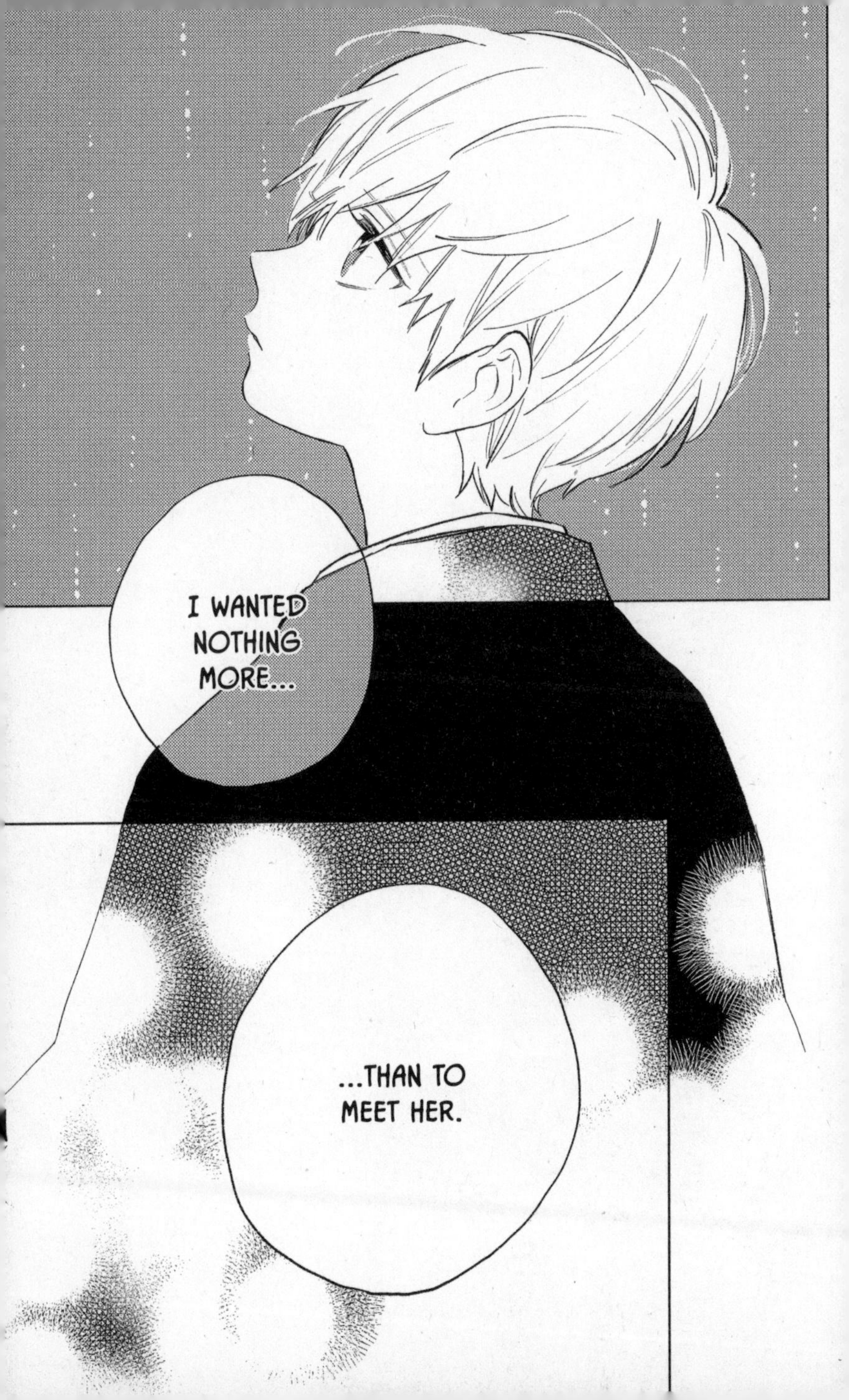
I WANTED NOTHING MORE...
...THAN TO MEET HER.

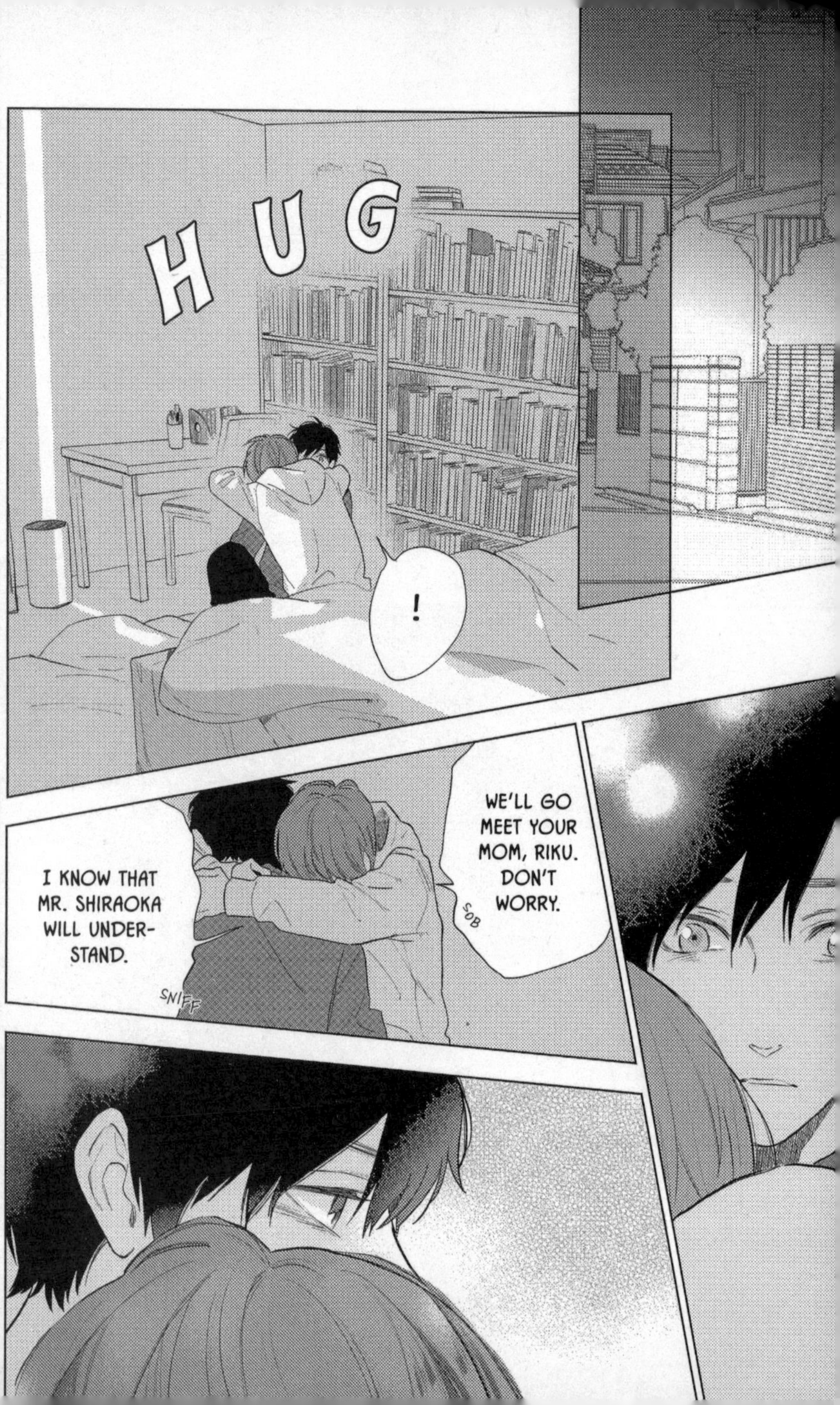
HUG
!
WE'LL GO MEET YOUR MOM, RIKU. DON'T WORRY.
SOB
I KNOW THAT MR. SHIRAOKA WILL UNDERSTAND.
SNIFF

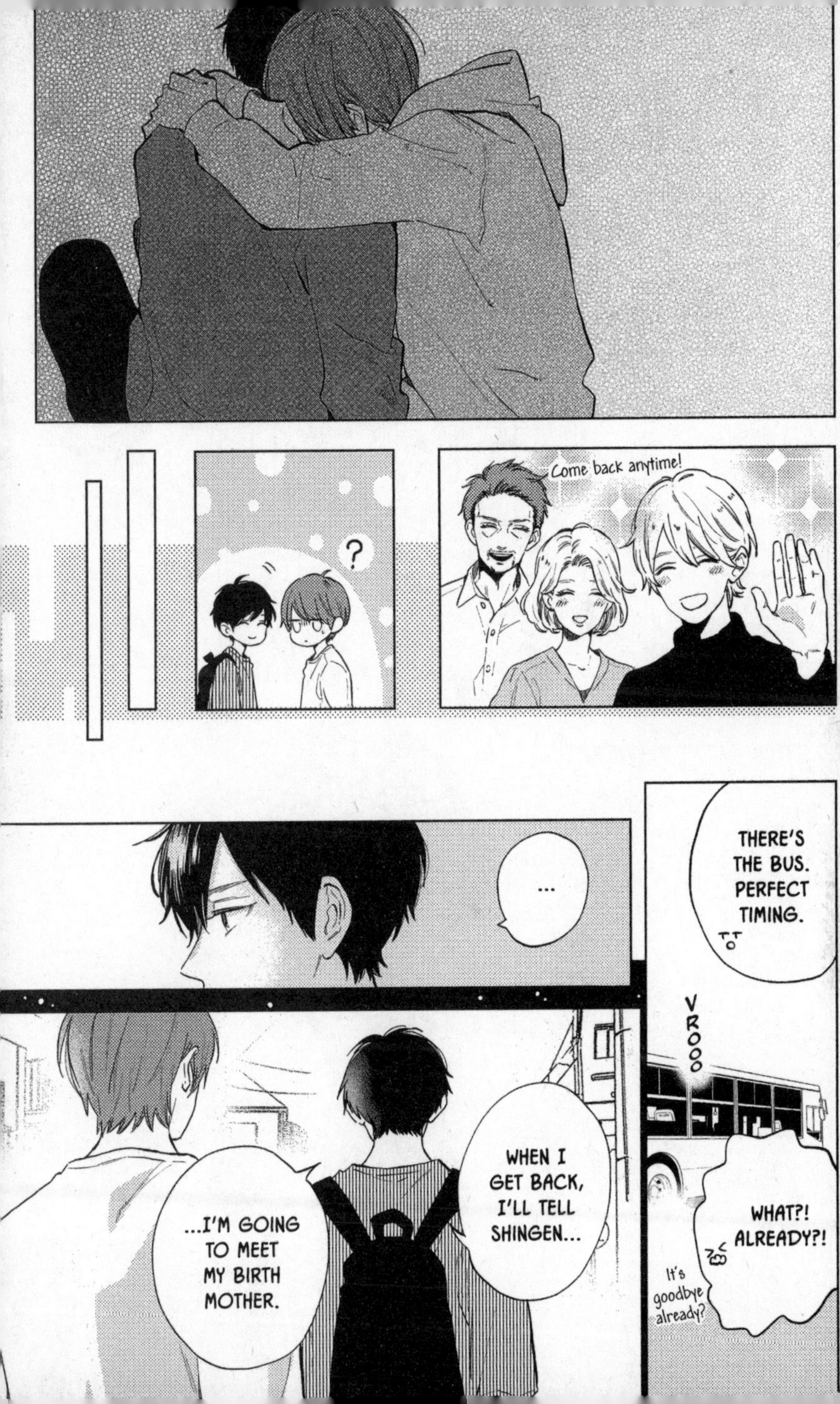
Come back anytime!
?
THERE'S THE BUS. PERFECT TIMING.
...
VROOO
WHAT?! ALREADY?!
It's goodbye already?
WHEN I GET BACK, I'LL TELL SHINGEN...
...I'M GOING TO MEET MY BIRTH MOTHER.

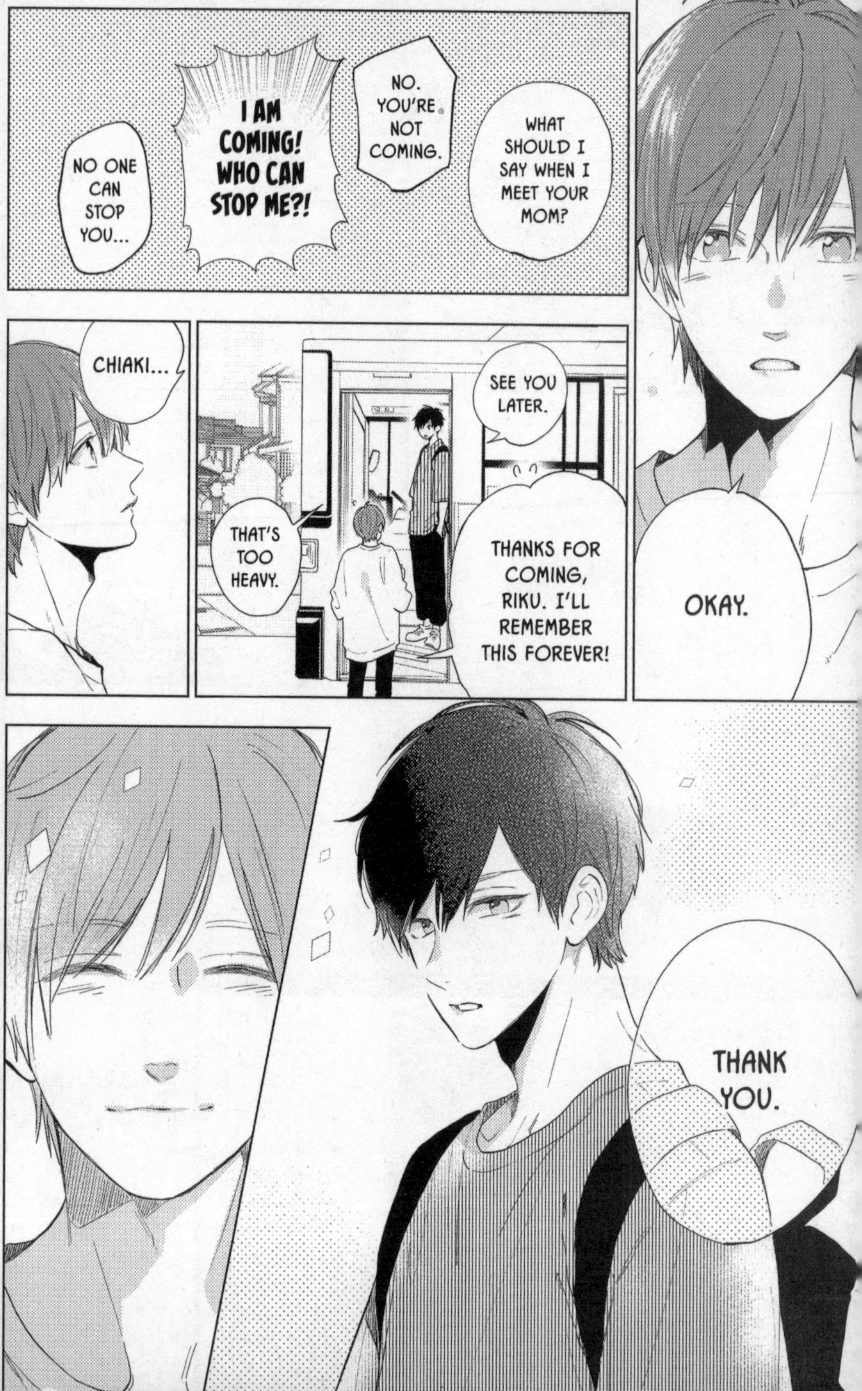
OKAY.
WHAT SHOULD I SAY WHEN I MEET YOUR MOM?
NO. YOU'RE NOT COMING.
I AM COMING! WHO CAN STOP ME?!
NO ONE CAN STOP YOU...
THANKS FOR COMING, RIKU. I'LL REMEMBER THIS FOREVER!
SEE YOU LATER.
THAT'S TOO HEAVY.
CHIAKI...
THANK YOU.

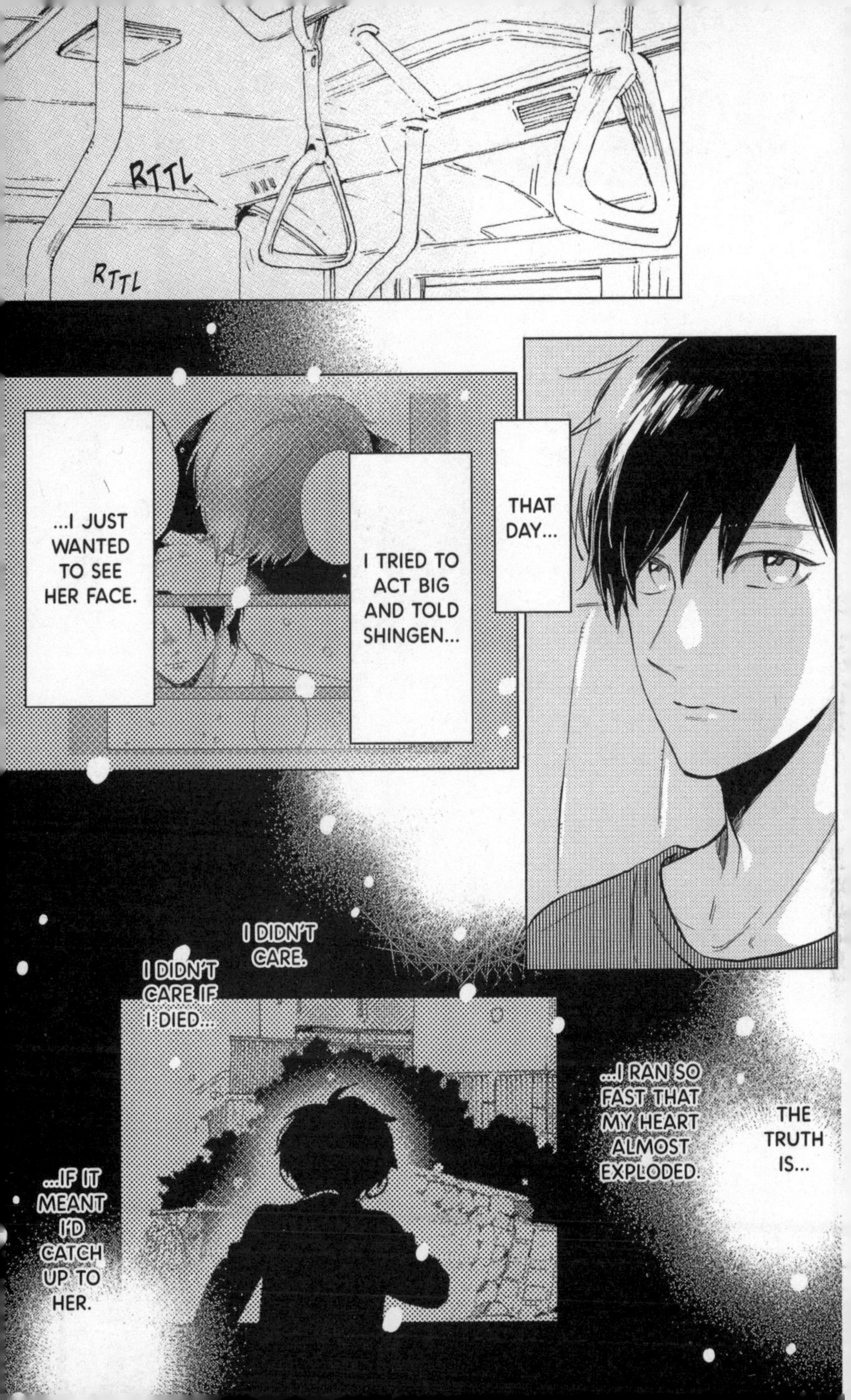
RTTL
RTTL
THAT DAY...
I TRIED TO ACT BIG AND TOLD SHINGEN...
...I JUST WANTED TO SEE HER FACE.
THE TRUTH IS...
...I RAN SO FAST THAT MY HEART ALMOST EXPLODED.
I DIDN'T CARE.
I DIDN'T CARE IF I DIED...
...IF IT MEANT I'D CATCH UP TO HER.

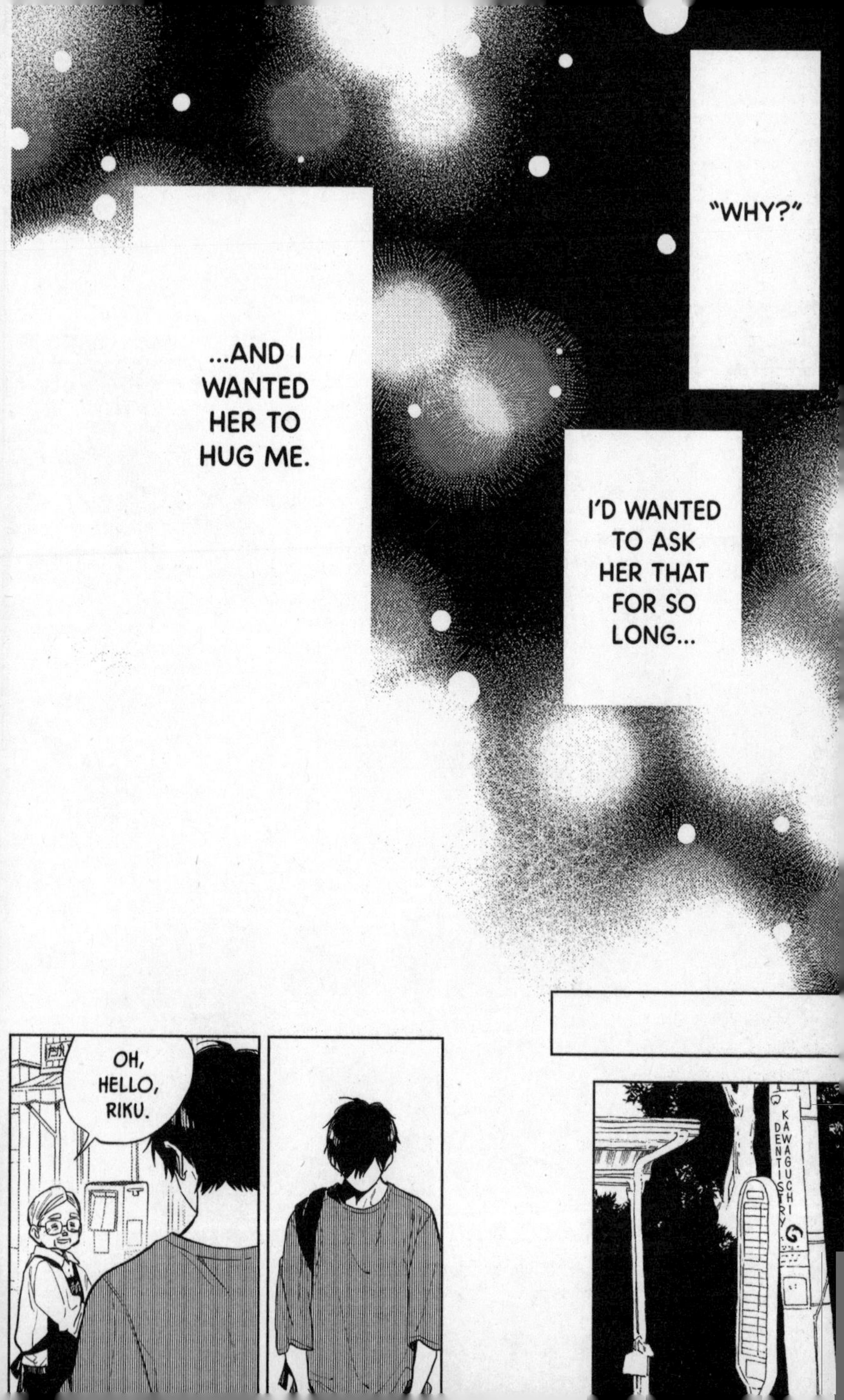
"WHY?"
I'D WANTED TO ASK HER THAT FOR SO LONG...
...AND I WANTED HER TO HUG ME.
KAWAGUCHI
DENTISTRY
OH, HELLO, RIKU.

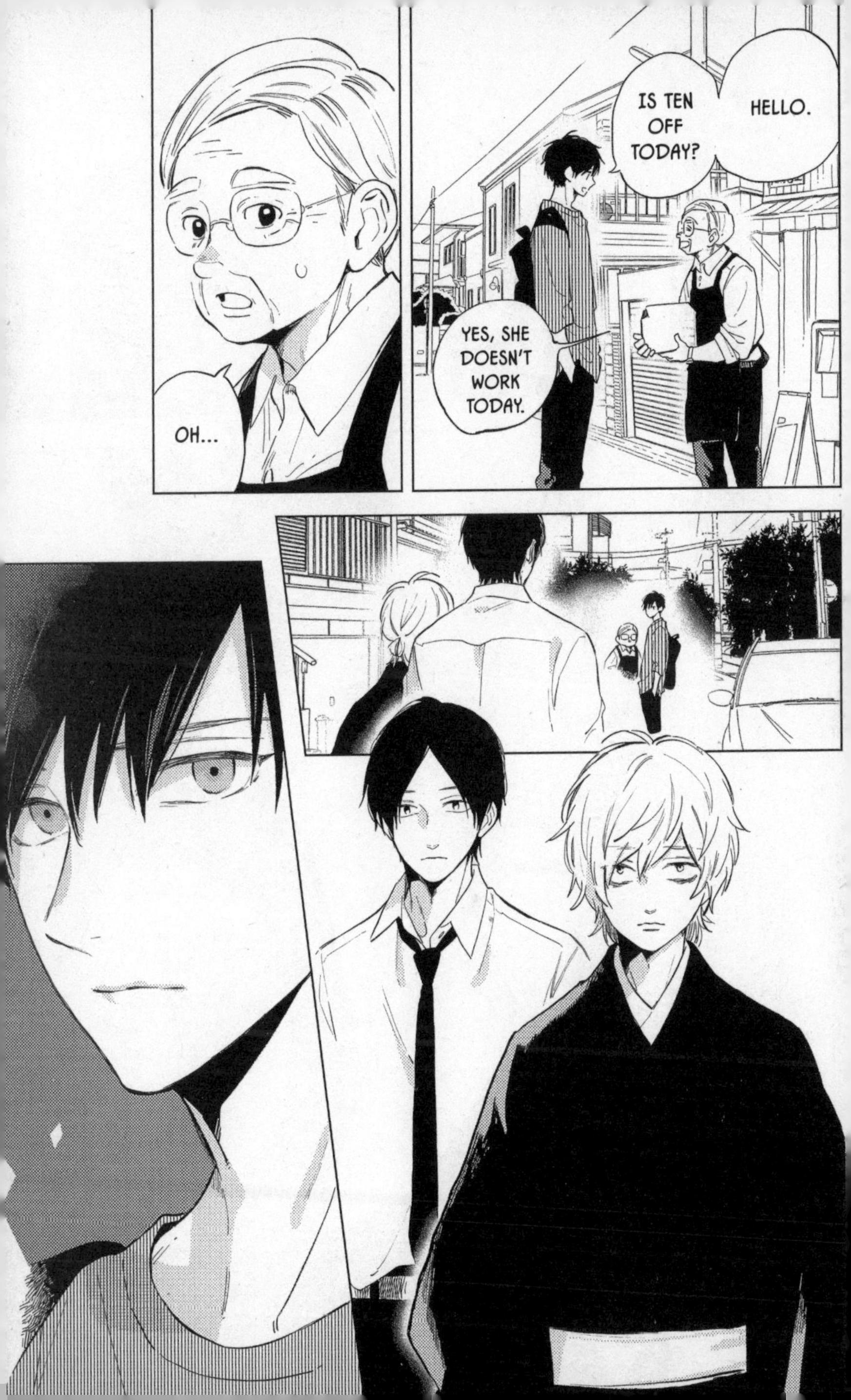
HELLO.
IS TEN OFF TODAY?
YES, SHE DOESN'T WORK TODAY.
OH...

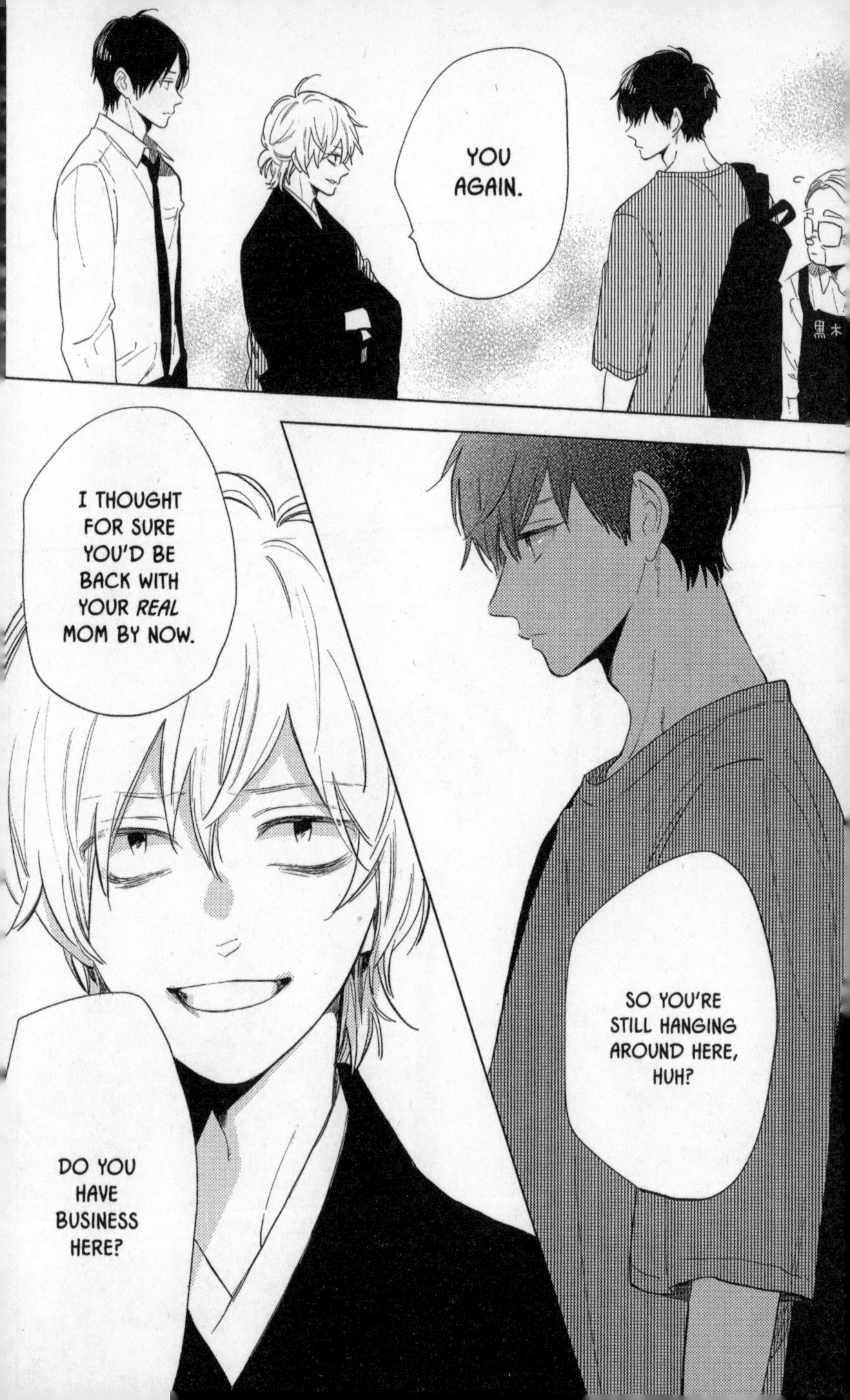
YOU AGAIN.
SO YOU'RE STILL HANGING AROUND HERE, HUH?
I THOUGHT FOR SURE YOU'D BE BACK WITH YOUR *REAL* MOM BY NOW.
DO YOU HAVE BUSINESS HERE?

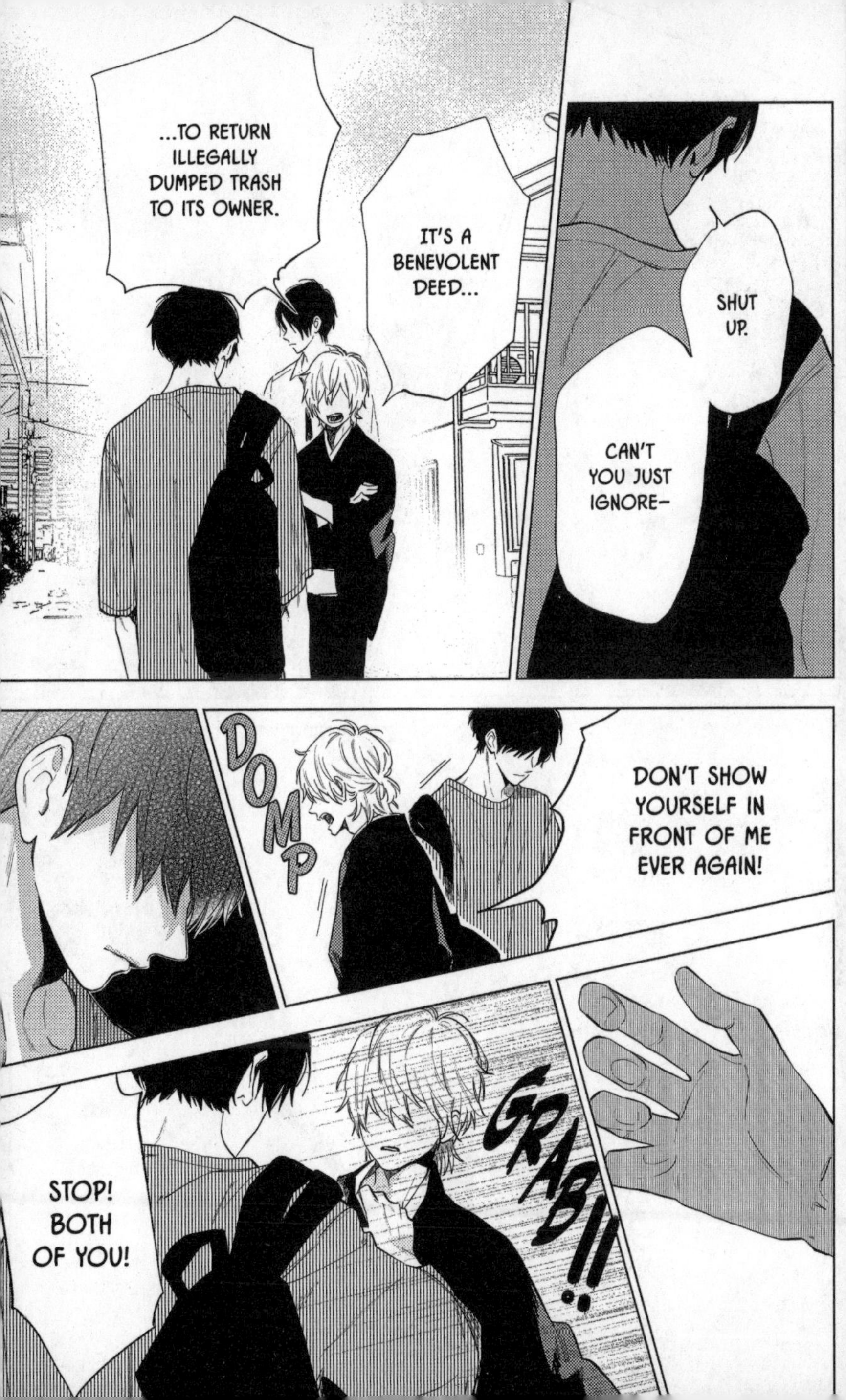
SHUT UP.
CAN'T YOU JUST IGNORE-
IT'S A BENEVOLENT DEED...
...TO RETURN ILLEGALLY DUMPED TRASH TO ITS OWNER.
DON'T SHOW YOURSELF IN FRONT OF ME EVER AGAIN!
DOMP
GRAB!!
STOP! BOTH OF YOU!

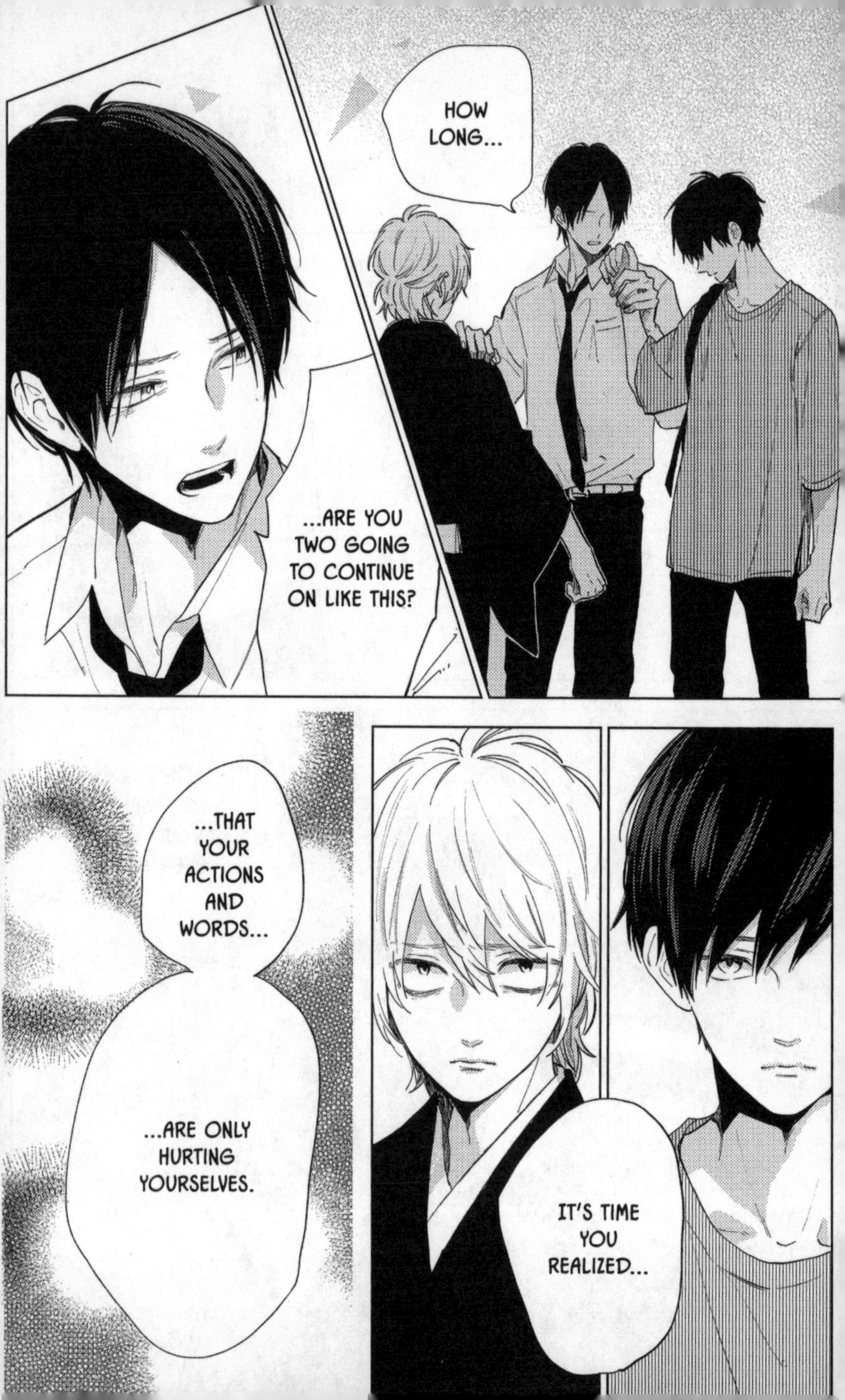
HOW LONG...
...ARE YOU TWO GOING TO CONTINUE ON LIKE THIS?
IT'S TIME YOU REALIZED...
...THAT YOUR ACTIONS AND WORDS...
...ARE ONLY HURTING YOURSELVES.

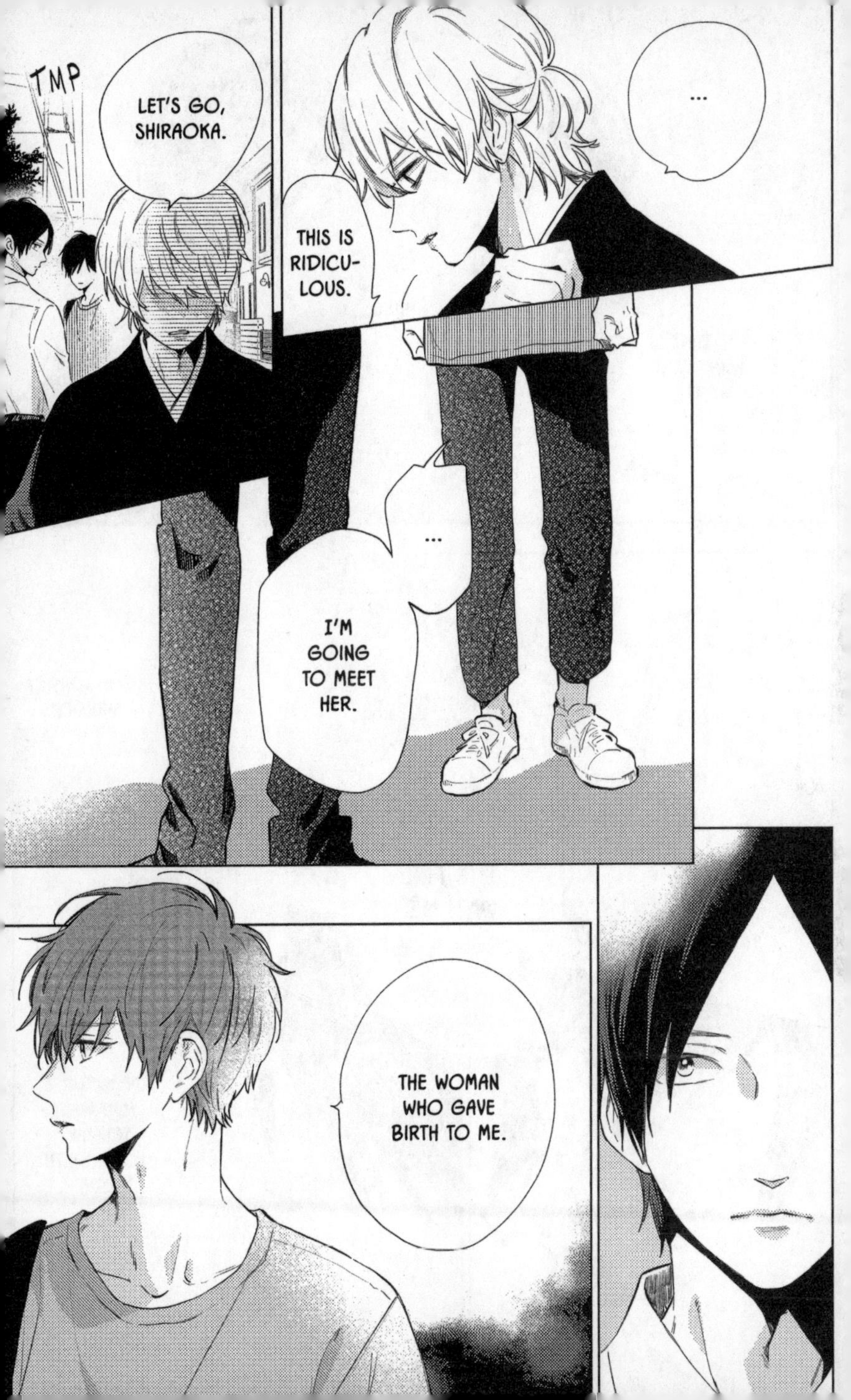
...
THIS IS RIDICULOUS.
TMP
LET'S GO, SHIRAOKA.
...
I'M GOING TO MEET HER.
THE WOMAN WHO GAVE BIRTH TO ME.

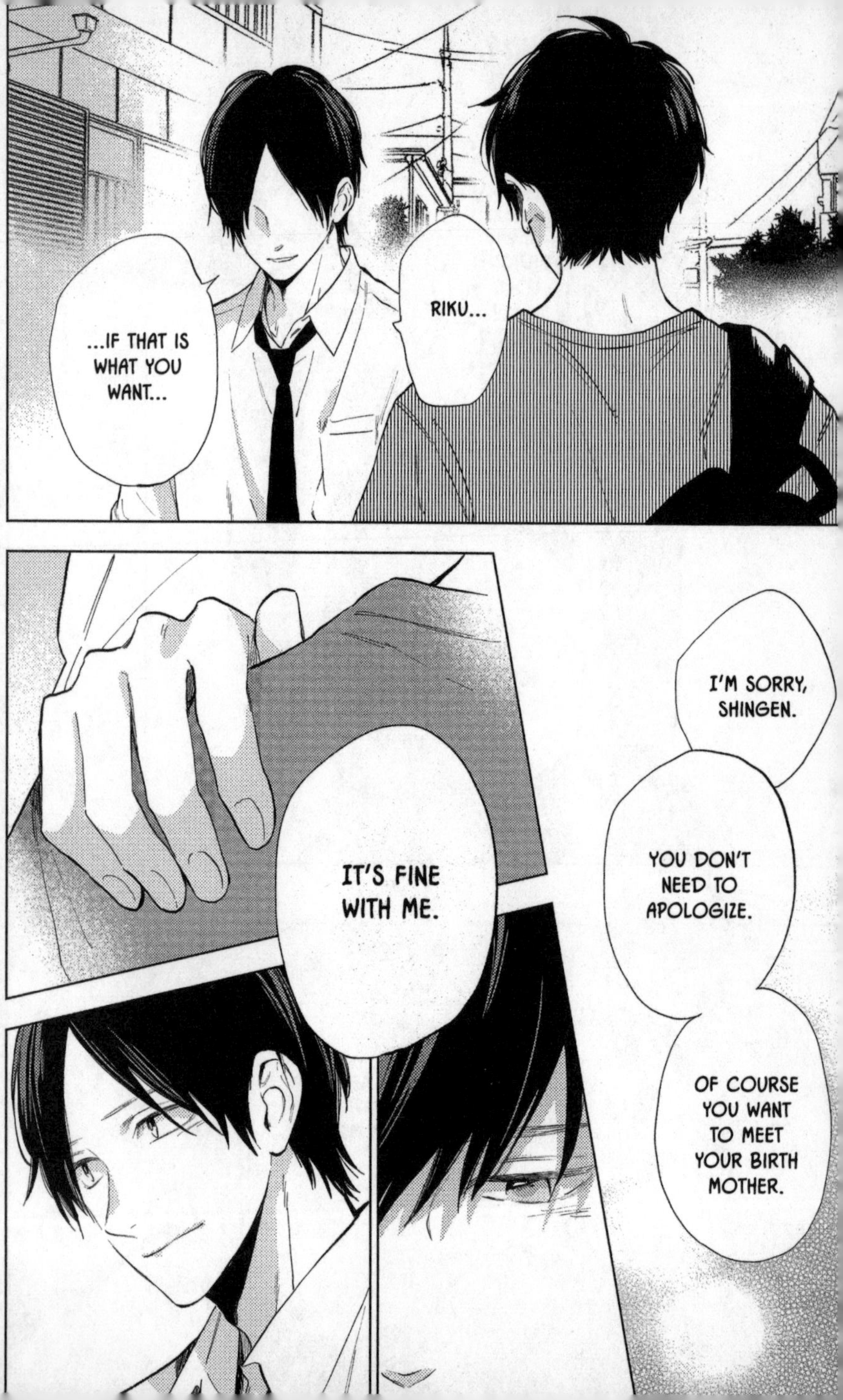
RIKU...
...IF THAT IS WHAT YOU WANT...
I'M SORRY, SHINGEN.
YOU DON'T NEED TO APOLOGIZE.
OF COURSE YOU WANT TO MEET YOUR BIRTH MOTHER.
IT'S FINE WITH ME.

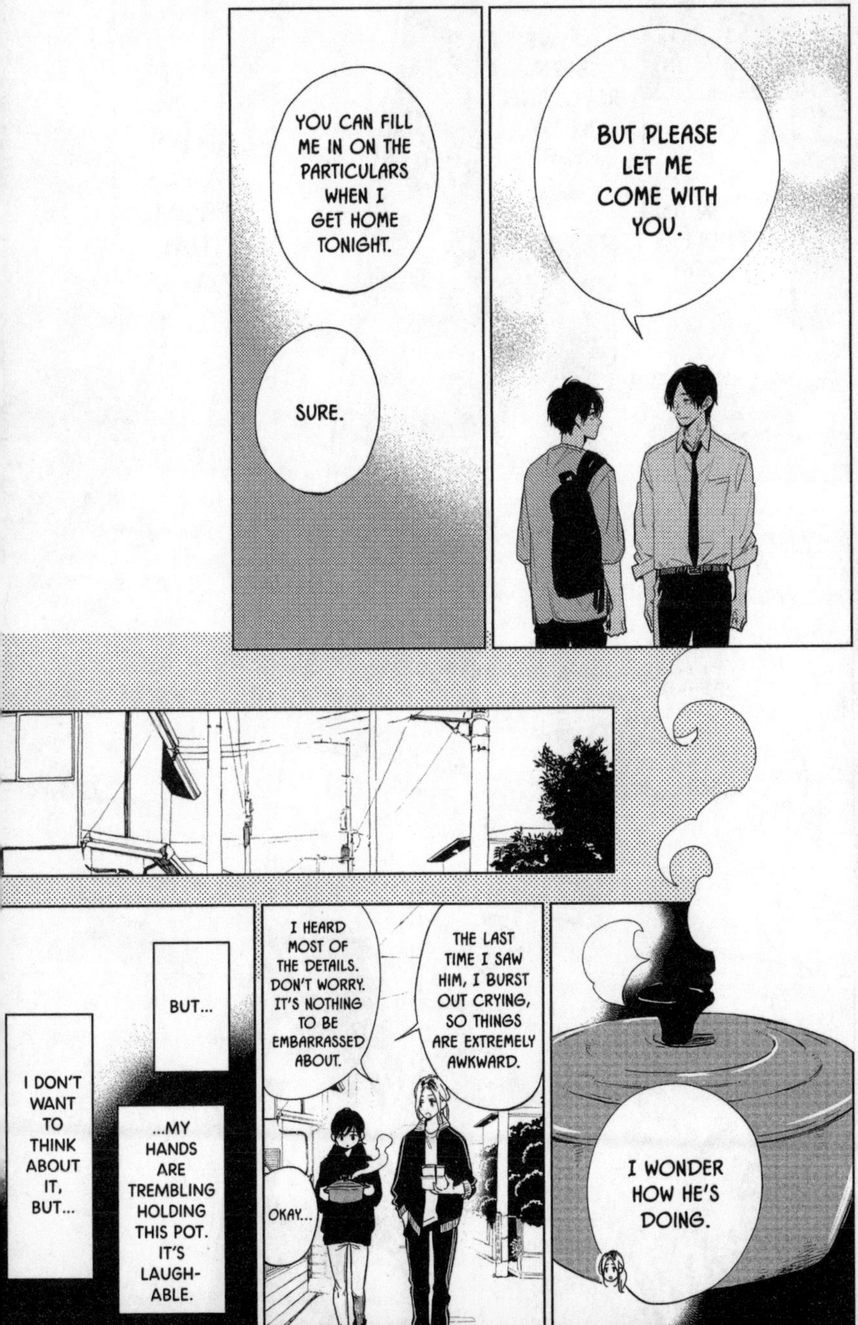
BUT PLEASE LET ME COME WITH YOU.
YOU CAN FILL ME IN ON THE PARTICULARS WHEN I GET HOME TONIGHT.
SURE.
I WONDER HOW HE'S DOING.
THE LAST TIME I SAW HIM, I BURST OUT CRYING, SO THINGS ARE EXTREMELY AWKWARD.
I HEARD MOST OF THE DETAILS. DON'T WORRY. IT'S NOTHING TO BE EMBARRASSED ABOUT.
OKAY...
BUT...
I DON'T WANT TO THINK ABOUT IT, BUT...
...MY HANDS ARE TREMBLING HOLDING THIS POT. IT'S LAUGHABLE.

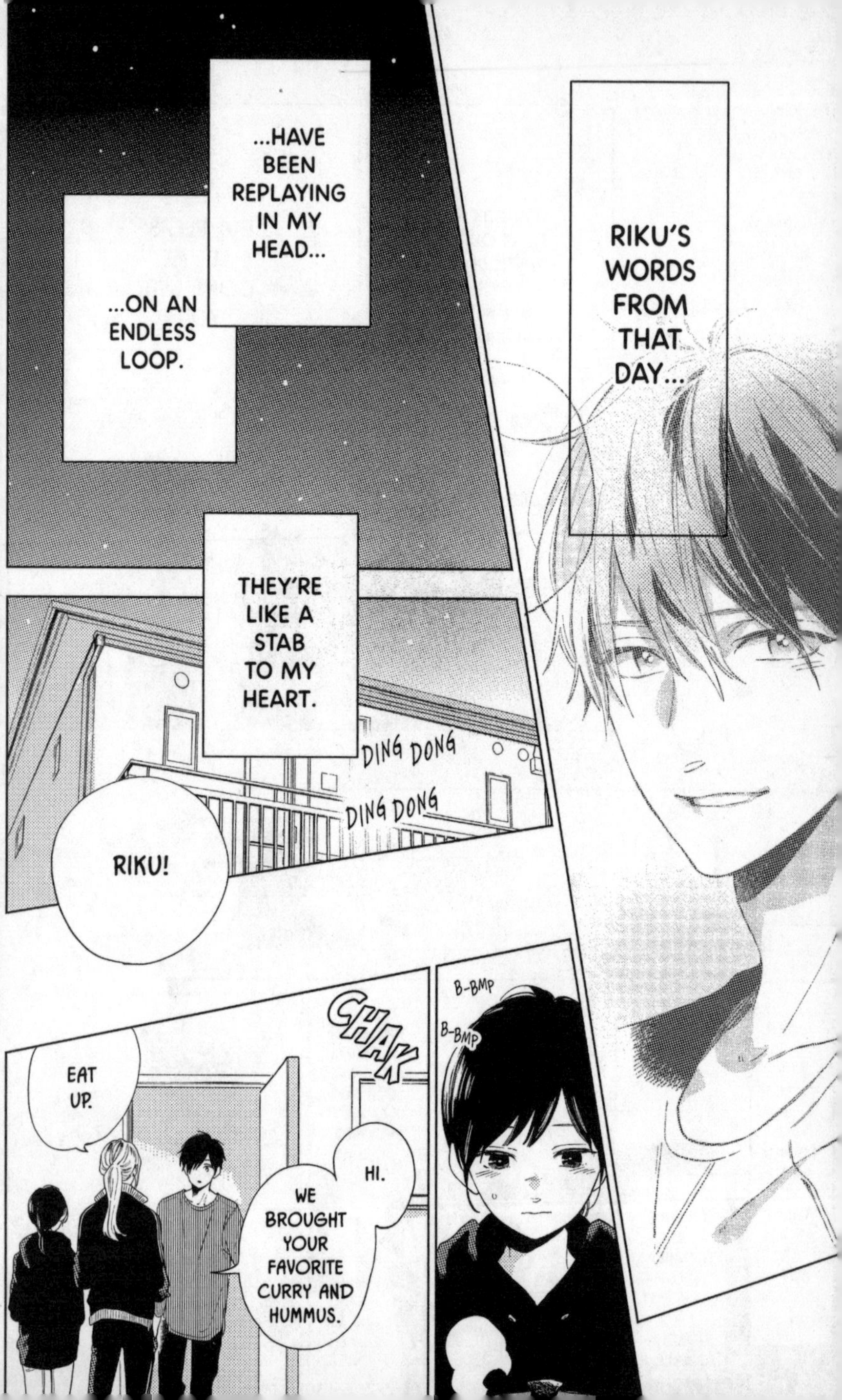
RIKU'S WORDS FROM THAT DAY...
...HAVE BEEN REPLAYING IN MY HEAD...
...ON AN ENDLESS LOOP.
THEY'RE LIKE A STAB TO MY HEART.
DING DONG
DING DONG
RIKU!
B-BMP
B-BMP
CHAK
HI.
WE BROUGHT YOUR FAVORITE CURRY AND HUMMUS.
EAT UP.

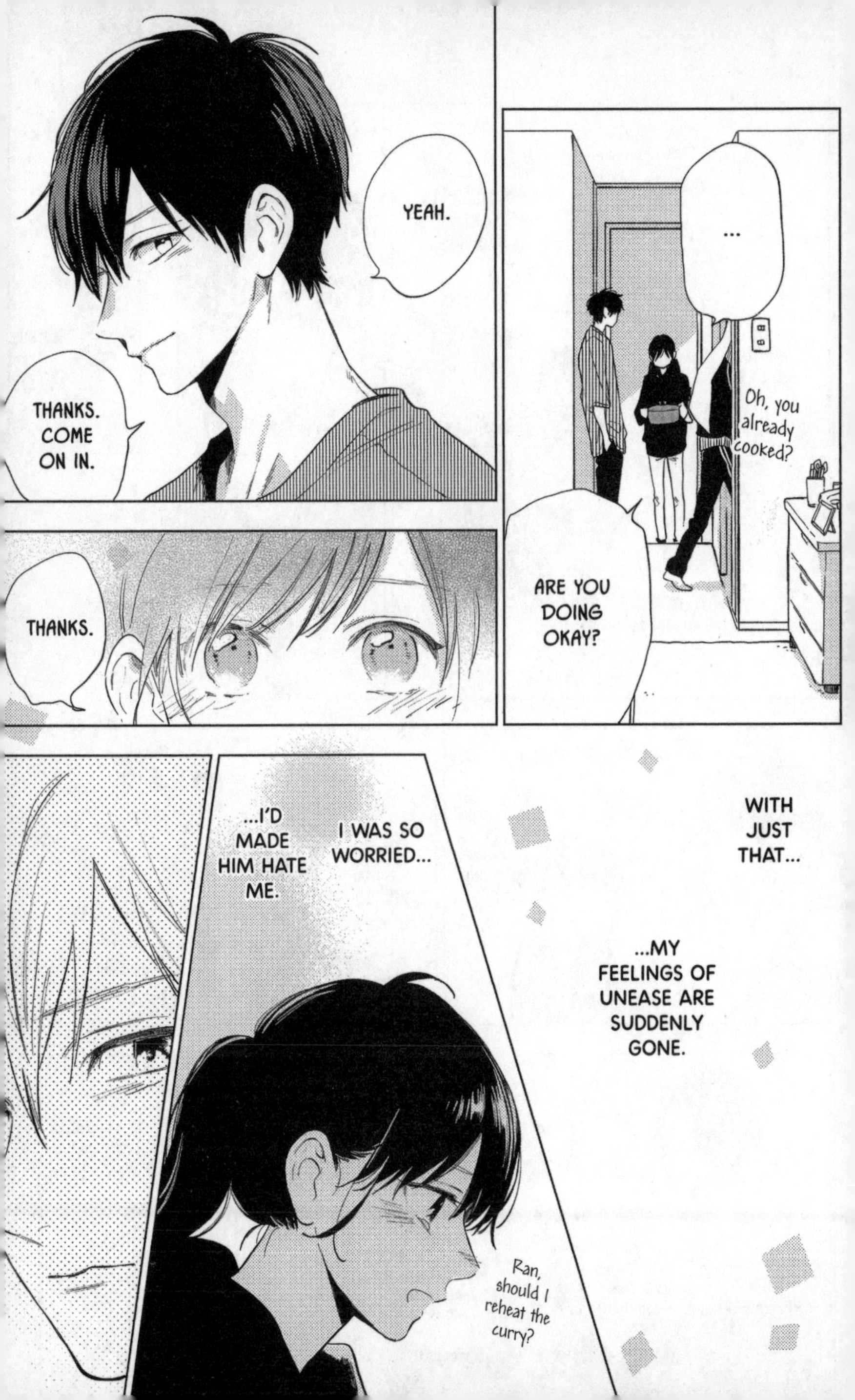
...
Oh, you already cooked?
ARE YOU DOING OKAY?
YEAH.
THANKS. COME ON IN.
THANKS.
WITH JUST THAT...
...MY FEELINGS OF UNEASE ARE SUDDENLY GONE.
I WAS SO WORRIED...
...I'D MADE HIM HATE ME.
Ran, should I reheat the curry?

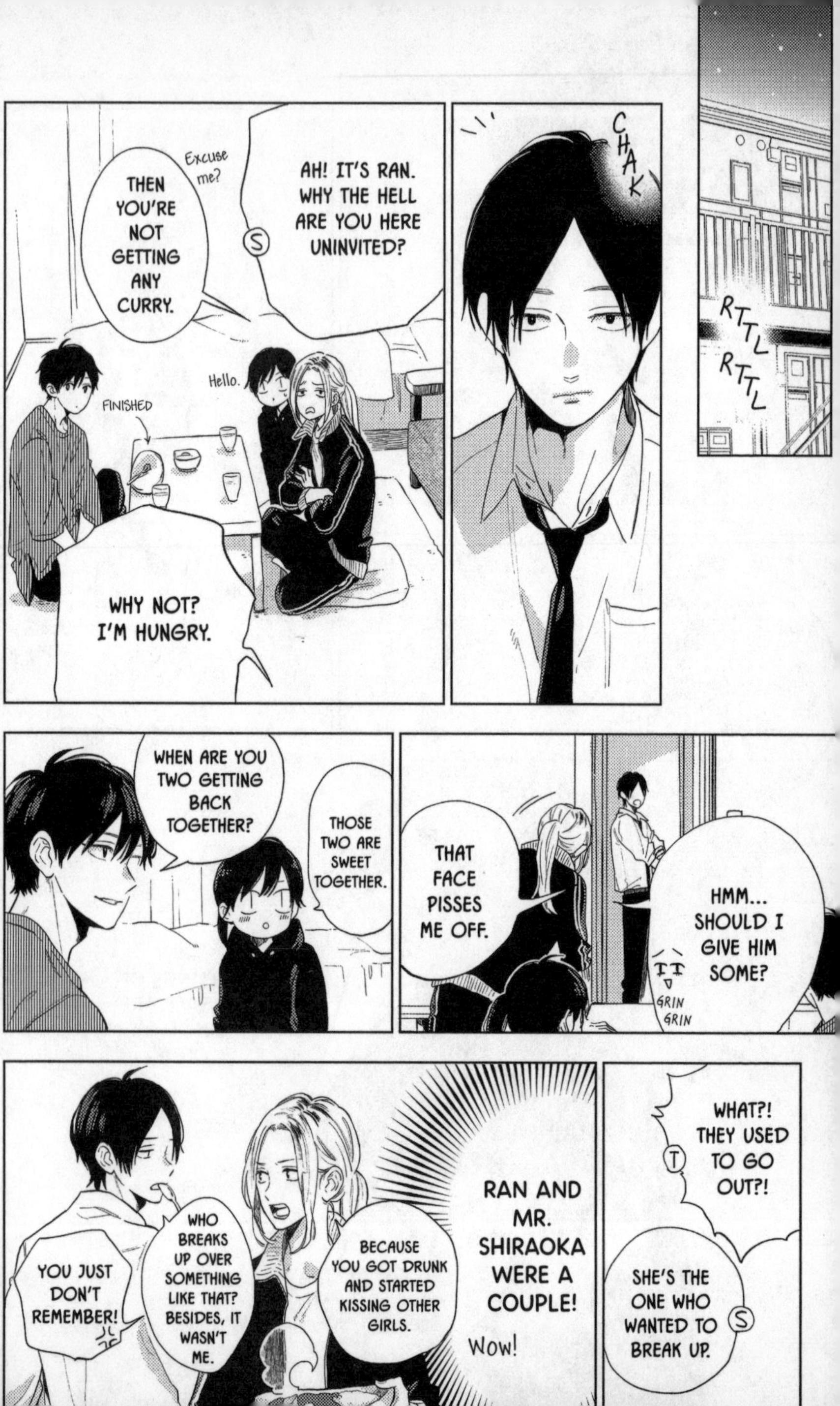
RTTL RTTL
CHAK
AH! IT'S RAN. WHY THE HELL ARE YOU HERE UNINVITED?
Excuse me?
THEN YOU'RE NOT GETTING ANY CURRY.
Hello.
FINISHED
WHY NOT? I'M HUNGRY.
HMM... SHOULD I GIVE HIM SOME?
GRIN GRIN
THAT FACE PISSES ME OFF.
THOSE TWO ARE SWEET TOGETHER.
WHEN ARE YOU TWO GETTING BACK TOGETHER?
WHAT?! THEY USED TO GO OUT?!
SHE'S THE ONE WHO WANTED TO BREAK UP.
RAN AND MR. SHIRAOKA WERE A COUPLE!
Wow!
BECAUSE YOU GOT DRUNK AND STARTED KISSING OTHER GIRLS.
WHO BREAKS UP OVER SOMETHING LIKE THAT? BESIDES, IT WASN'T ME.
YOU JUST DON'T REMEMBER!

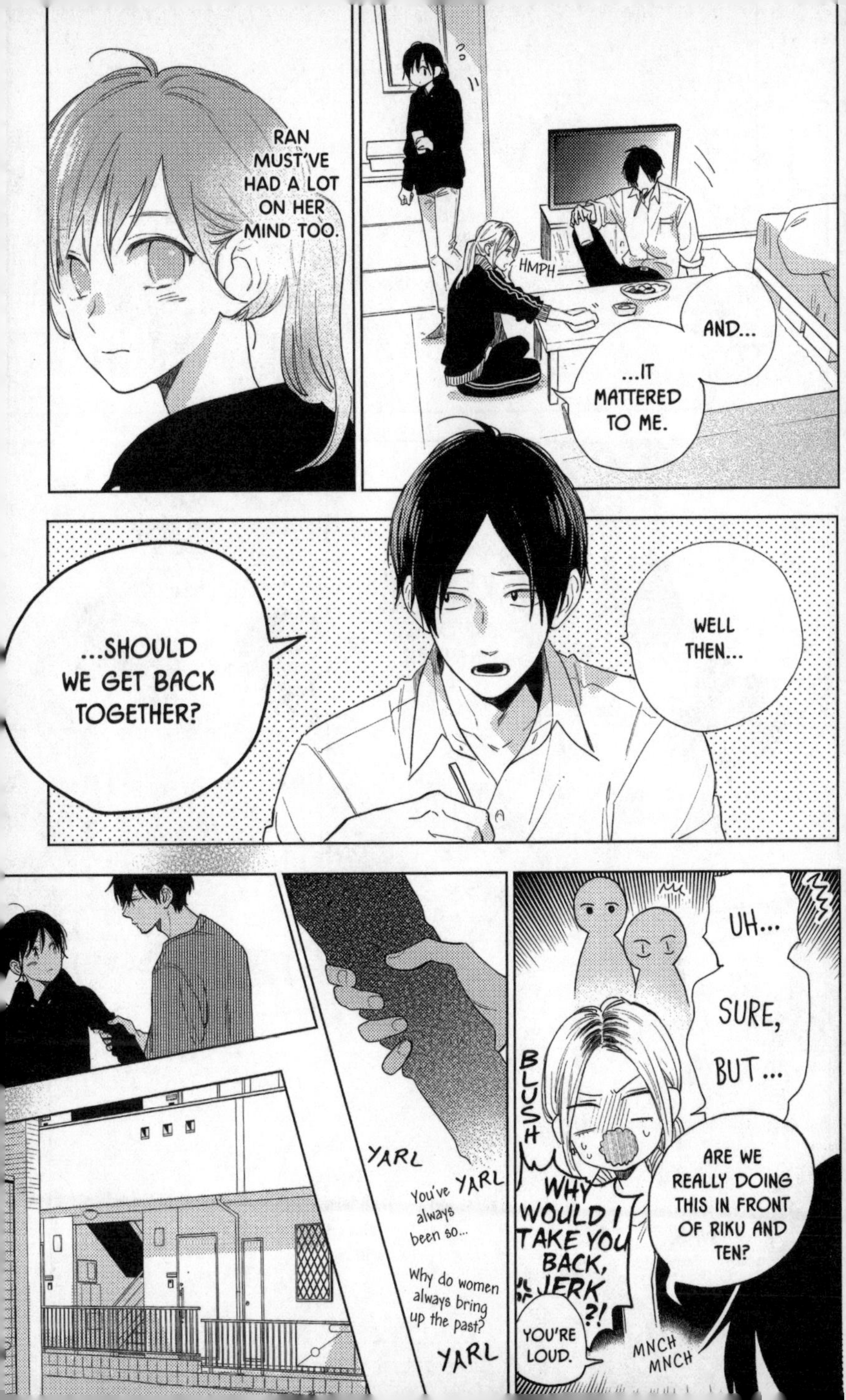
HMPH
AND...
...IT MATTERED TO ME.
RAN MUST'VE HAD A LOT ON HER MIND TOO.
WELL THEN...
...SHOULD WE GET BACK TOGETHER?
UH...
SURE, BUT...
ARE WE REALLY DOING THIS IN FRONT OF RIKU AND TEN?
BLUSH
WHY WOULD I TAKE YOU BACK, JERK?!
YOU'RE LOUD.
MNCH MNCH
YARL
You've always been so...
YARL
Why do women always bring up the past?
YARL

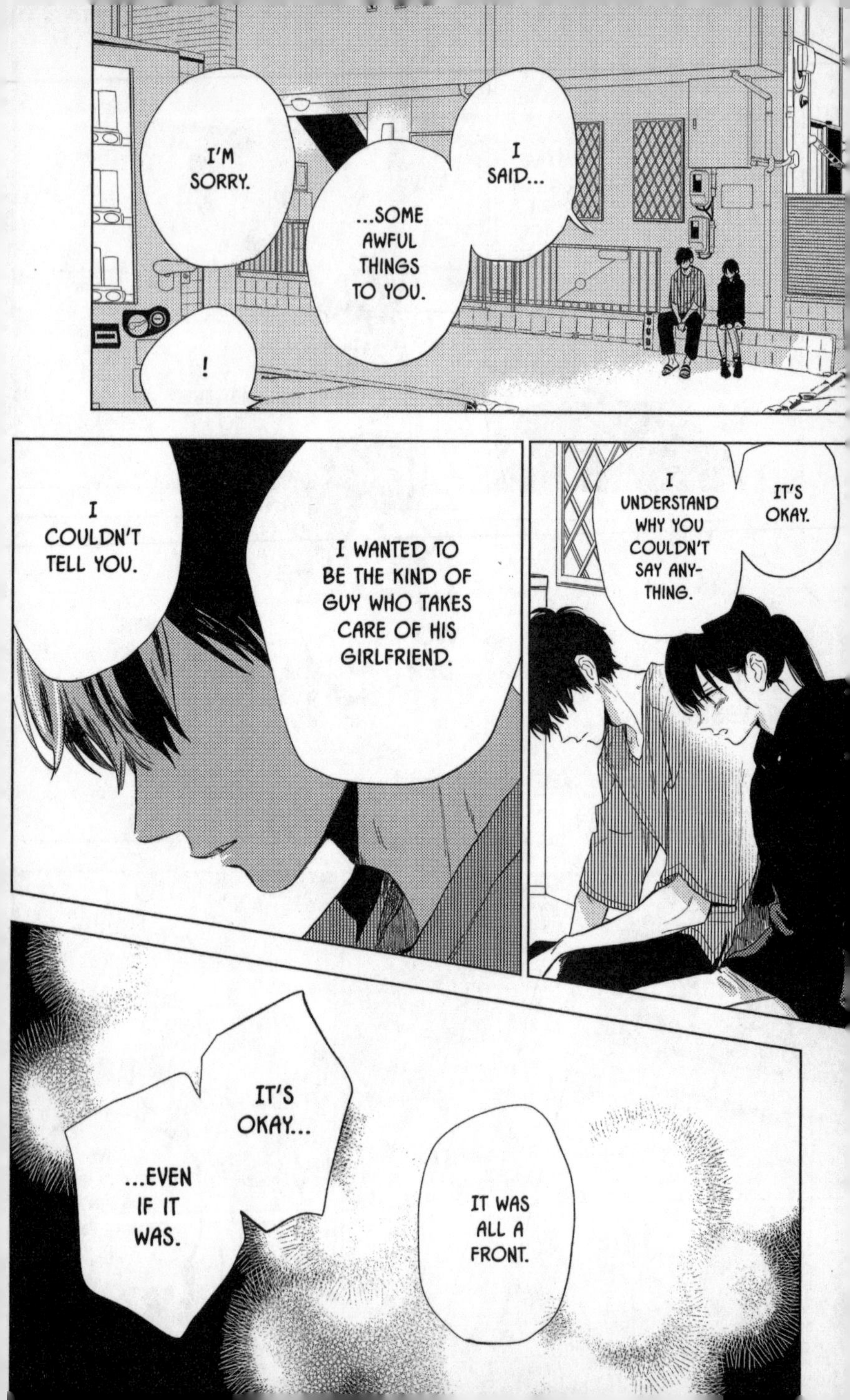
I SAID...
...SOME AWFUL THINGS TO YOU.
I'M SORRY.
!
IT'S OKAY.
I UNDERSTAND WHY YOU COULDN'T SAY ANY-THING.
I WANTED TO BE THE KIND OF GUY WHO TAKES CARE OF HIS GIRLFRIEND.
I COULDN'T TELL YOU.
IT WAS ALL A FRONT.
IT'S OKAY...
...EVEN IF IT WAS.

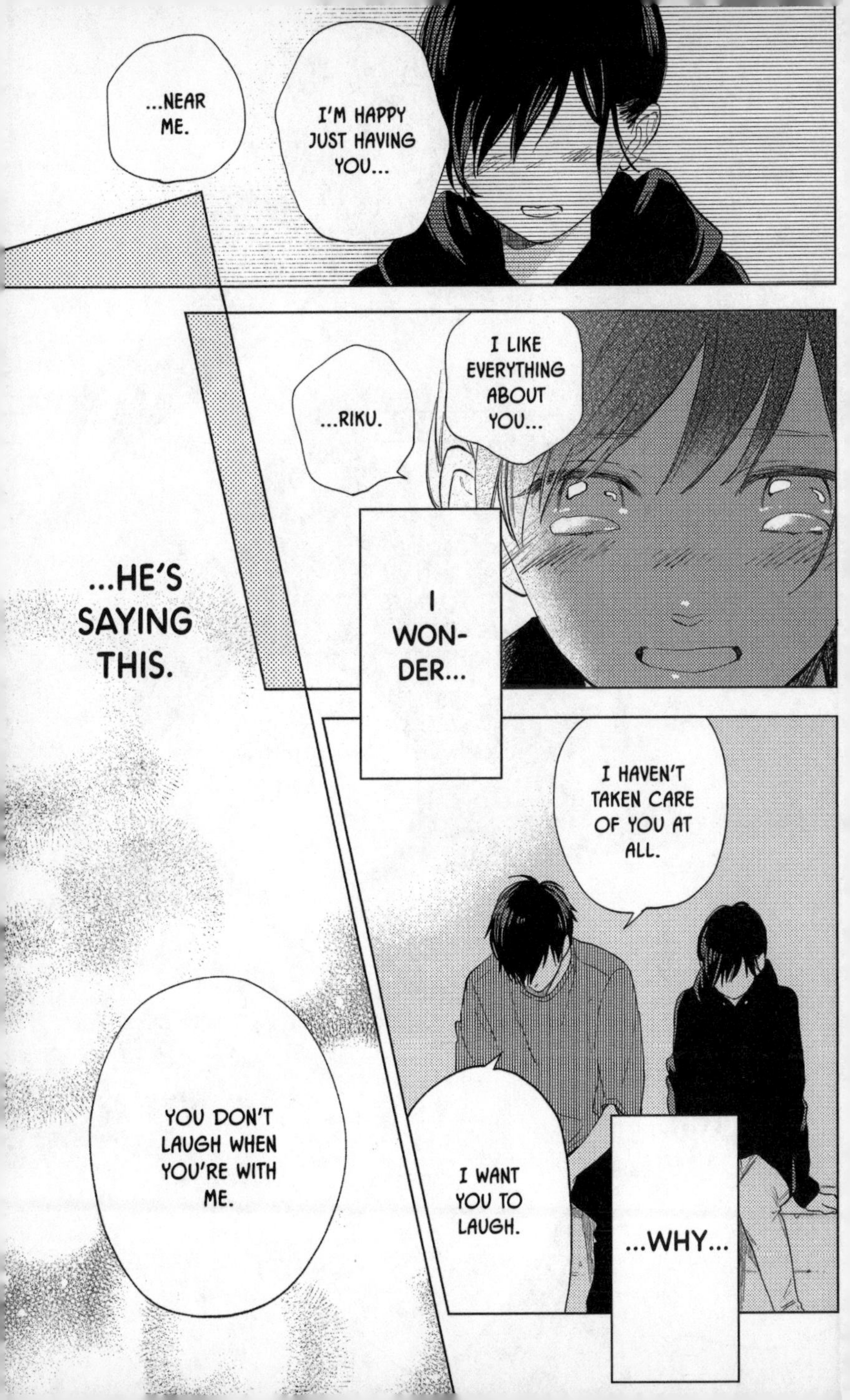
I'M HAPPY JUST HAVING YOU...
...NEAR ME.
I LIKE EVERYTHING ABOUT YOU...
...RIKU.
I WONDER...
I HAVEN'T TAKEN CARE OF YOU AT ALL.
I WANT YOU TO LAUGH.
...WHY...
...HE'S SAYING THIS.
YOU DON'T LAUGH WHEN YOU'RE WITH ME.

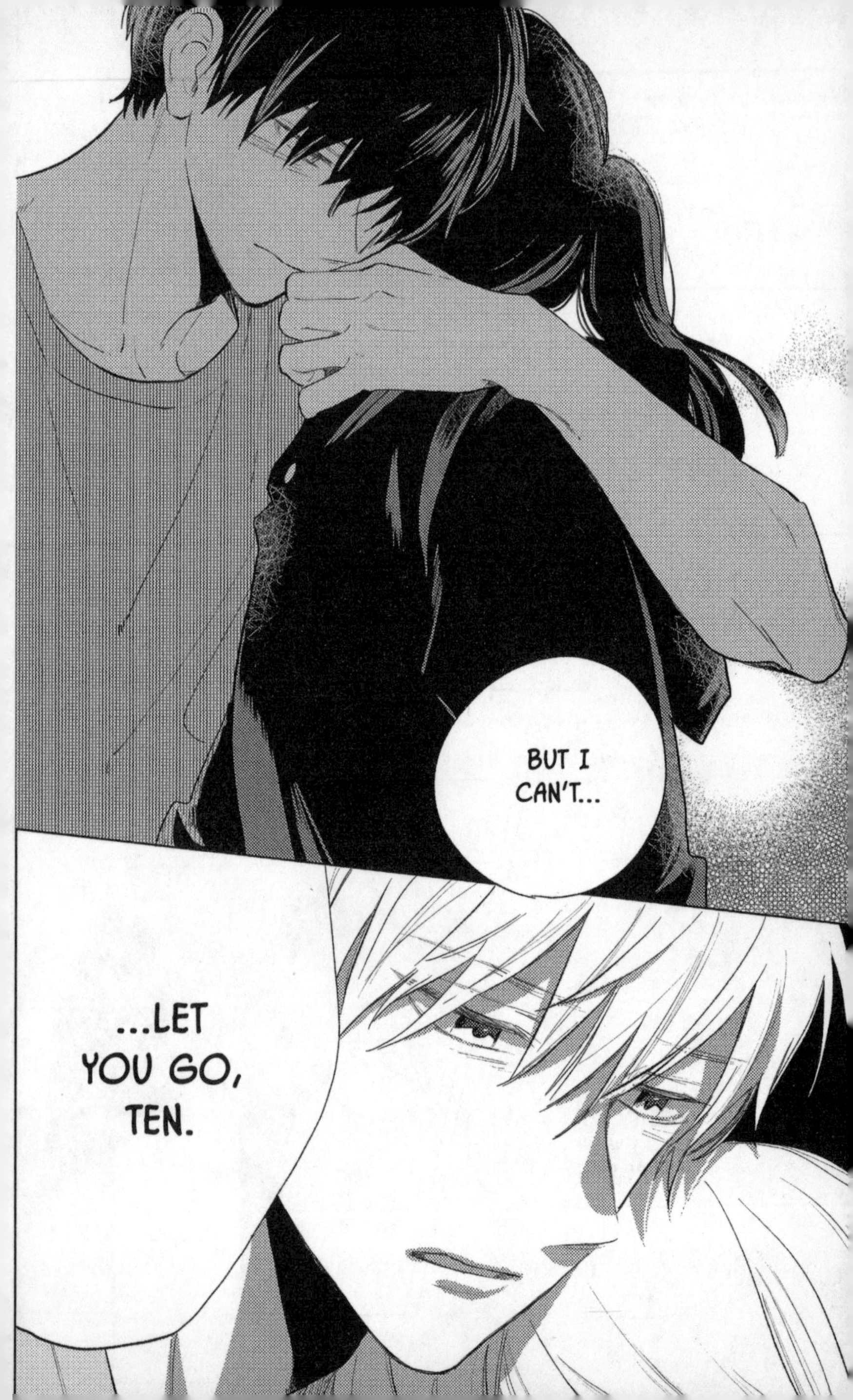
BUT I CAN'T...
...LET YOU GO, TEN.

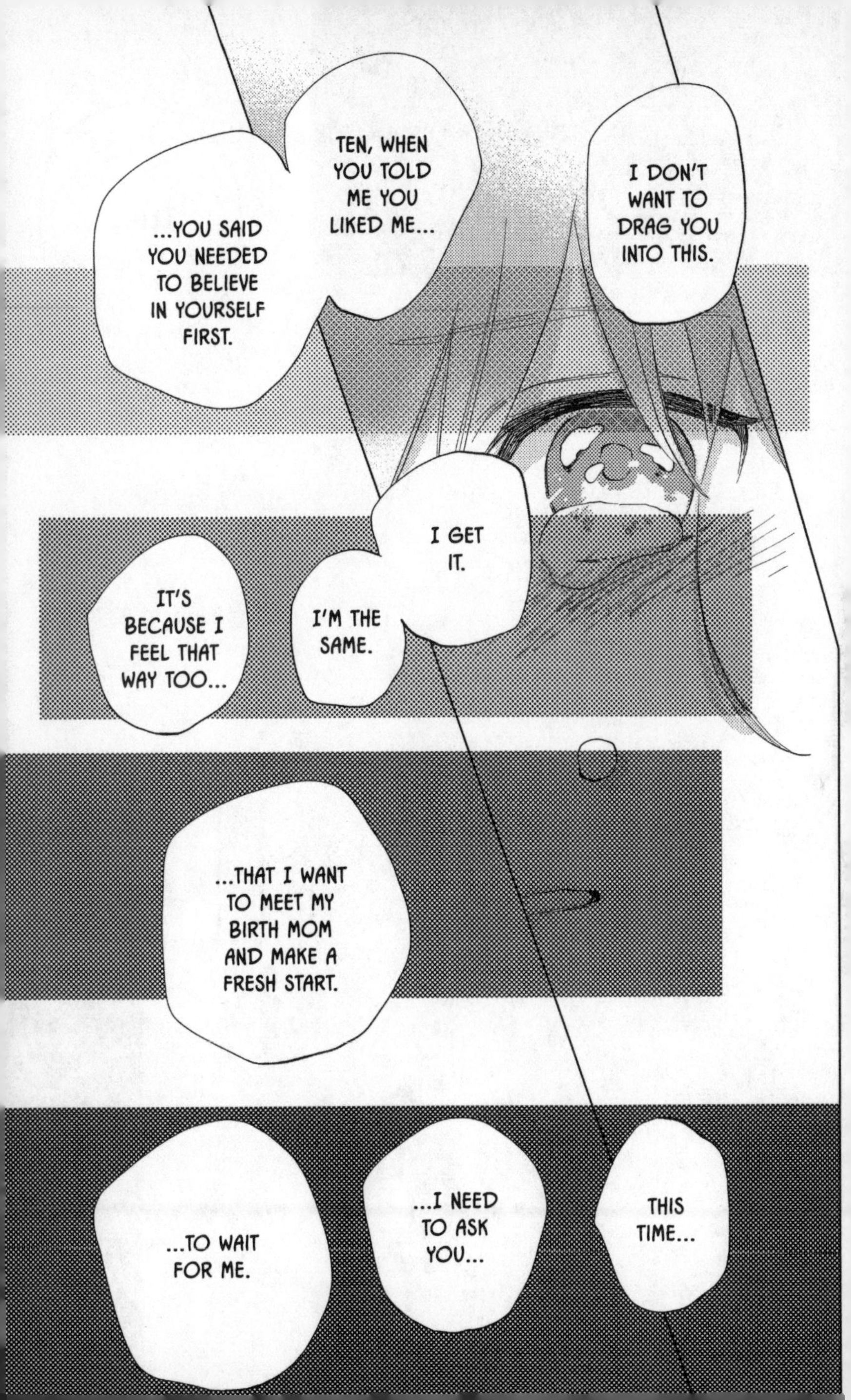
I DON'T WANT TO DRAG YOU INTO THIS.
TEN, WHEN YOU TOLD ME YOU LIKED ME...
...YOU SAID YOU NEEDED TO BELIEVE IN YOURSELF FIRST.
I GET IT.
I'M THE SAME.
IT'S BECAUSE I FEEL THAT WAY TOO...
...THAT I WANT TO MEET MY BIRTH MOM AND MAKE A FRESH START.
THIS TIME...
...I NEED TO ASK YOU...
...TO WAIT FOR ME.

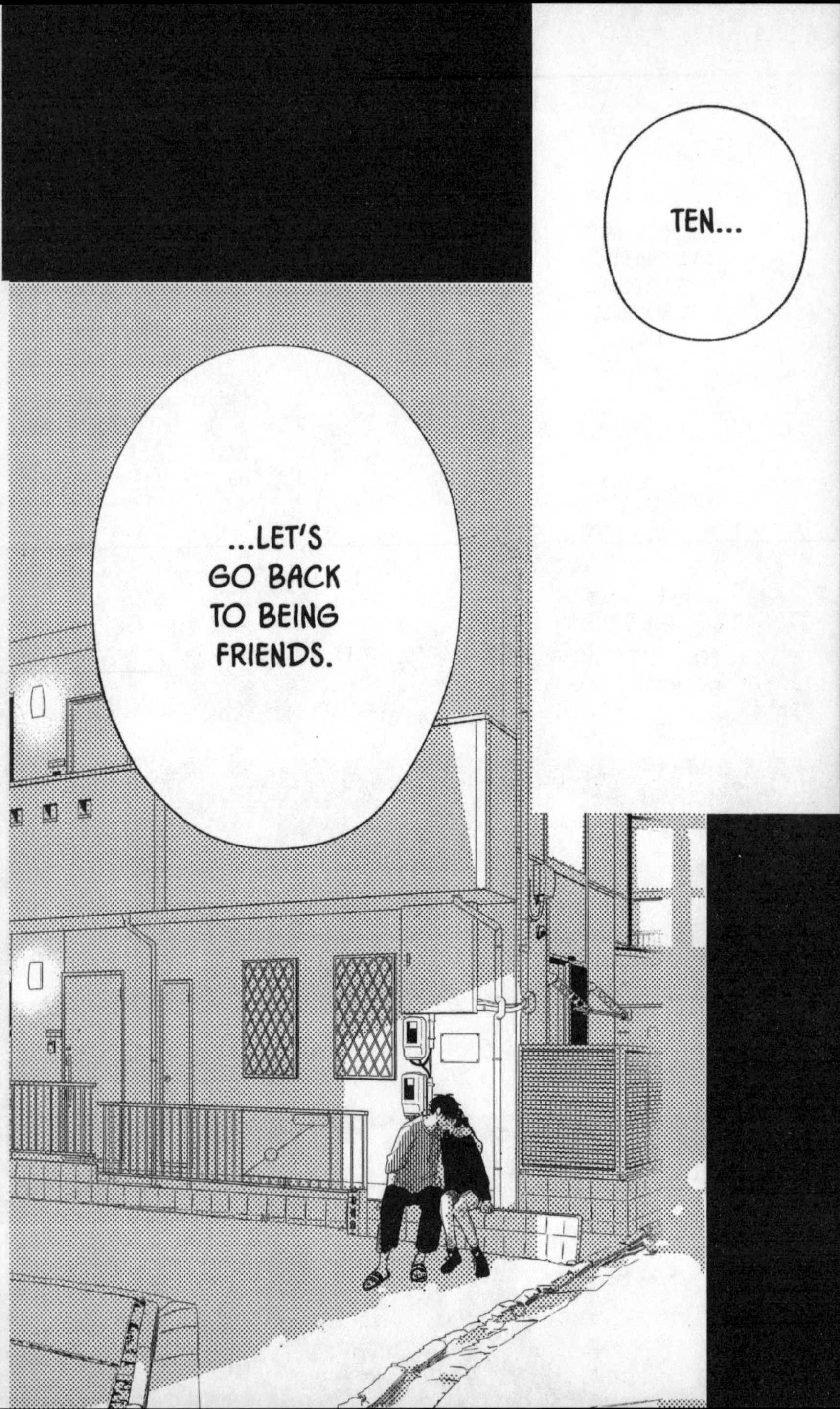
TEN...
...LET'S GO BACK TO BEING FRIENDS.

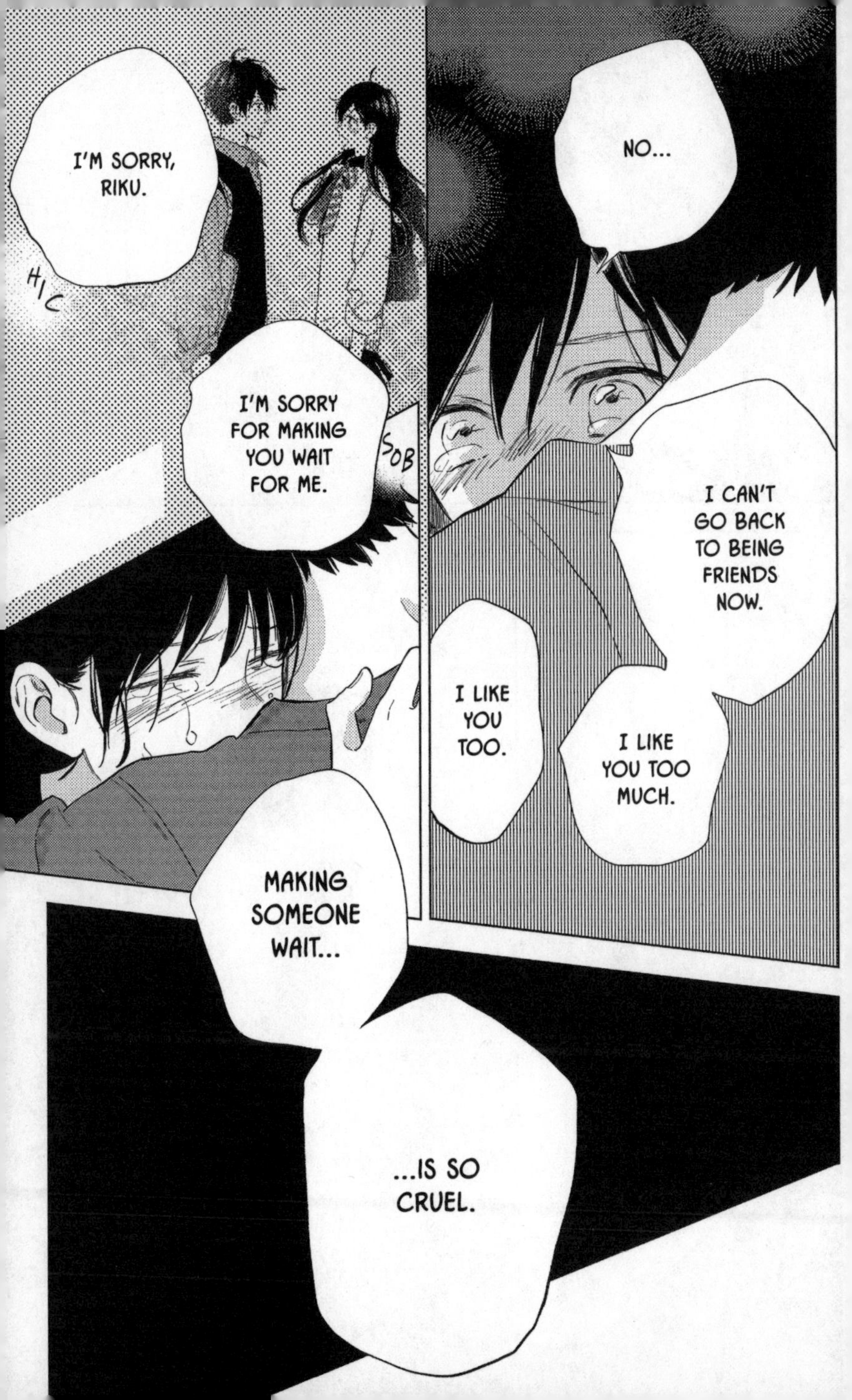
NO...
I CAN'T GO BACK TO BEING FRIENDS NOW.
I LIKE YOU TOO.
I LIKE YOU TOO MUCH.
I'M SORRY, RIKU.
HIC
I'M SORRY FOR MAKING YOU WAIT FOR ME.
SOB
MAKING SOMEONE WAIT...
...IS SO CRUEL.

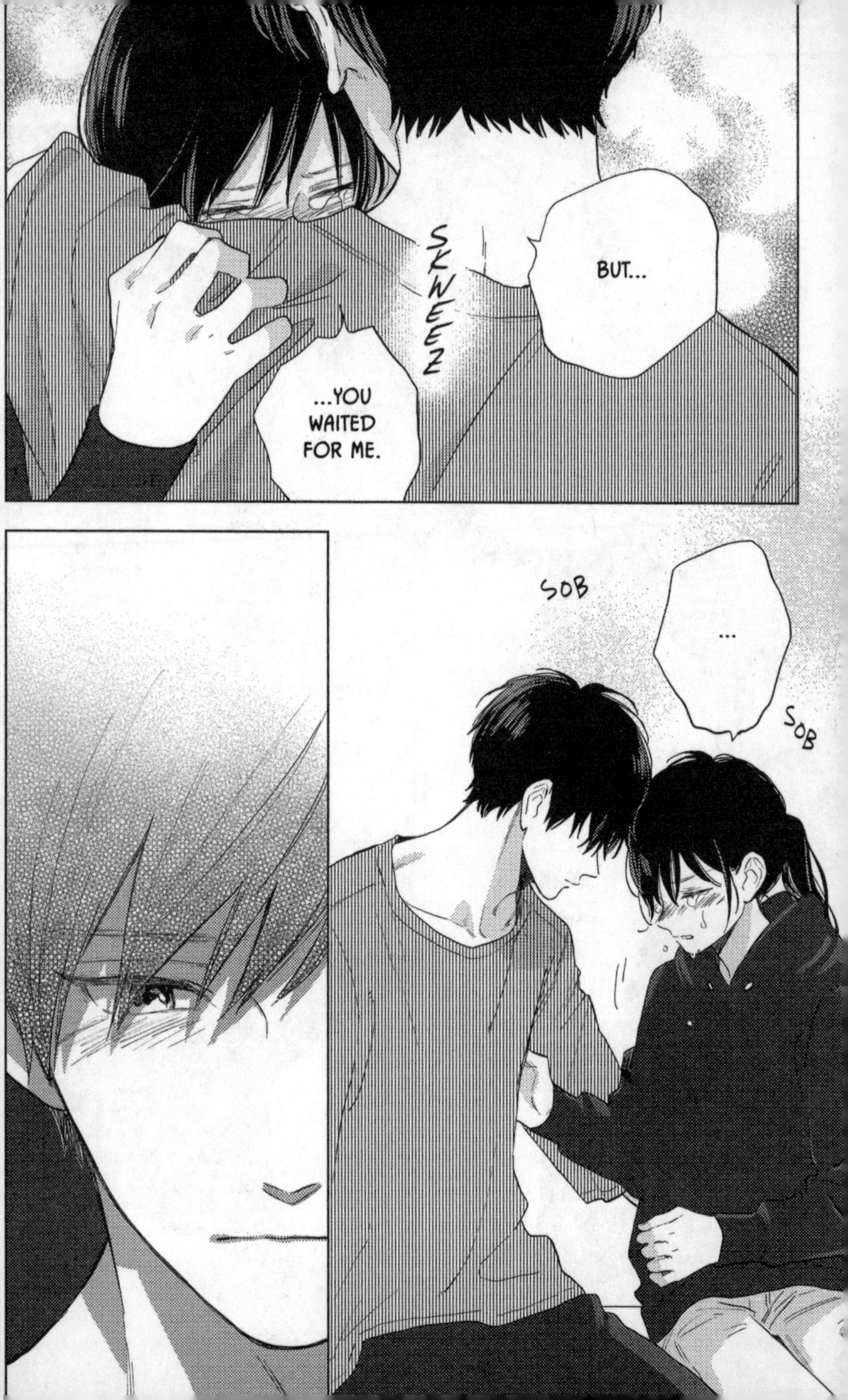
BUT...
SKWEEZ
...YOU WAITED FOR ME.
...
SOB
SOB

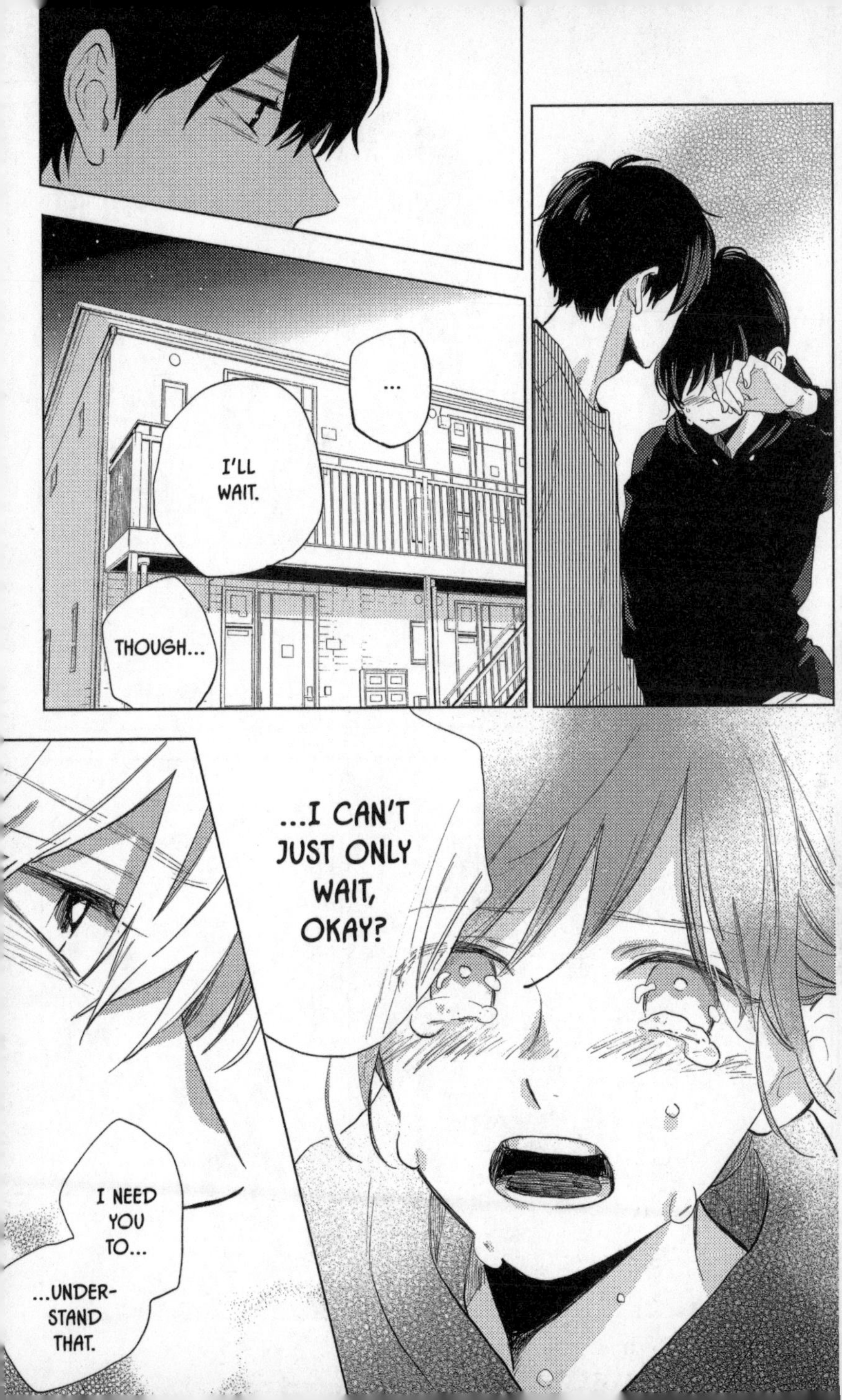
...
I'LL WAIT.
THOUGH...
...I CAN'T JUST ONLY WAIT, OKAY?
I NEED YOU TO...
...UNDER-STAND THAT.

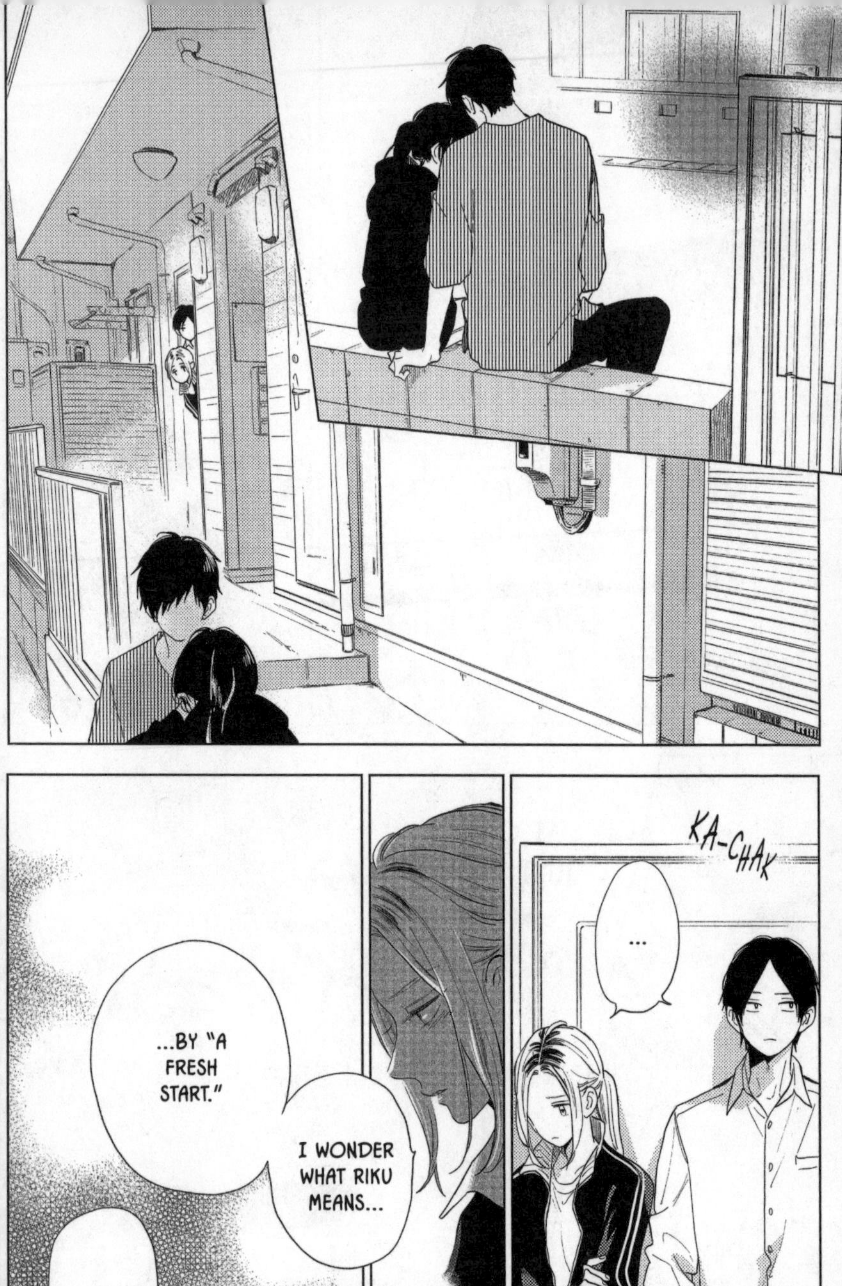
KA-CHAK
...
I WONDER WHAT RIKU MEANS...
...BY "A FRESH START."
...

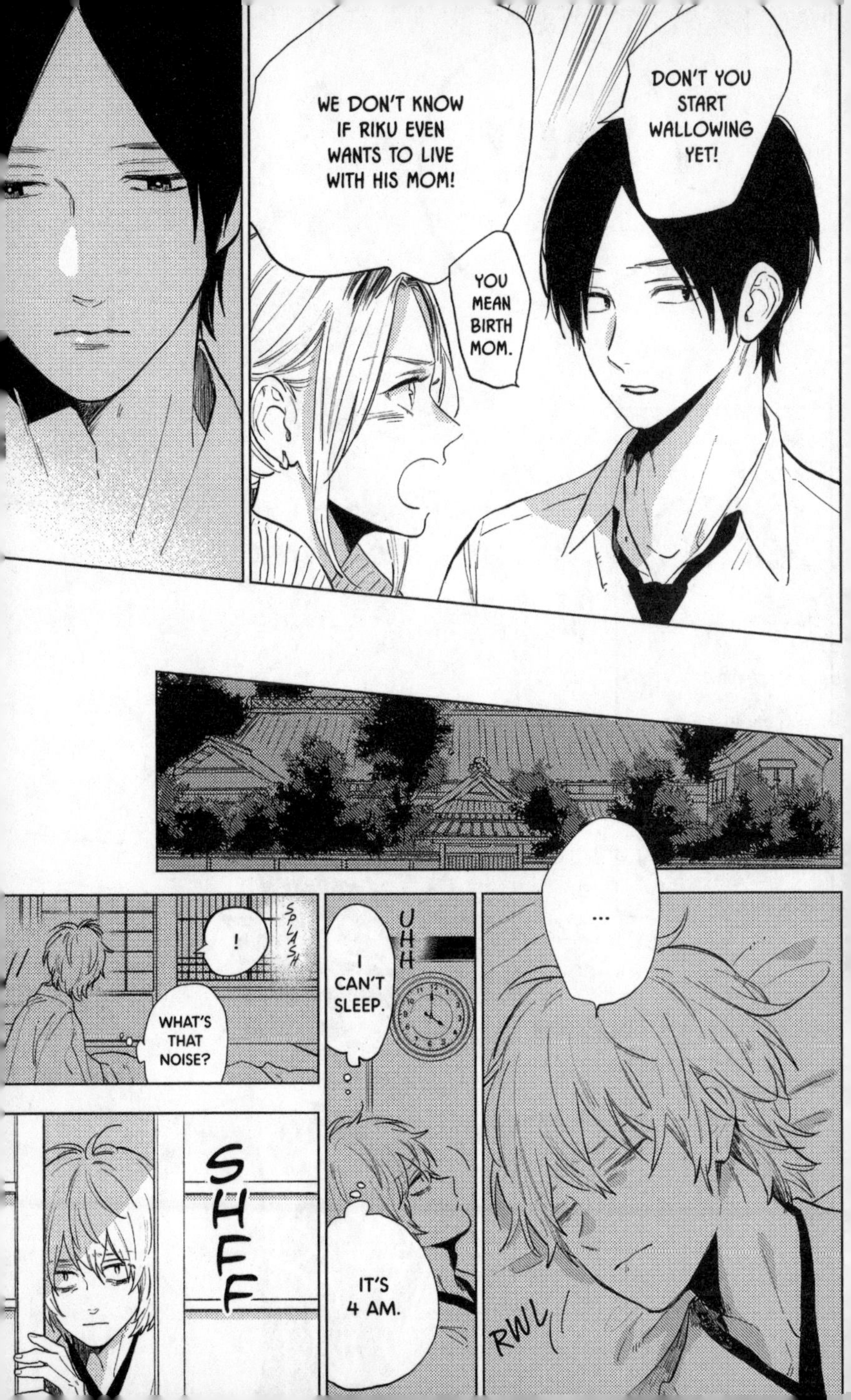
DON'T YOU START WALLOWING YET!
WE DON'T KNOW IF RIKU EVEN WANTS TO LIVE WITH HIS MOM!
YOU MEAN BIRTH MOM.
...
RWL
UHH
I CAN'T SLEEP.
IT'S 4 AM.
SPLASH
!
WHAT'S THAT NOISE?
SHFF

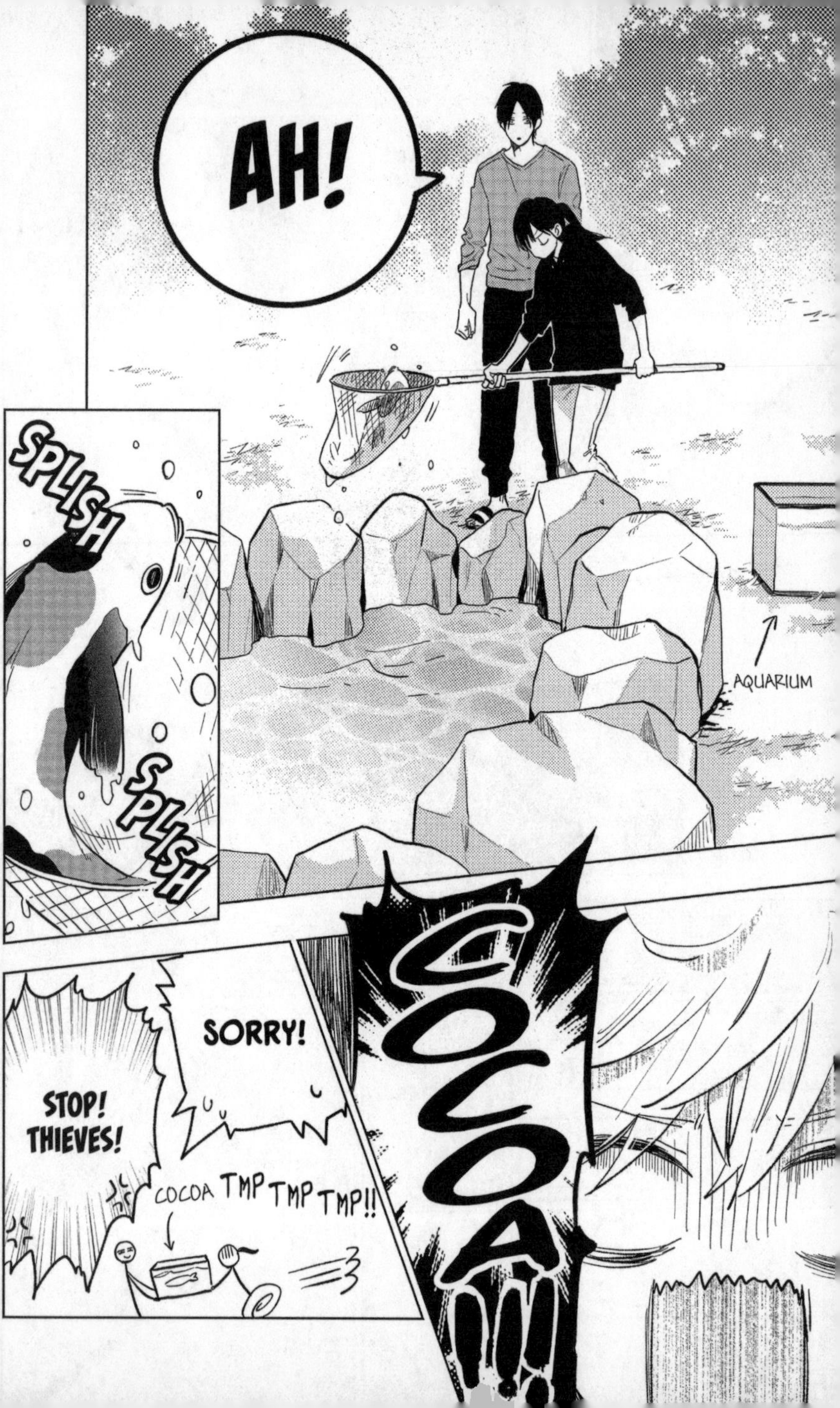
AH!
AQUARIUM
SPLISH
SPLISH
COCOA!!
SORRY!
STOP! THIEVES!
COCOA
TMP TMP TMP!!

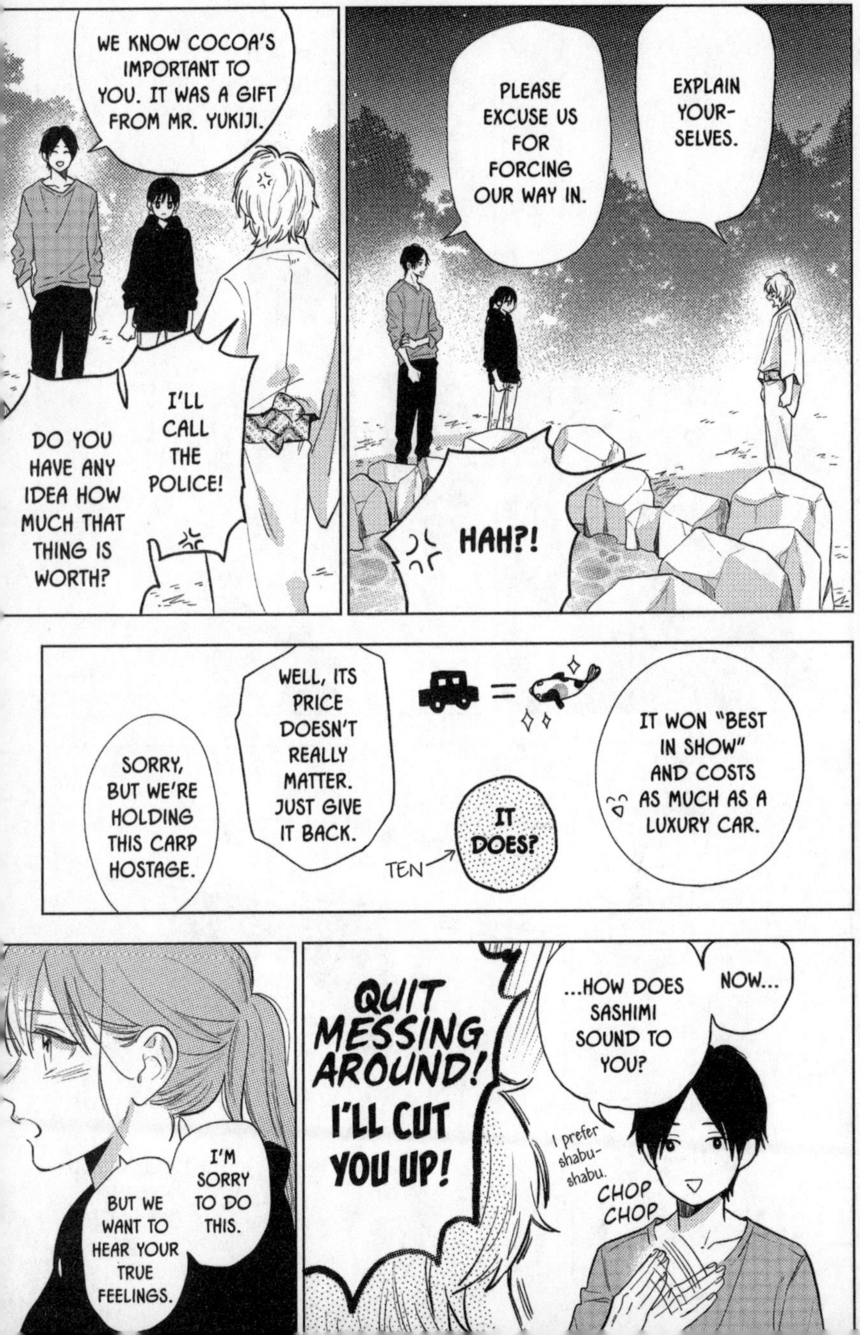
EXPLAIN YOURSELVES.
PLEASE EXCUSE US FOR FORCING OUR WAY IN.
HAH?!
WE KNOW COCOA'S IMPORTANT TO YOU. IT WAS A GIFT FROM MR. YUKIJI.
I'LL CALL THE POLICE!
DO YOU HAVE ANY IDEA HOW MUCH THAT THING IS WORTH?
IT WON "BEST IN SHOW" AND COSTS AS MUCH AS A LUXURY CAR.
IT DOES?
TEN
WELL, ITS PRICE DOESN'T REALLY MATTER. JUST GIVE IT BACK.
SORRY, BUT WE'RE HOLDING THIS CARP HOSTAGE.
NOW...
...HOW DOES SASHIMI SOUND TO YOU?
QUIT MESSING AROUND! I'LL CUT YOU UP!
I prefer shabu-shabu.
CHOP CHOP
I'M SORRY TO DO THIS.
BUT WE WANT TO HEAR YOUR TRUE FEELINGS.

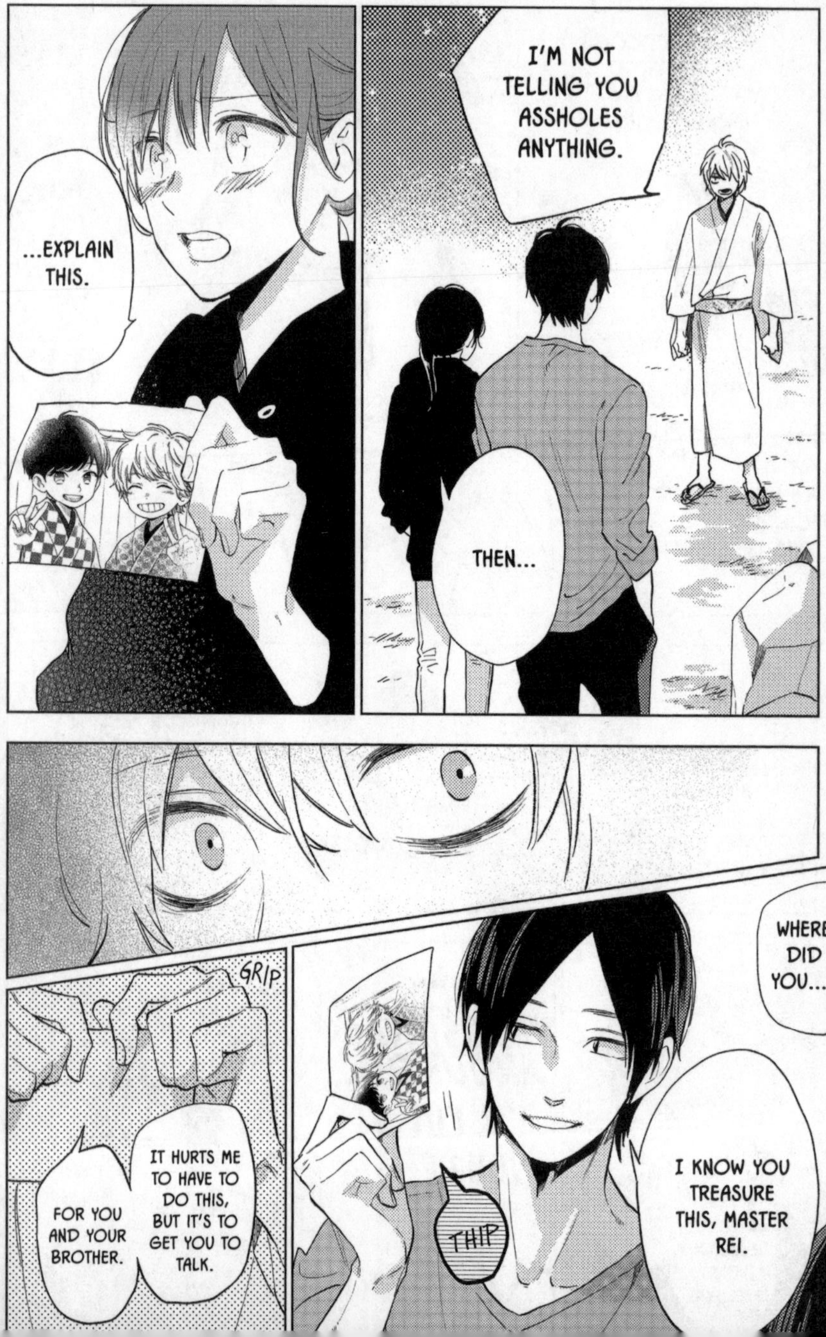
I'M NOT TELLING YOU ASSHOLES ANYTHING.
THEN...
...EXPLAIN THIS.
WHERE DID YOU...?
I KNOW YOU TREASURE THIS, MASTER REI.
THIP
GRIP
IT HURTS ME TO HAVE TO DO THIS, BUT IT'S TO GET YOU TO TALK.
FOR YOU AND YOUR BROTHER.

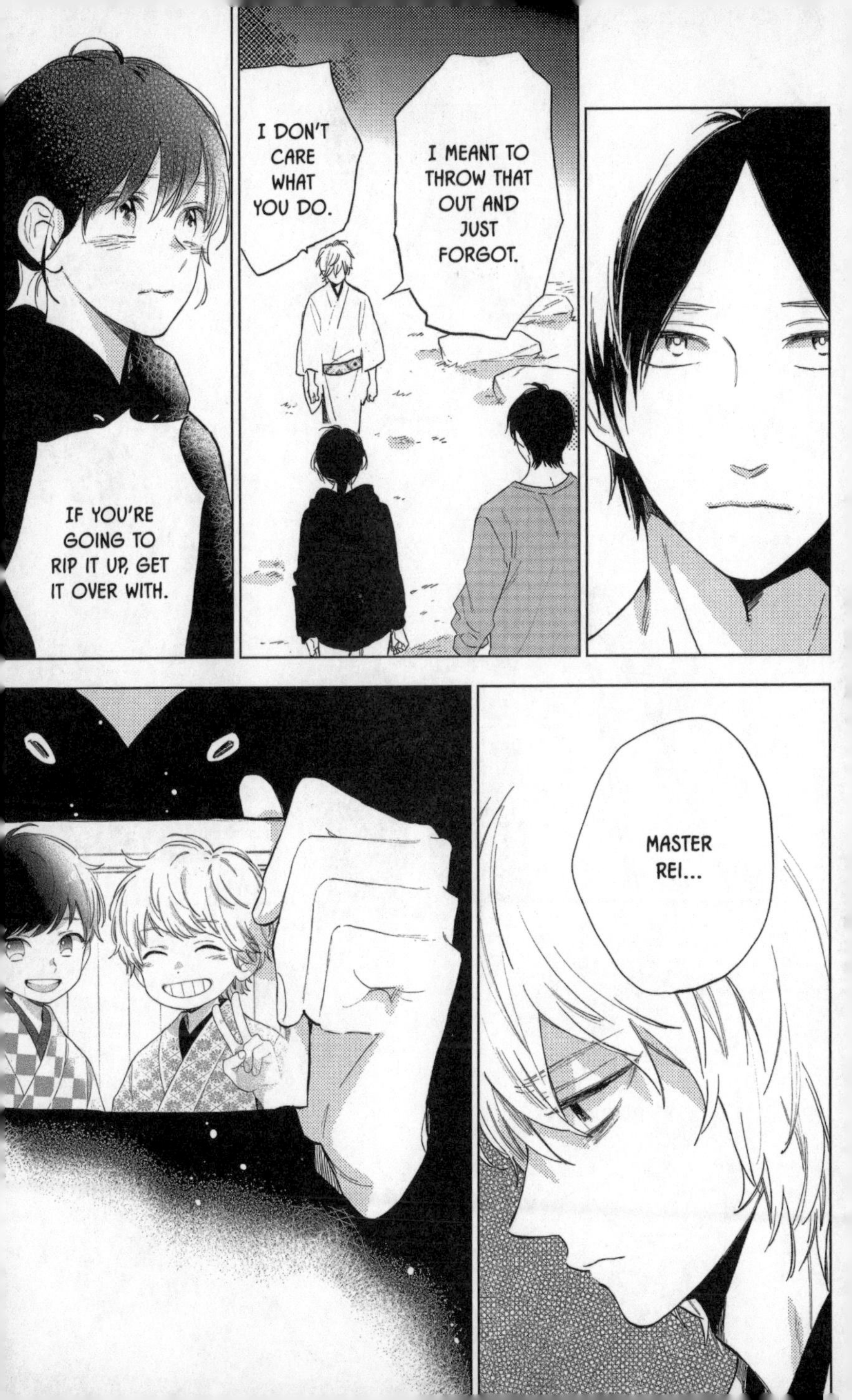
I MEANT TO THROW THAT OUT AND JUST FORGOT.
I DON'T CARE WHAT YOU DO.
IF YOU'RE GOING TO RIP IT UP, GET IT OVER WITH.
MASTER REI...

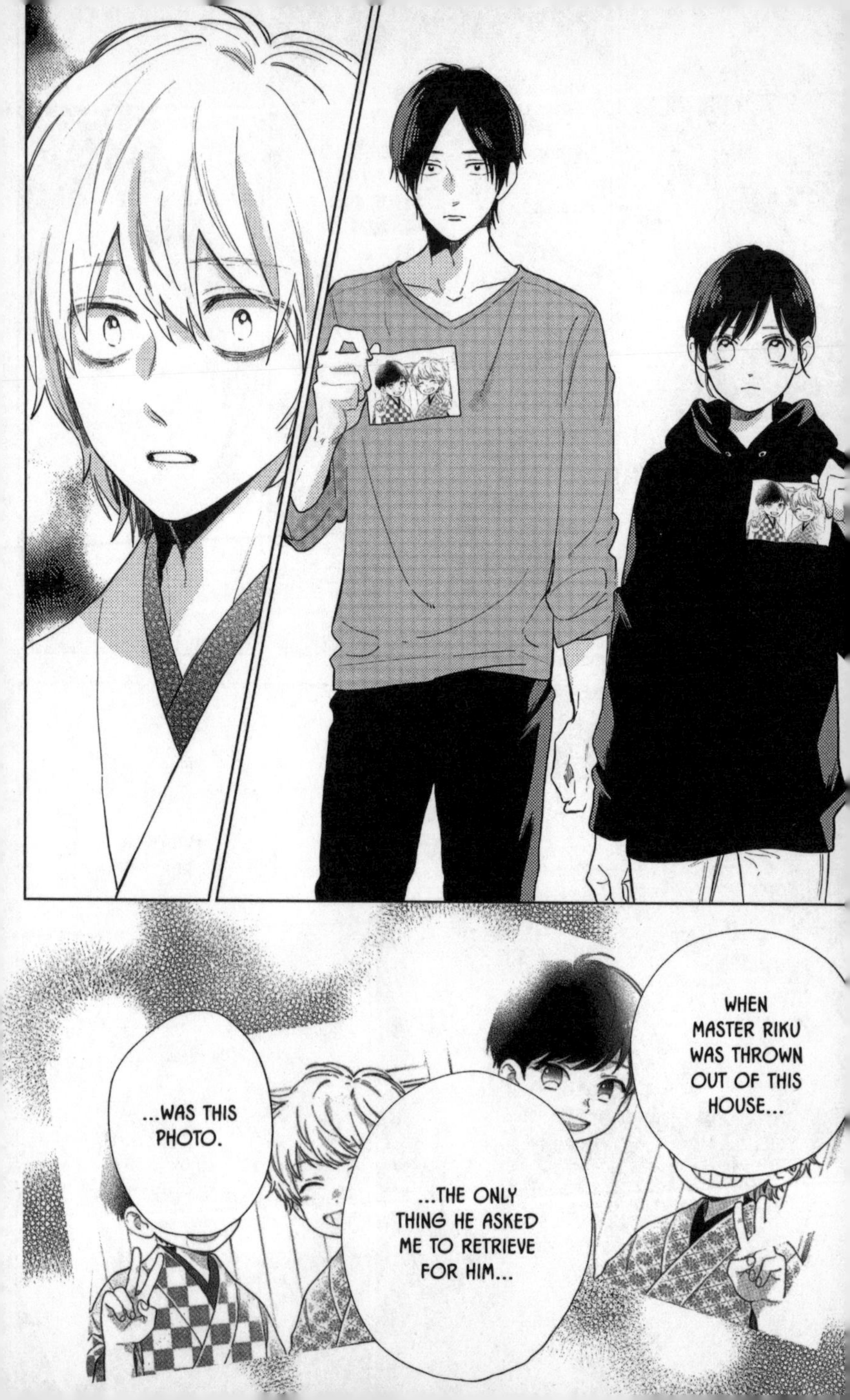
WHEN MASTER RIKU WAS THROWN OUT OF THIS HOUSE...
...THE ONLY THING HE ASKED ME TO RETRIEVE FOR HIM...
...WAS THIS PHOTO.

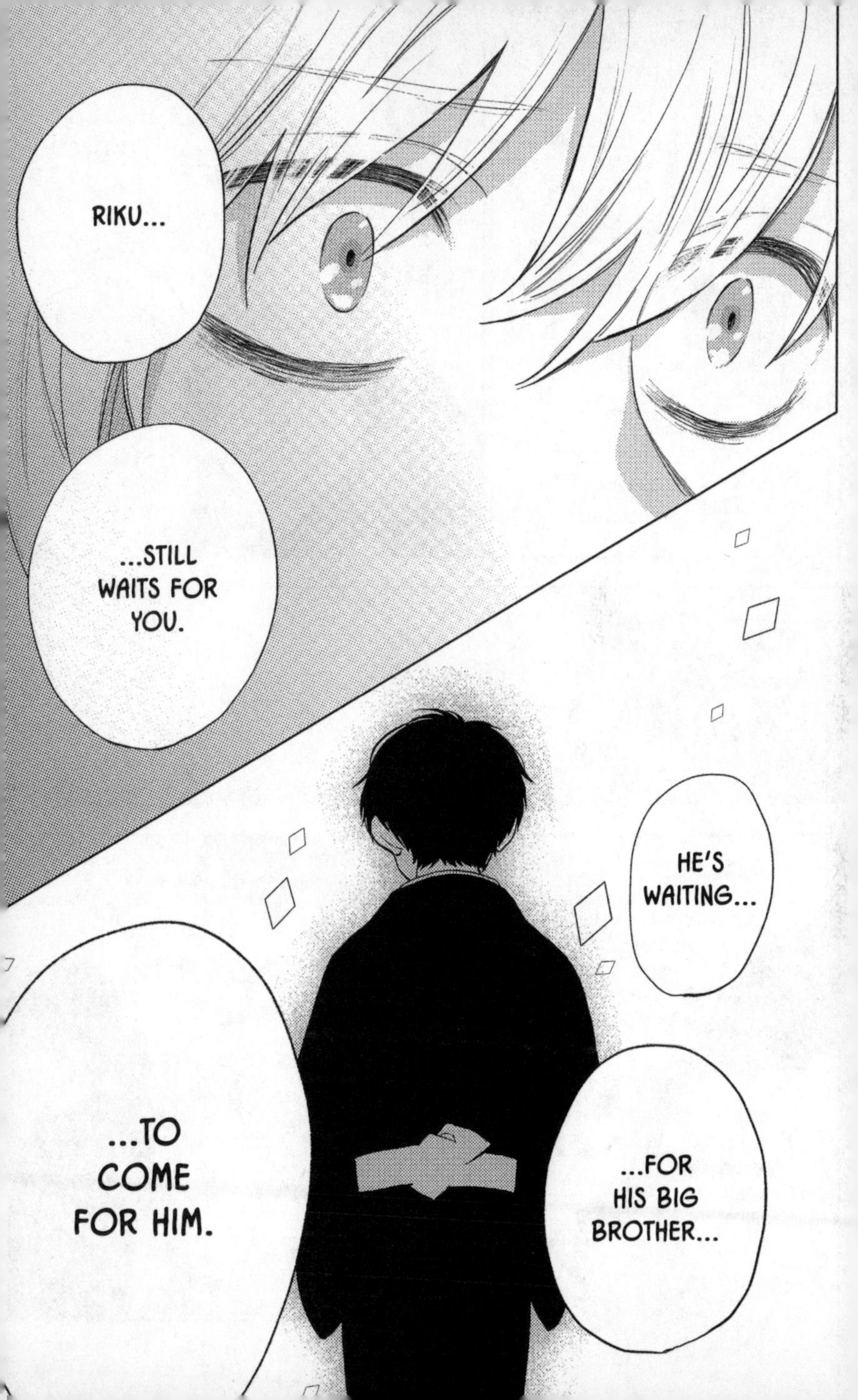
RIKU...
...STILL WAITS FOR YOU.
HE'S WAITING...
...FOR HIS BIG BROTHER...
...TO COME FOR HIM.

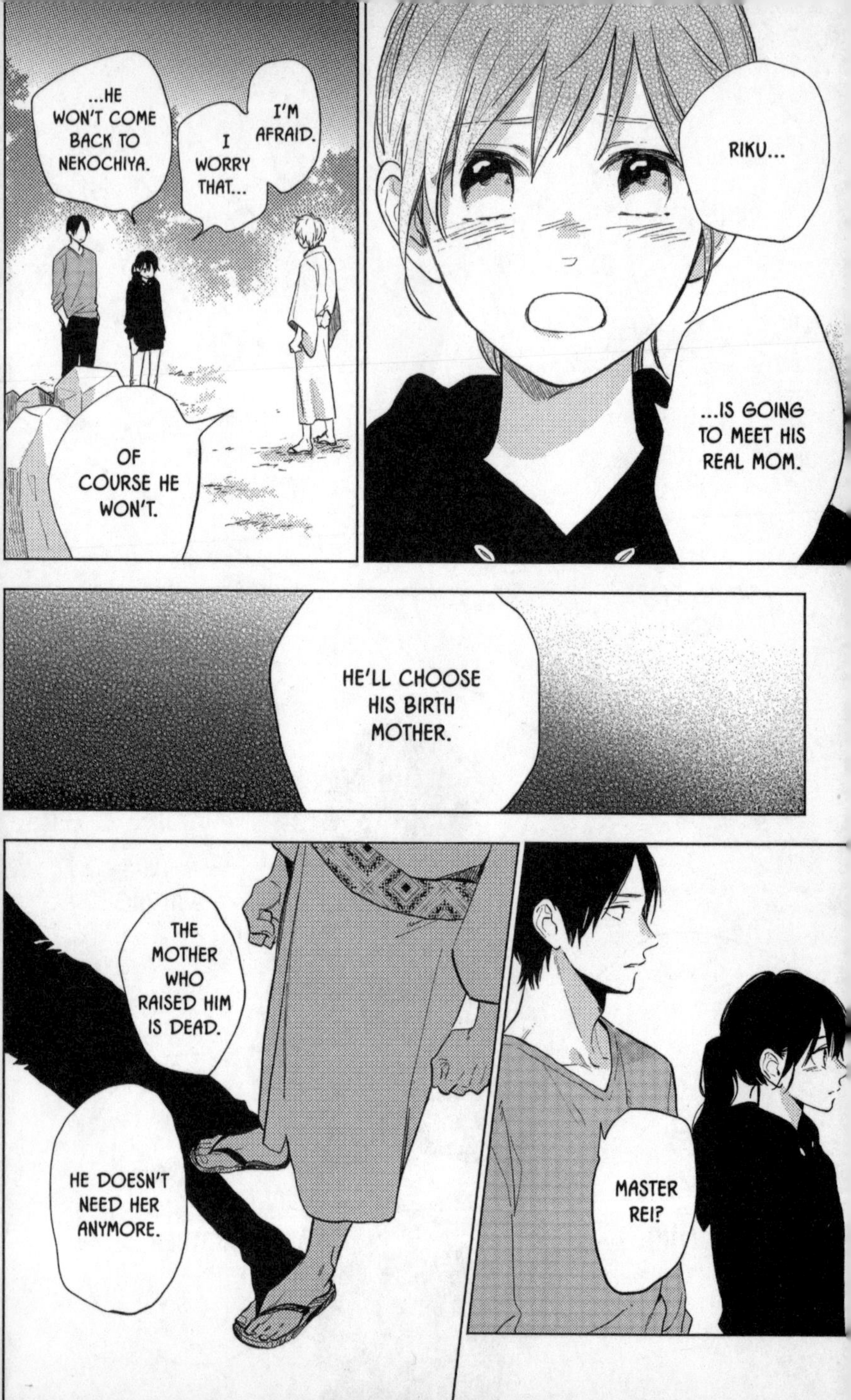
RIKU...
...IS GOING TO MEET HIS REAL MOM.
I'M AFRAID.
I WORRY THAT...
...HE WON'T COME BACK TO NEKOCHIYA.
OF COURSE HE WON'T.
HE'LL CHOOSE HIS BIRTH MOTHER.
MASTER REI?
THE MOTHER WHO RAISED HIM IS DEAD.
HE DOESN'T NEED HER ANYMORE.

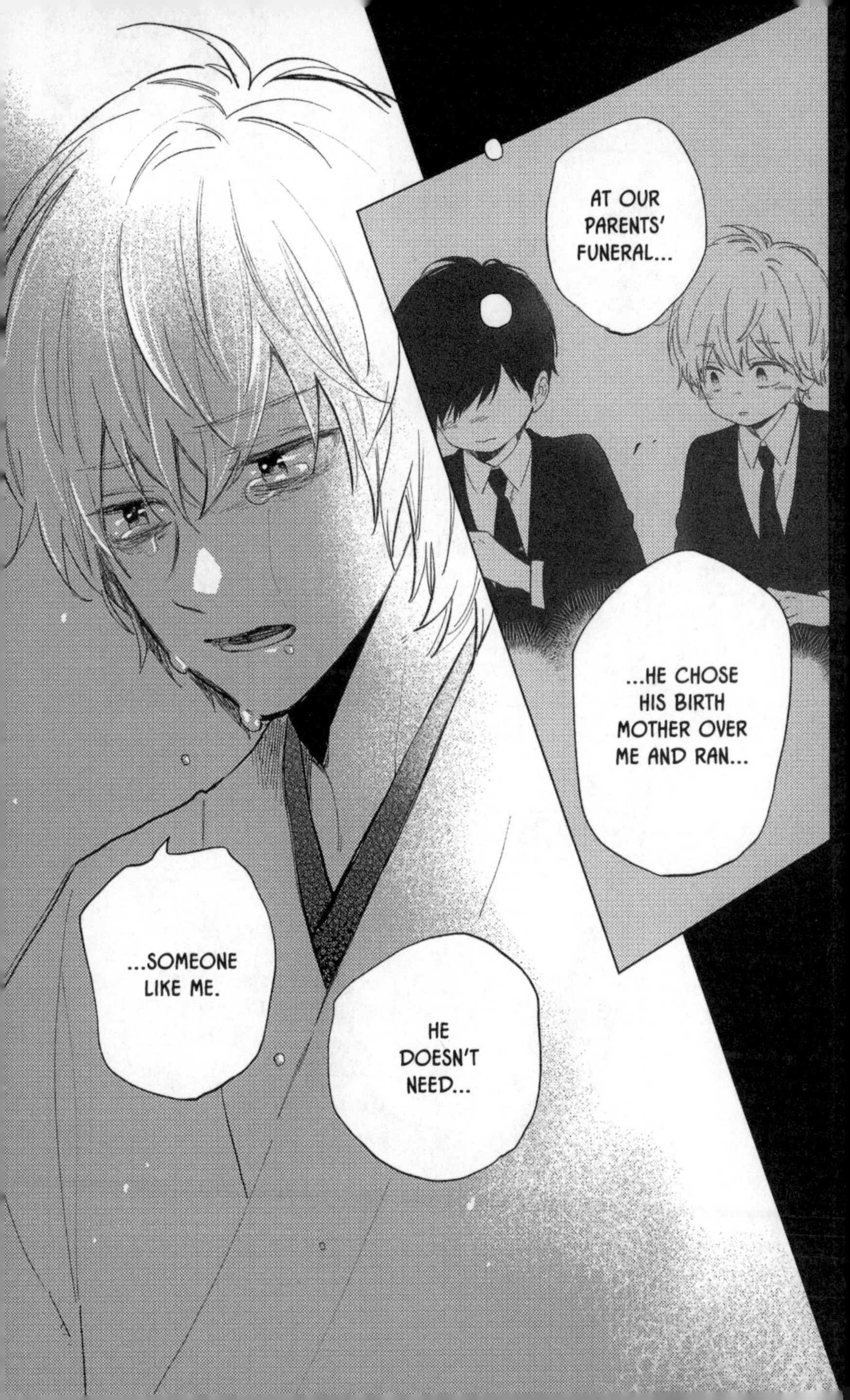
AT OUR PARENTS' FUNERAL...
...HE CHOSE HIS BIRTH MOTHER OVER ME AND RAN...
HE DOESN'T NEED...
...SOMEONE LIKE ME.

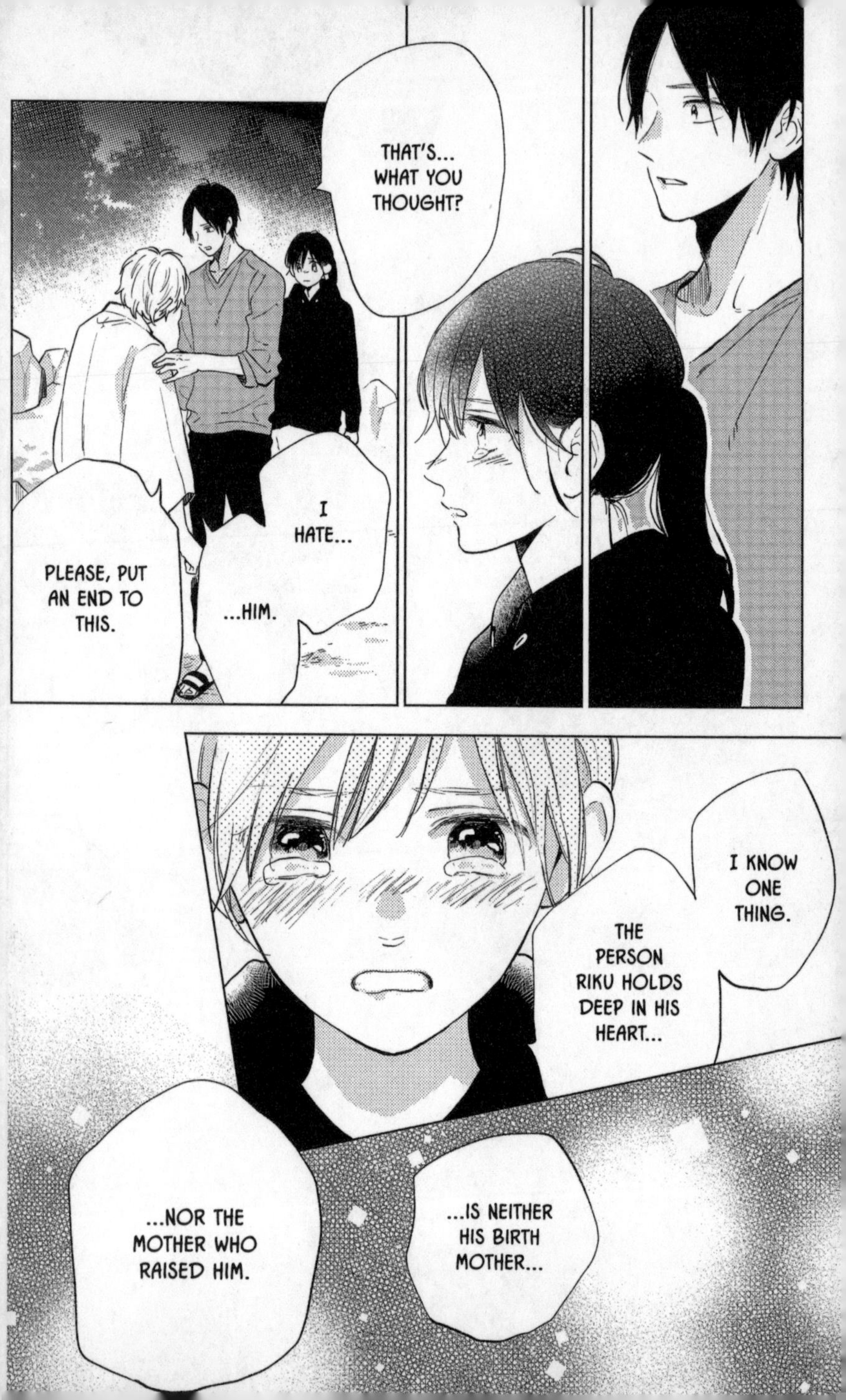
THAT'S... WHAT YOU THOUGHT?
I HATE...
...HIM.
PLEASE, PUT AN END TO THIS.
I KNOW ONE THING.
THE PERSON RIKU HOLDS DEEP IN HIS HEART...
...IS NEITHER HIS BIRTH MOTHER...
...NOR THE MOTHER WHO RAISED HIM.

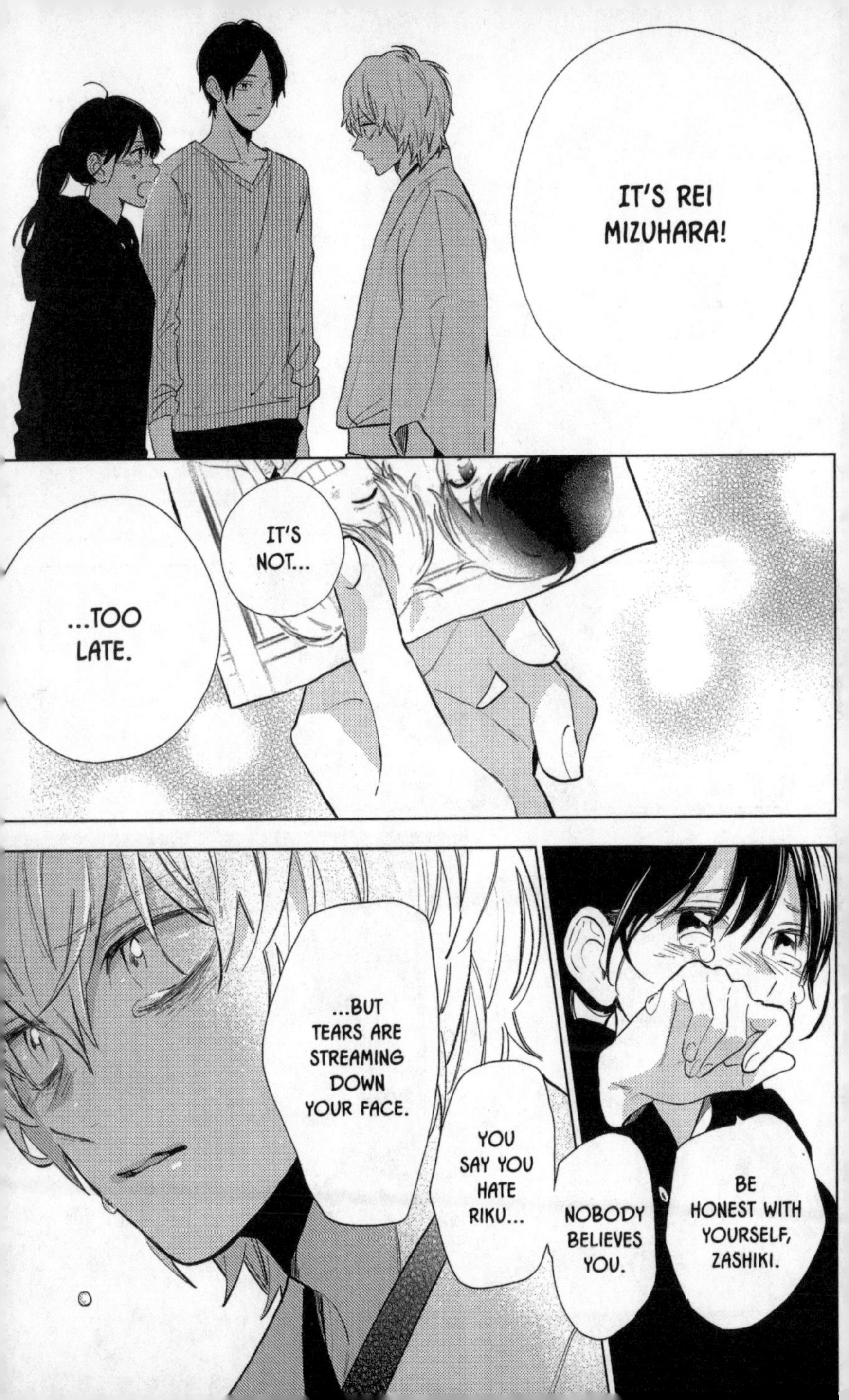
IT'S REI MIZUHARA!
IT'S NOT...
...TOO LATE.
YOU SAY YOU HATE RIKU...
...BUT TEARS ARE STREAMING DOWN YOUR FACE.
NOBODY BELIEVES YOU.
BE HONEST WITH YOURSELF, ZASHIKI.

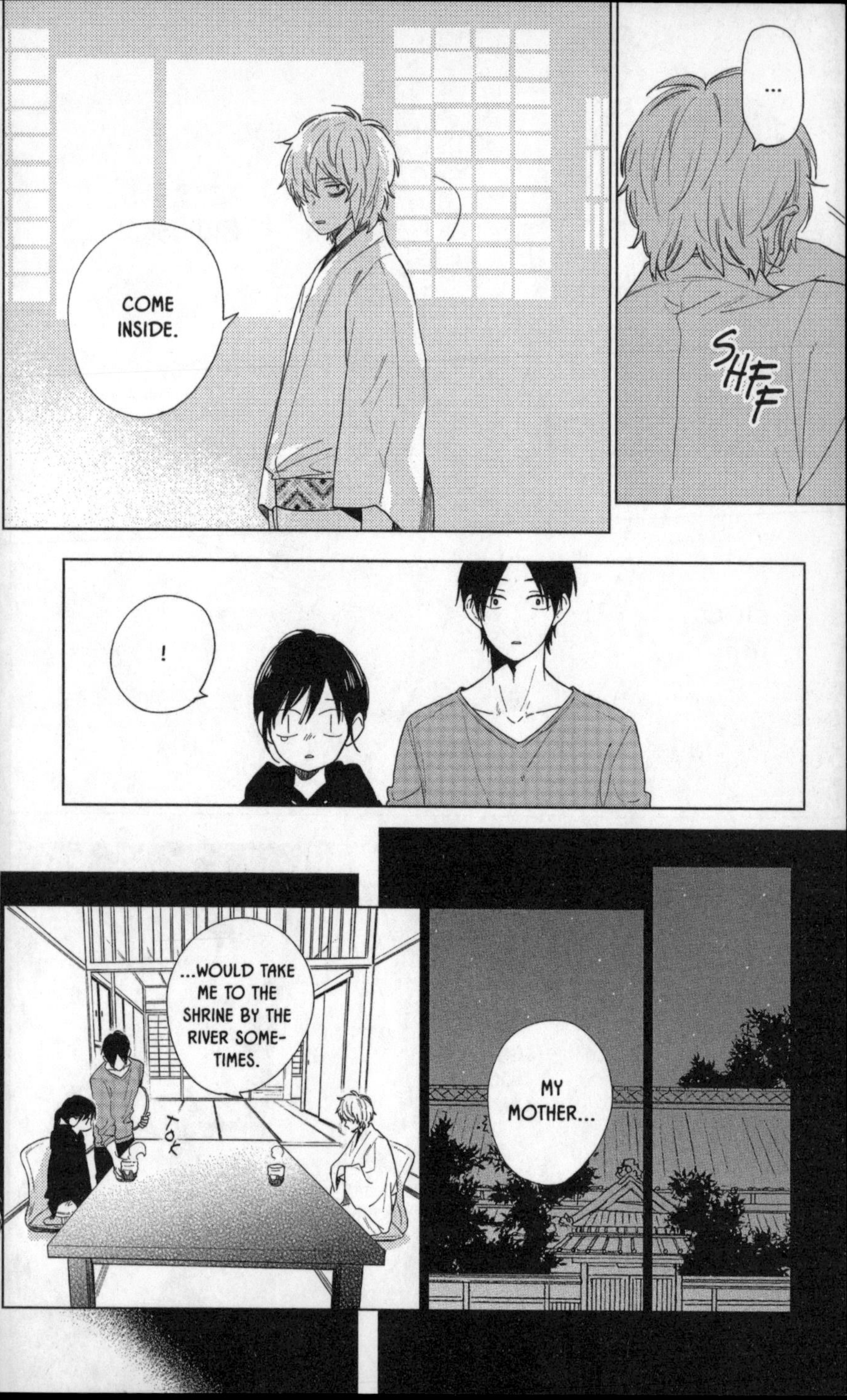
...
SHFF
COME INSIDE.
!
MY MOTHER...
...WOULD TAKE ME TO THE SHRINE BY THE RIVER SOMETIMES.
TOK

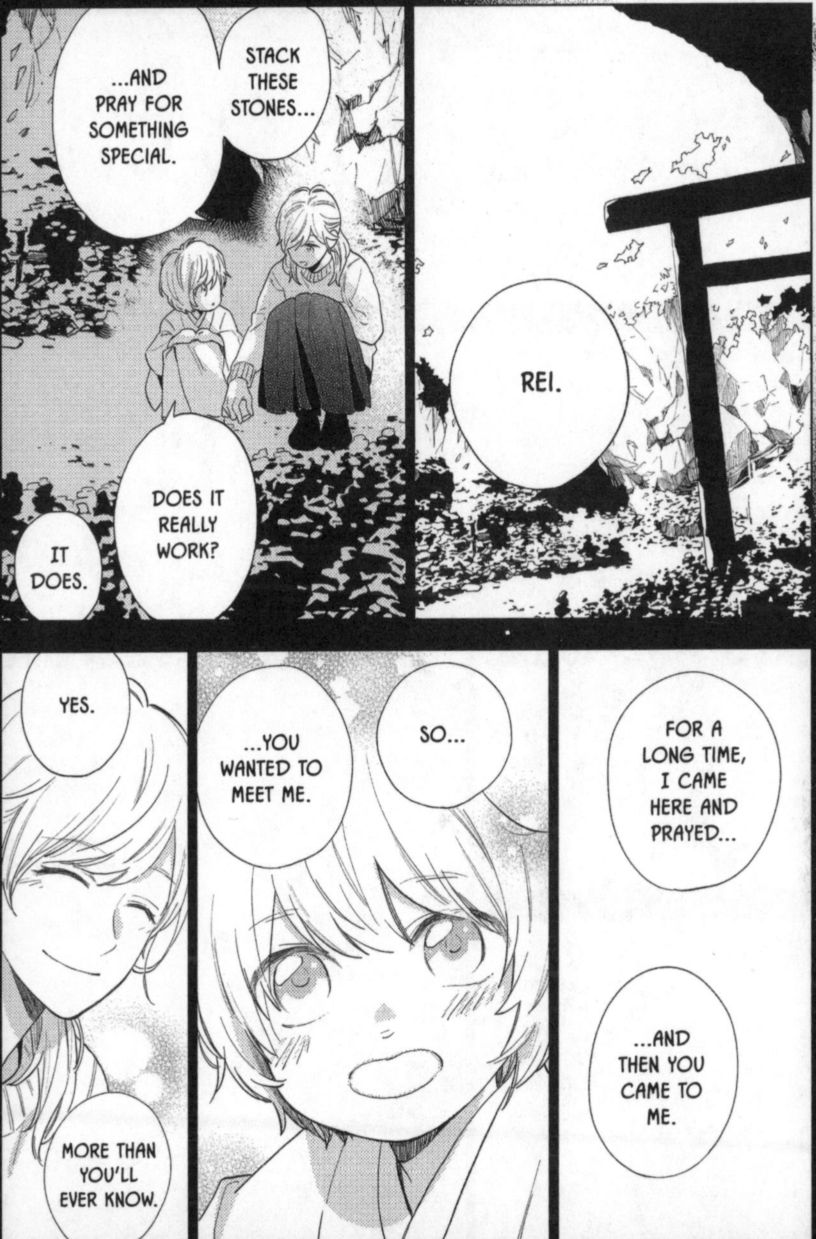
REI.
STACK THESE STONES...
...AND PRAY FOR SOMETHING SPECIAL.
DOES IT REALLY WORK?
IT DOES.
FOR A LONG TIME, I CAME HERE AND PRAYED...
...AND THEN YOU CAME TO ME.
SO...
...YOU WANTED TO MEET ME.
YES.
MORE THAN YOU'LL EVER KNOW.

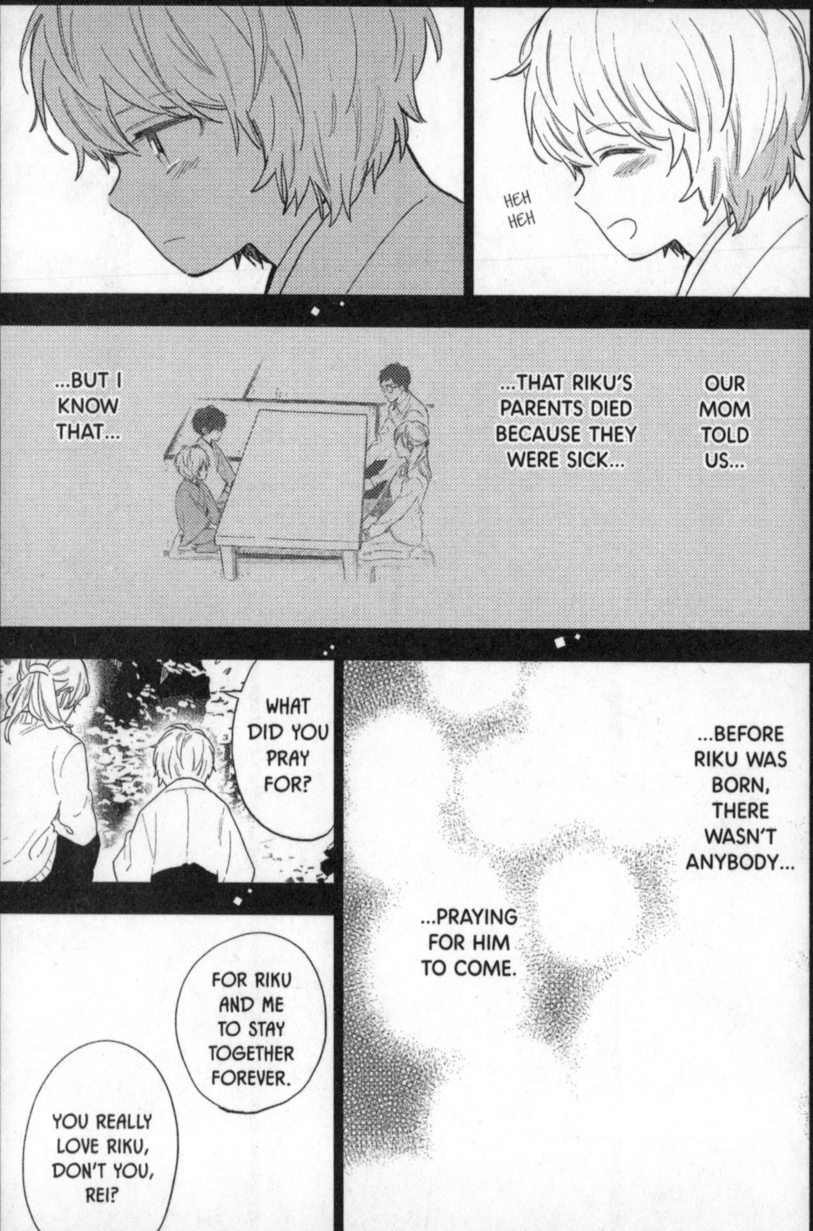
HEH HEH
OUR MOM TOLD US...
...THAT RIKU'S PARENTS DIED BECAUSE THEY WERE SICK...
...BUT I KNOW THAT...
...BEFORE RIKU WAS BORN, THERE WASN'T ANYBODY...
...PRAYING FOR HIM TO COME.
WHAT DID YOU PRAY FOR?
FOR RIKU AND ME TO STAY TOGETHER FOREVER.
YOU REALLY LOVE RIKU, DON'T YOU, REI?

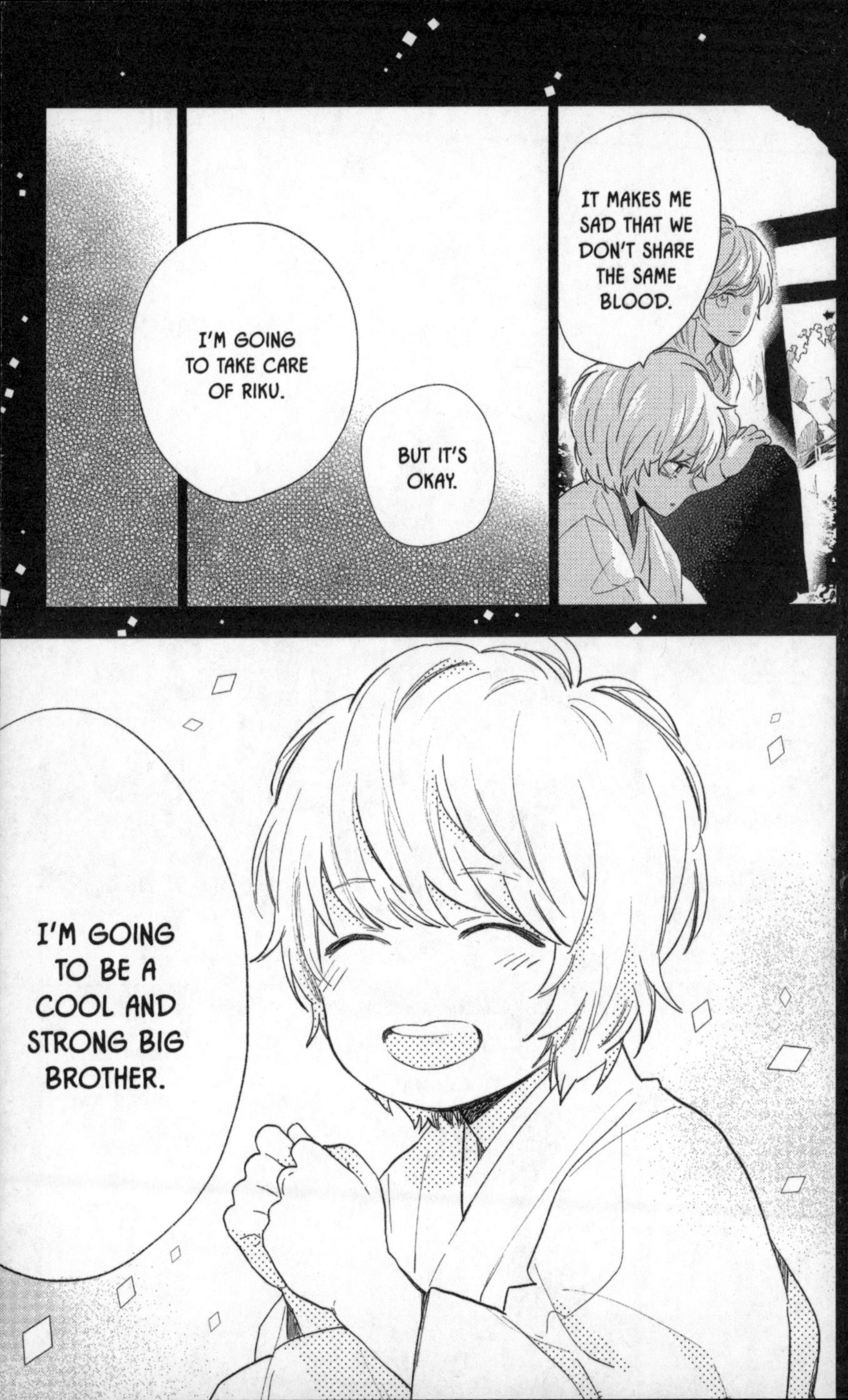
IT MAKES ME SAD THAT WE DON'T SHARE THE SAME BLOOD.
BUT IT'S OKAY.
I'M GOING TO TAKE CARE OF RIKU.
I'M GOING TO BE A COOL AND STRONG BIG BROTHER.

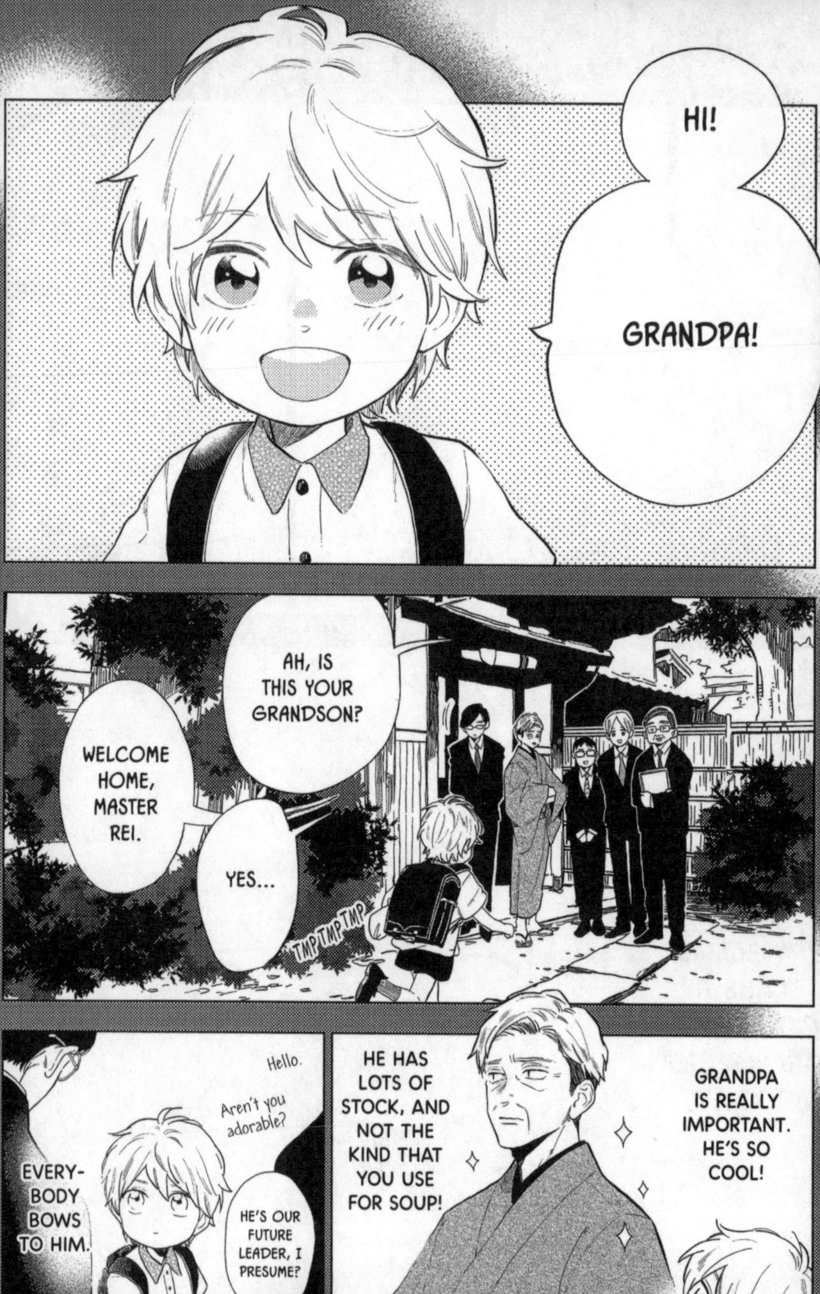
HI!
GRANDPA!
AH, IS THIS YOUR GRANDSON?
WELCOME HOME, MASTER REI.
YES...
TMP TMP TMP
GRANDPA IS REALLY IMPORTANT. HE'S SO COOL!
HE HAS LOTS OF STOCK, AND NOT THE KIND THAT YOU USE FOR SOUP!
Hello.
Aren't you adorable?
HE'S OUR FUTURE LEADER, I PRESUME?
EVERY-BODY BOWS TO HIM.

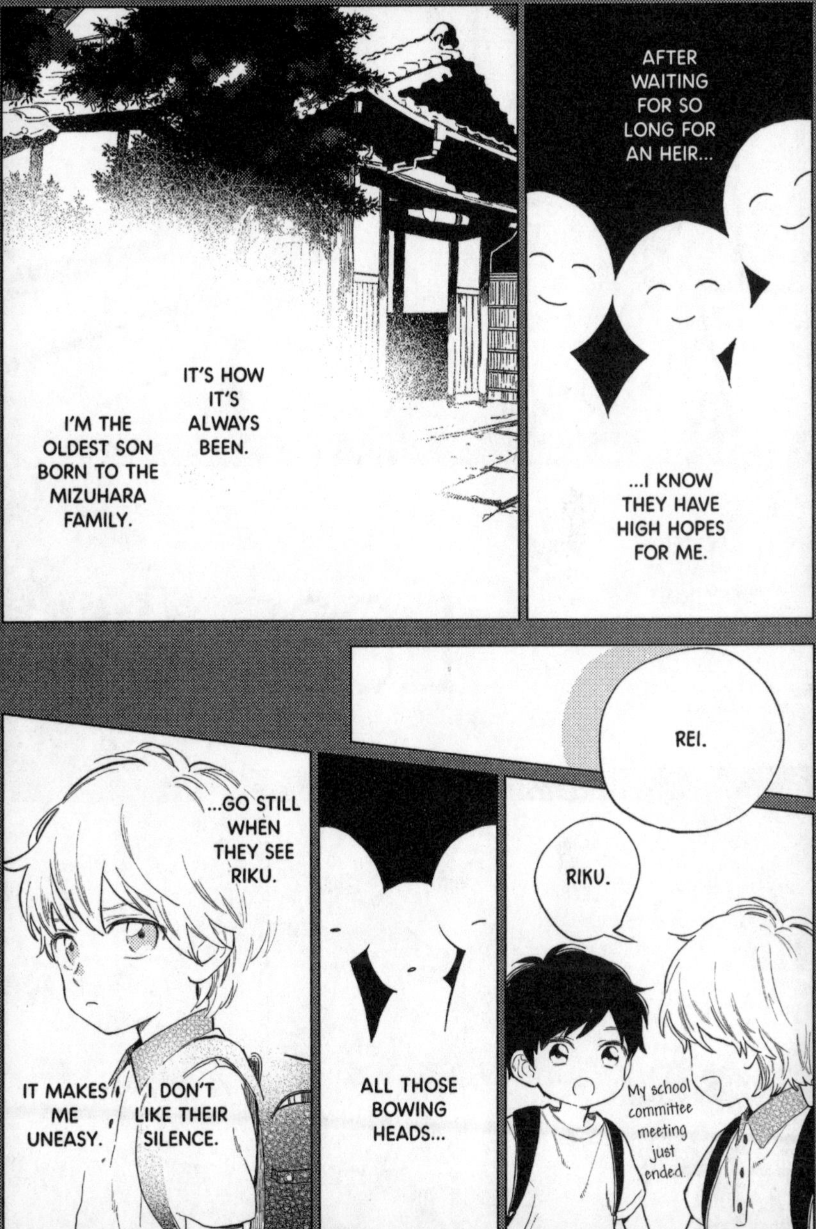

AFTER WAITING FOR SO LONG FOR AN HEIR...
...I KNOW THEY HAVE HIGH HOPES FOR ME.
IT'S HOW IT'S ALWAYS BEEN.
I'M THE OLDEST SON BORN TO THE MIZUHARA FAMILY.
REI.
RIKU.
My school committee meeting just ended.
ALL THOSE BOWING HEADS...
...GO STILL WHEN THEY SEE RIKU.
I DON'T LIKE THEIR SILENCE.
IT MAKES ME UNEASY.

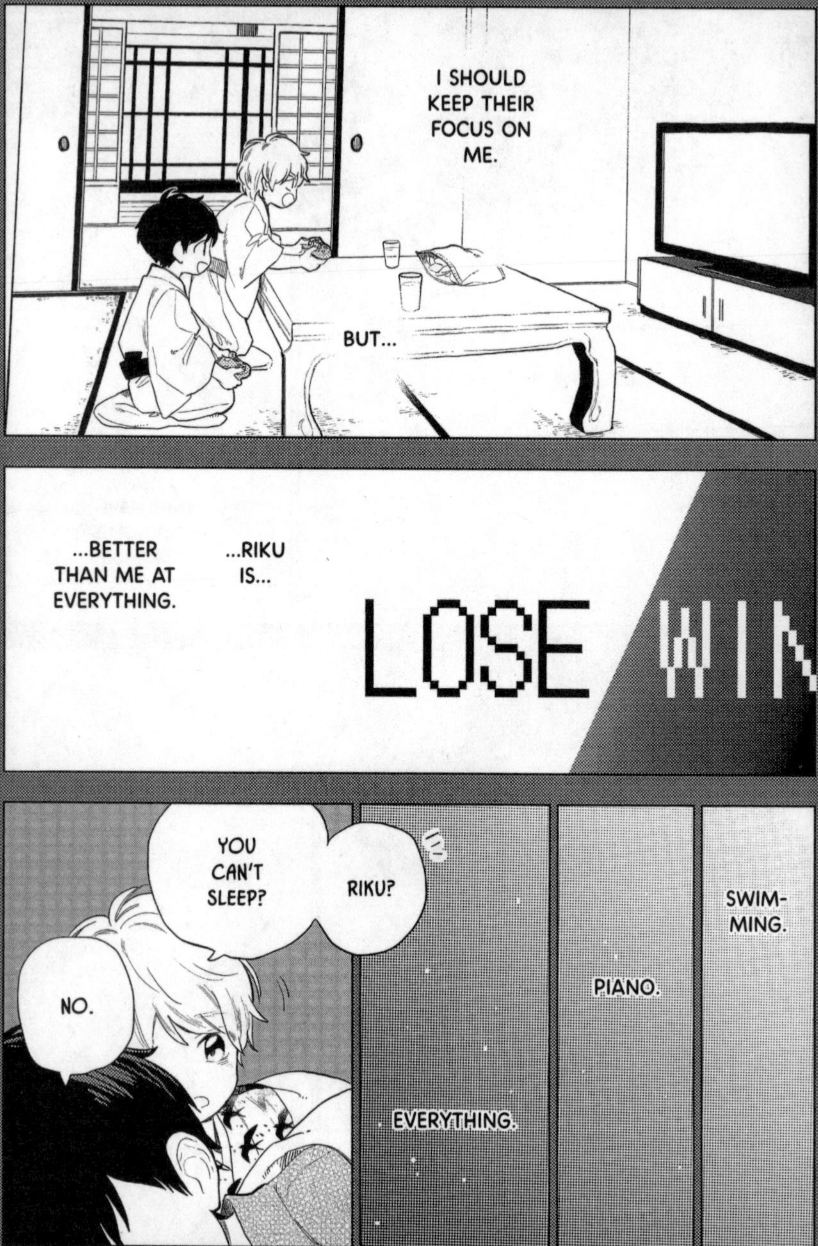
I SHOULD KEEP THEIR FOCUS ON ME.
BUT...
...RIKU IS...
...BETTER THAN ME AT EVERYTHING.
WIN
LOSE
SWIM-MING.
PIANO.
EVERYTHING.
RIKU?
YOU CAN'T SLEEP?
NO.

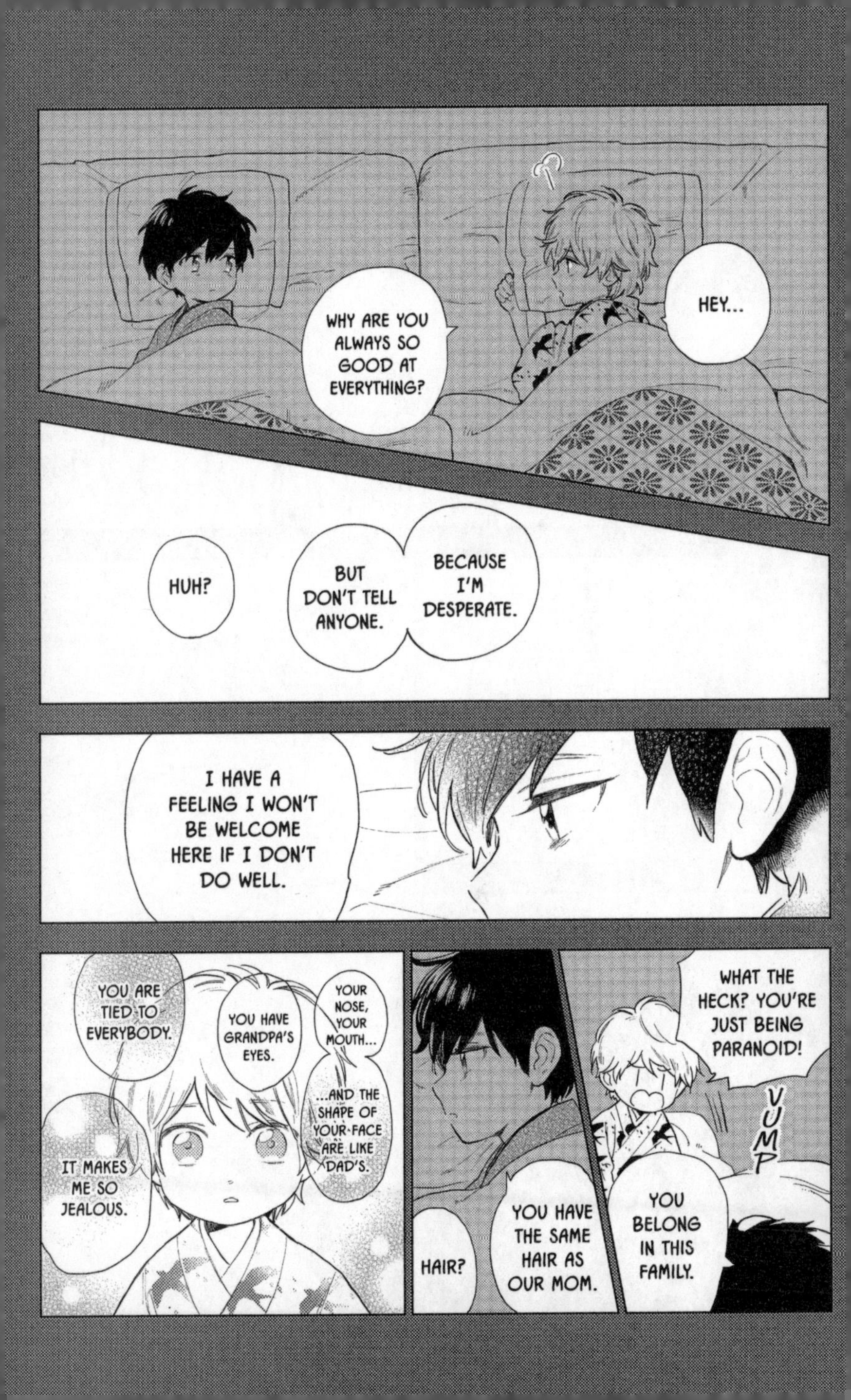
HEY...
WHY ARE YOU ALWAYS SO GOOD AT EVERYTHING?
BECAUSE I'M DESPERATE.
BUT DON'T TELL ANYONE.
HUH?
I HAVE A FEELING I WON'T BE WELCOME HERE IF I DON'T DO WELL.
WHAT THE HECK? YOU'RE JUST BEING PARANOID!
VUMP
YOU BELONG IN THIS FAMILY.
YOU HAVE THE SAME HAIR AS OUR MOM.
HAIR?
YOUR NOSE, YOUR MOUTH...
...AND THE SHAPE OF YOUR FACE ARE LIKE DAD'S.
YOU HAVE GRANDPA'S EYES.
YOU ARE TIED TO EVERYBODY.
IT MAKES ME SO JEALOUS.

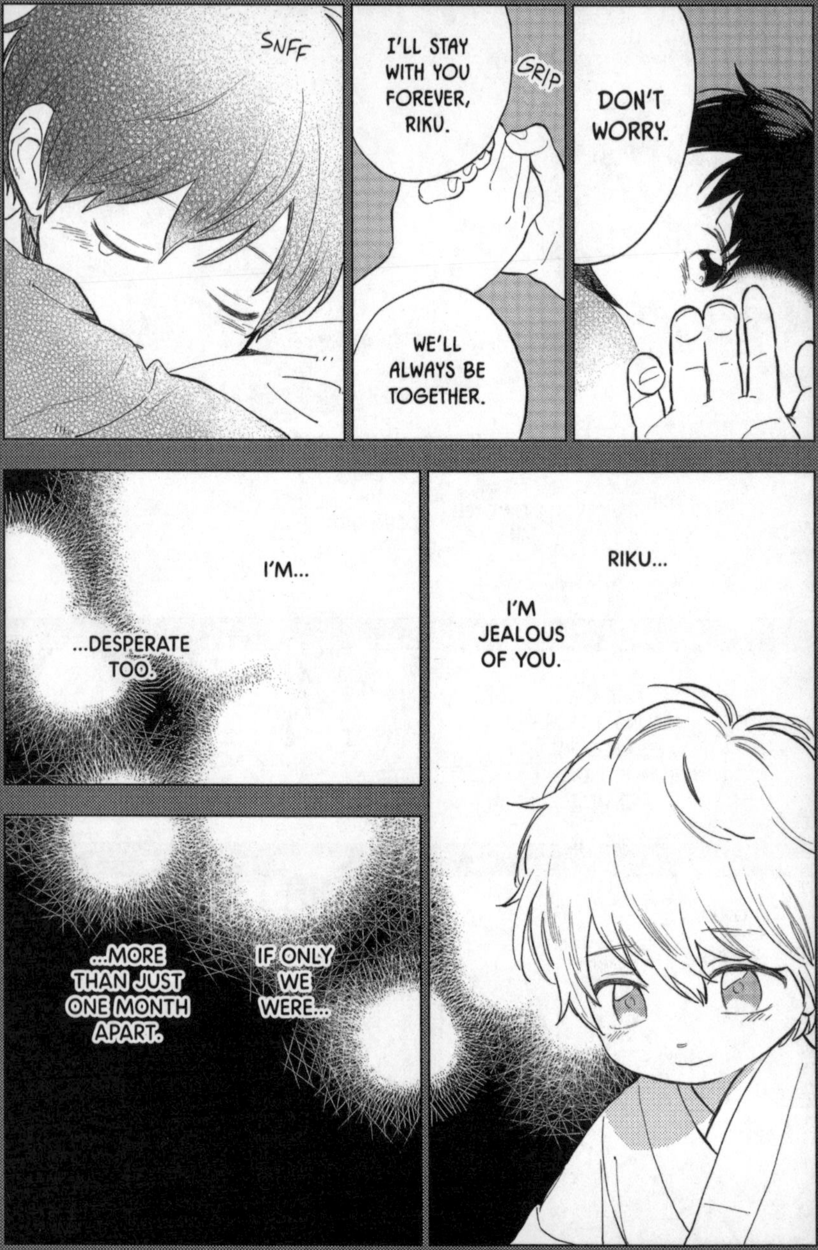
DON'T WORRY.
I'LL STAY WITH YOU FOREVER, RIKU.
GRIP
WE'LL ALWAYS BE TOGETHER.
SNFF
RIKU...
I'M JEALOUS OF YOU.
I'M...
...DESPERATE TOO.
IF ONLY WE WERE...
...MORE THAN JUST ONE MONTH APART.

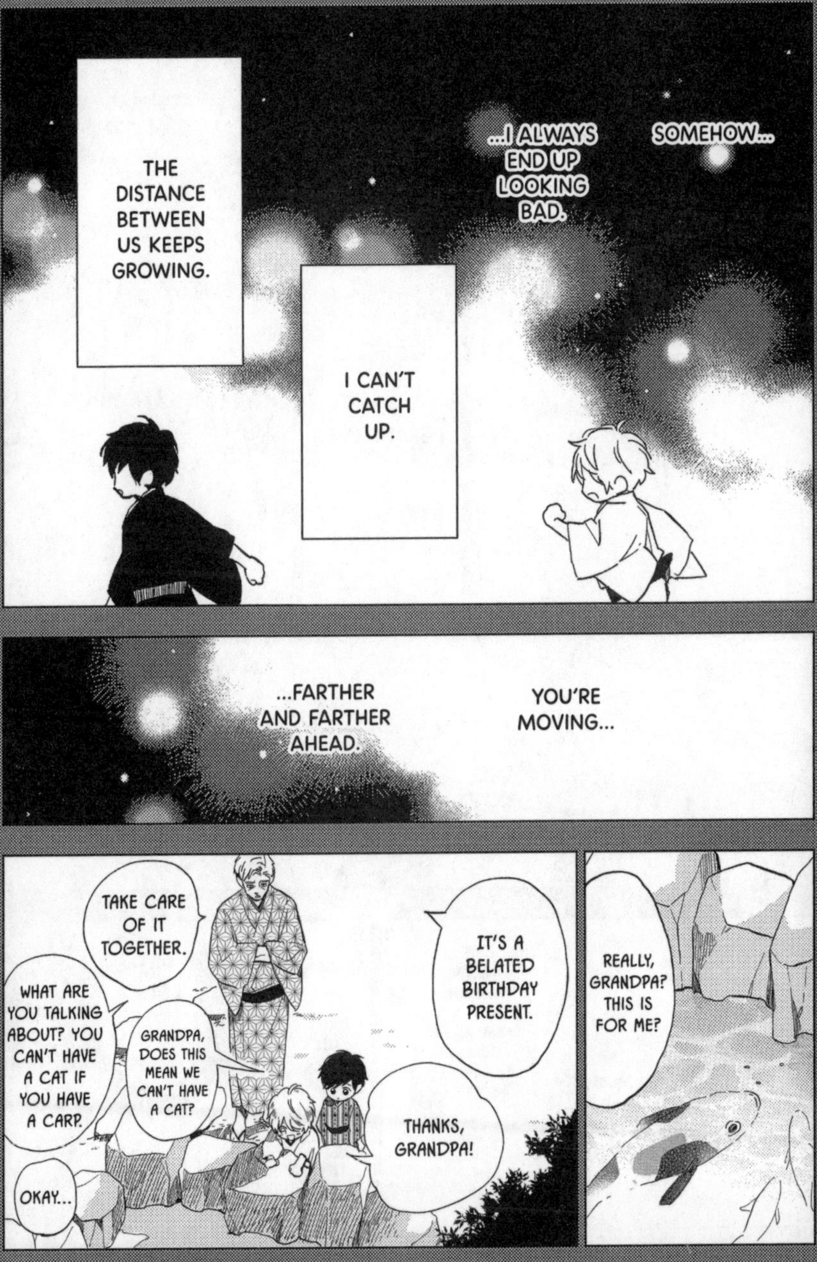

SOMEHOW...
...I ALWAYS END UP LOOKING BAD.
THE DISTANCE BETWEEN US KEEPS GROWING.
I CAN'T CATCH UP.
YOU'RE MOVING...
...FARTHER AND FARTHER AHEAD.
REALLY, GRANDPA? THIS IS FOR ME?
IT'S A BELATED BIRTHDAY PRESENT.
TAKE CARE OF IT TOGETHER.
THANKS, GRANDPA!
GRANDPA, DOES THIS MEAN WE CAN'T HAVE A CAT?
WHAT ARE YOU TALKING ABOUT? YOU CAN'T HAVE A CAT IF YOU HAVE A CARP.
OKAY...

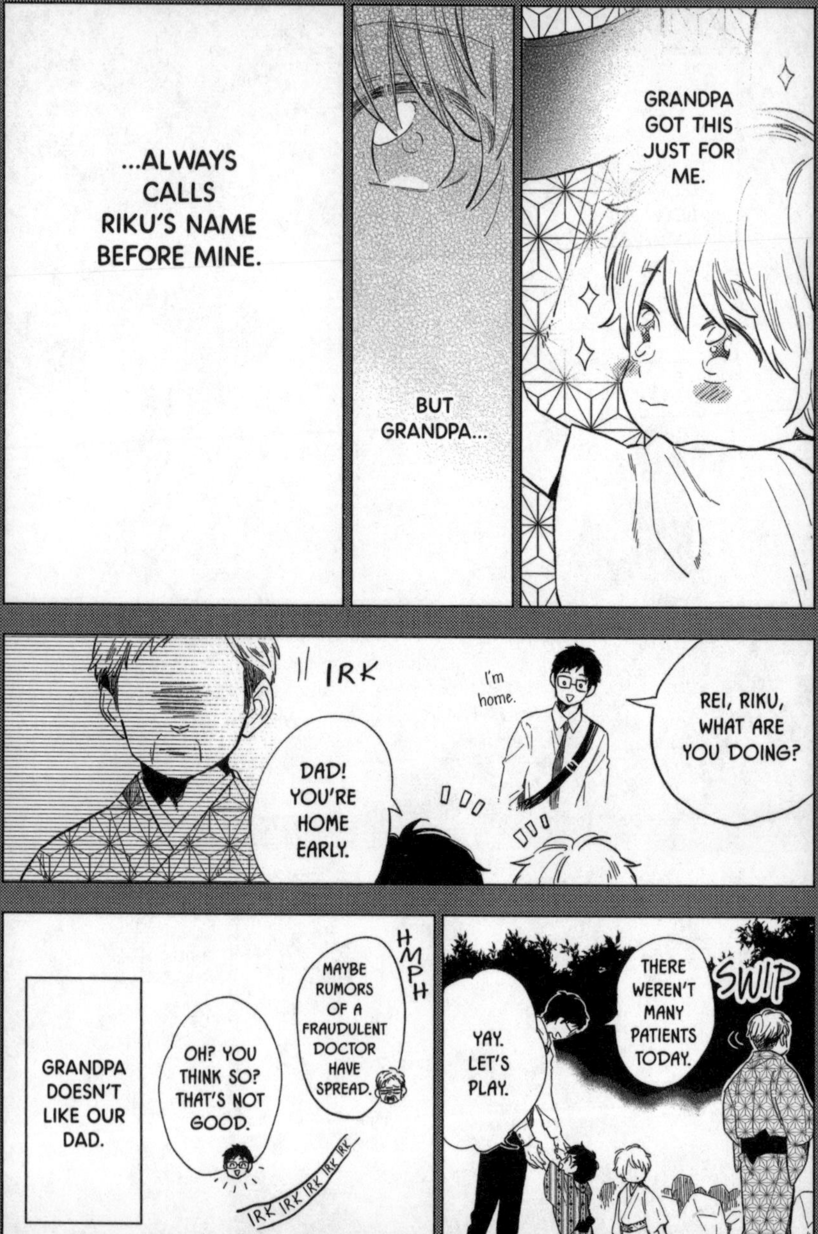
GRANDPA GOT THIS JUST FOR ME.
BUT GRANDPA...
...ALWAYS CALLS RIKU'S NAME BEFORE MINE.
REI, RIKU, WHAT ARE YOU DOING?
I'm home.
DAD! YOU'RE HOME EARLY.
IRK
SWIP
THERE WEREN'T MANY PATIENTS TODAY.
YAY. LET'S PLAY.
HMPH
MAYBE RUMORS OF A FRAUDULENT DOCTOR HAVE SPREAD.
OH? YOU THINK SO? THAT'S NOT GOOD.
IRK IRK IRK IRK IRK
GRANDPA DOESN'T LIKE OUR DAD.

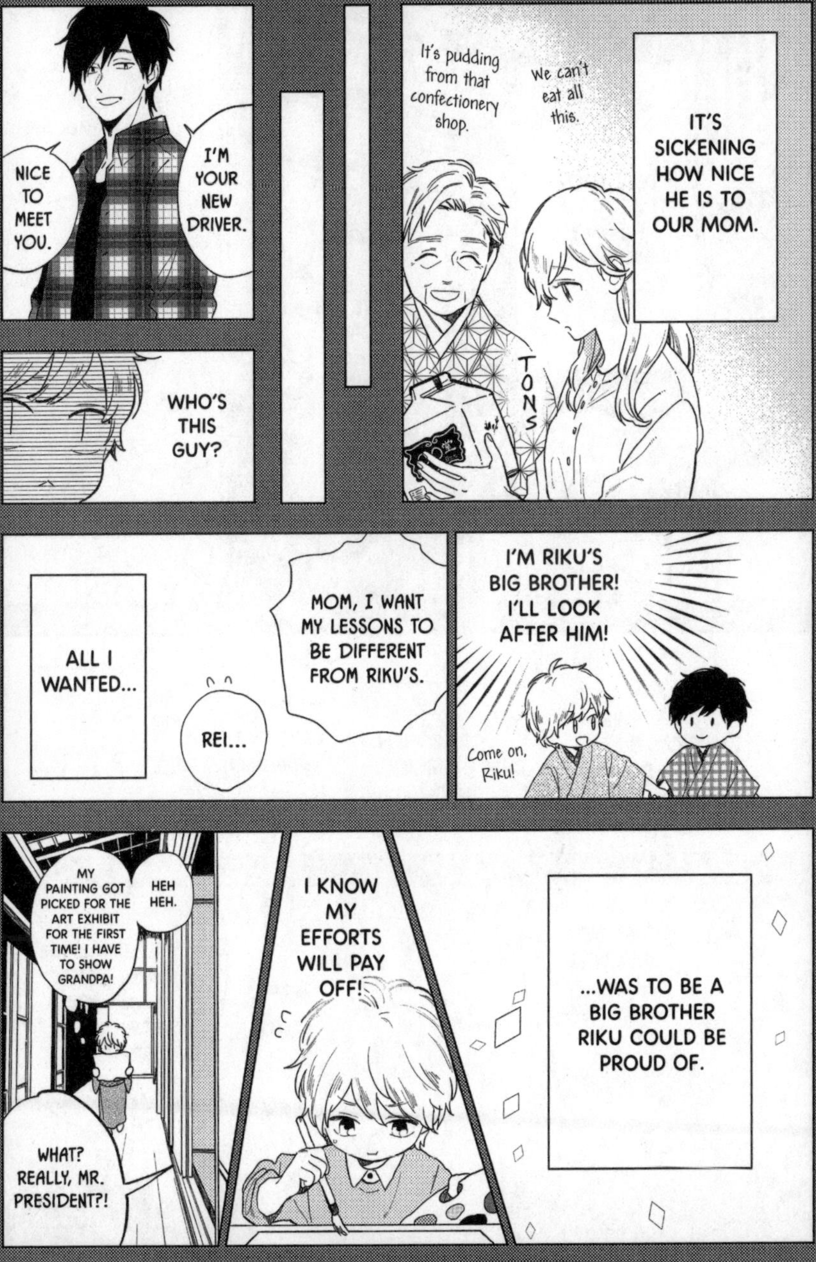
IT'S SICKENING HOW NICE HE IS TO OUR MOM.
We can't eat all this.
It's pudding from that confectionery shop.
TONS
I'M YOUR NEW DRIVER.
NICE TO MEET YOU.
WHO'S THIS GUY?
I'M RIKU'S BIG BROTHER! I'LL LOOK AFTER HIM!
Come on, Riku!
MOM, I WANT MY LESSONS TO BE DIFFERENT FROM RIKU'S.
REI...
ALL I WANTED...
...WAS TO BE A BIG BROTHER RIKU COULD BE PROUD OF.
I KNOW MY EFFORTS WILL PAY OFF!
HEH HEH.
MY PAINTING GOT PICKED FOR THE ART EXHIBIT FOR THE FIRST TIME! I HAVE TO SHOW GRANDPA!
WHAT? REALLY, MR. PRESIDENT?!

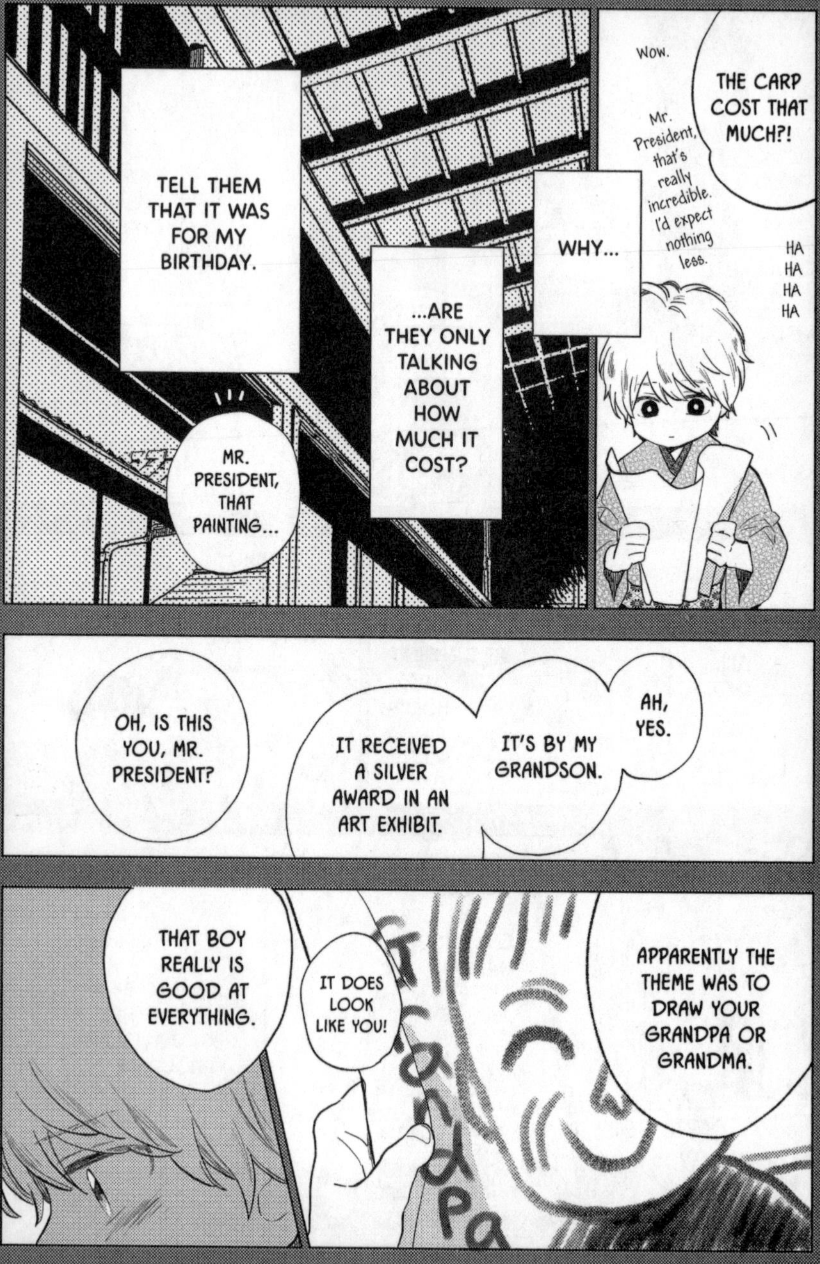
THE CARP COST THAT MUCH?!
Wow.
Mr. President, that's really incredible. I'd expect nothing less.
HA HA HA HA
WHY...
...ARE THEY ONLY TALKING ABOUT HOW MUCH IT COST?
TELL THEM THAT IT WAS FOR MY BIRTHDAY.
MR. PRESIDENT, THAT PAINTING...
AH, YES.
IT'S BY MY GRANDSON.
IT RECEIVED A SILVER AWARD IN AN ART EXHIBIT.
OH, IS THIS YOU, MR. PRESIDENT?
APPARENTLY THE THEME WAS TO DRAW YOUR GRANDPA OR GRANDMA.
IT DOES LOOK LIKE YOU!
THAT BOY REALLY IS GOOD AT EVERYTHING.

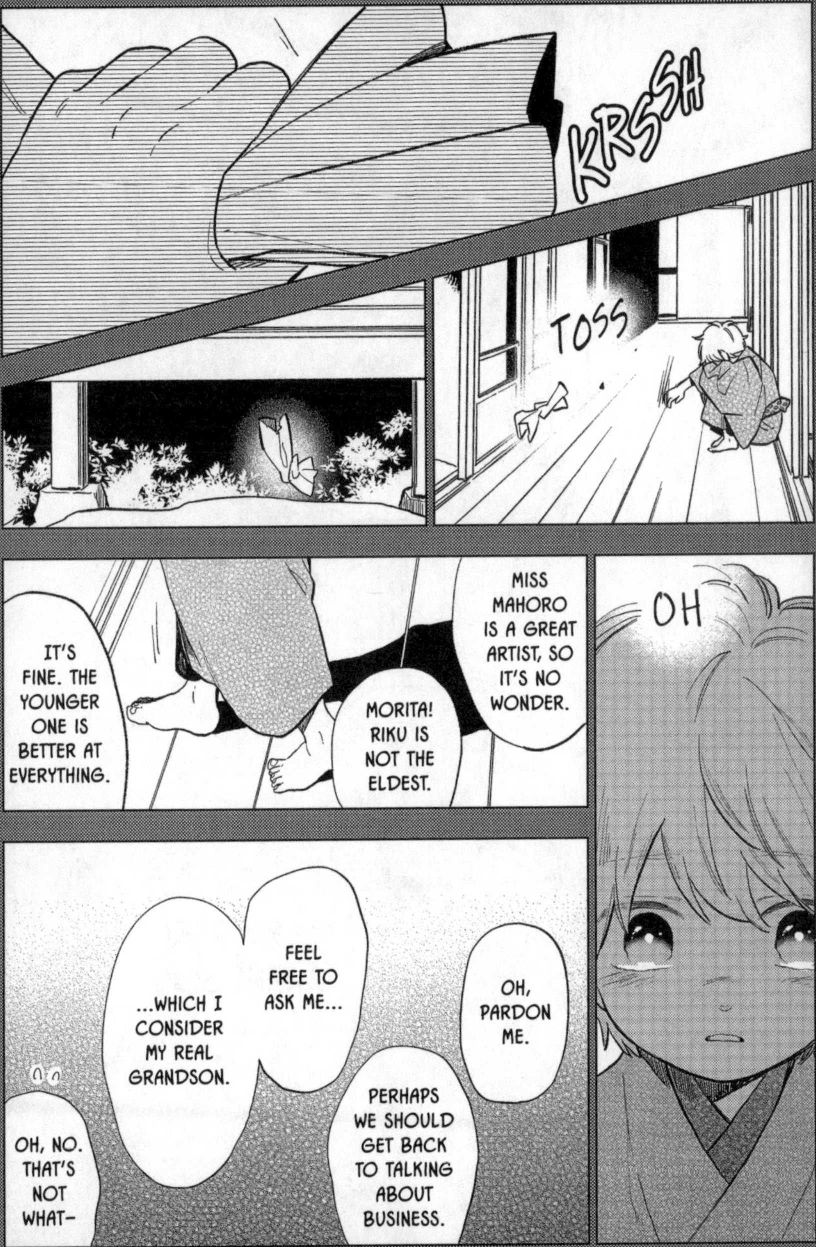
KRSSH
TOSS
OH
MISS MAHORO IS A GREAT ARTIST, SO IT'S NO WONDER.
MORITA! RIKU IS NOT THE ELDEST.
IT'S FINE. THE YOUNGER ONE IS BETTER AT EVERYTHING.
OH, PARDON ME.
FEEL FREE TO ASK ME...
...WHICH I CONSIDER MY REAL GRANDSON.
PERHAPS WE SHOULD GET BACK TO TALKING ABOUT BUSINESS.
OH, NO. THAT'S NOT WHAT–

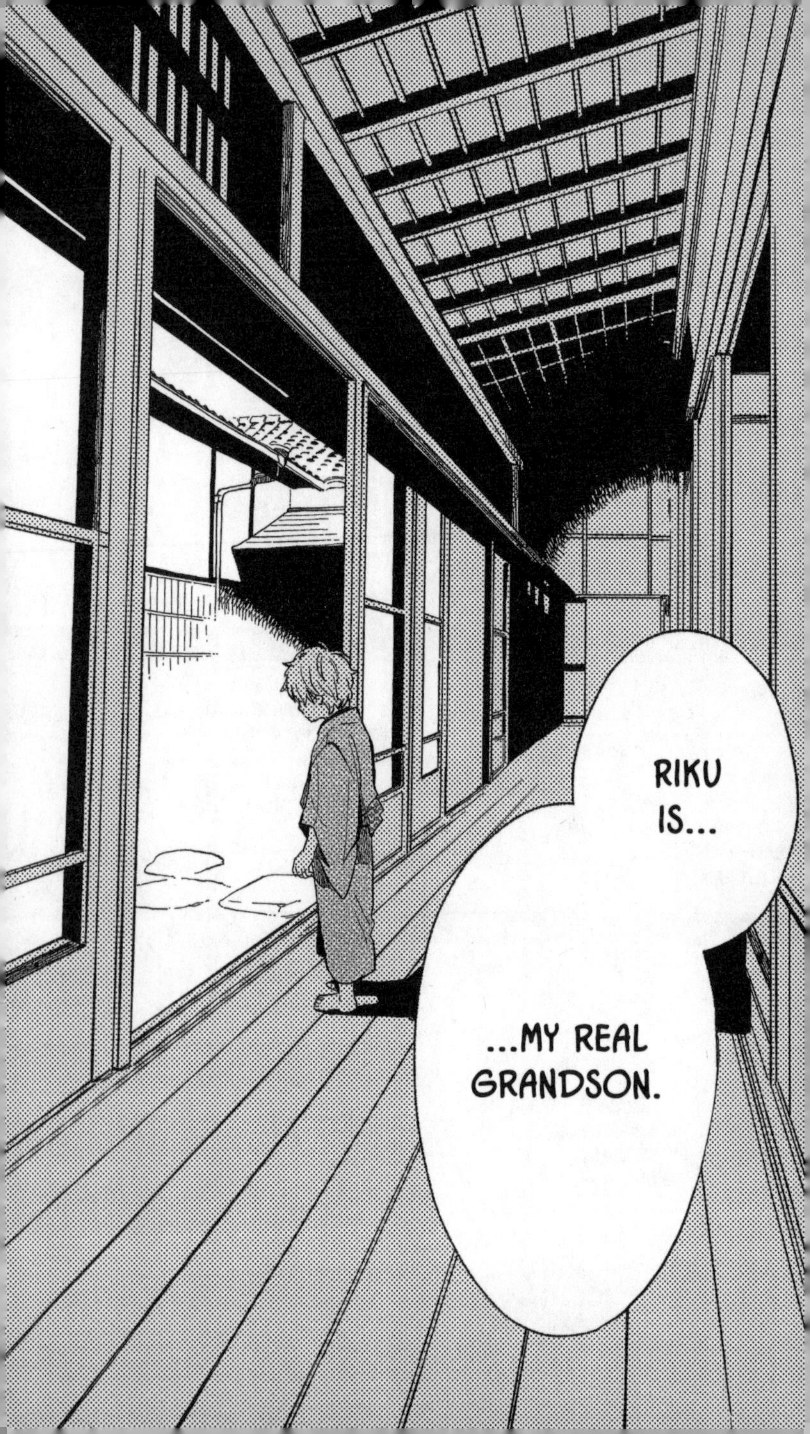
RIKU IS...
...MY REAL GRANDSON.

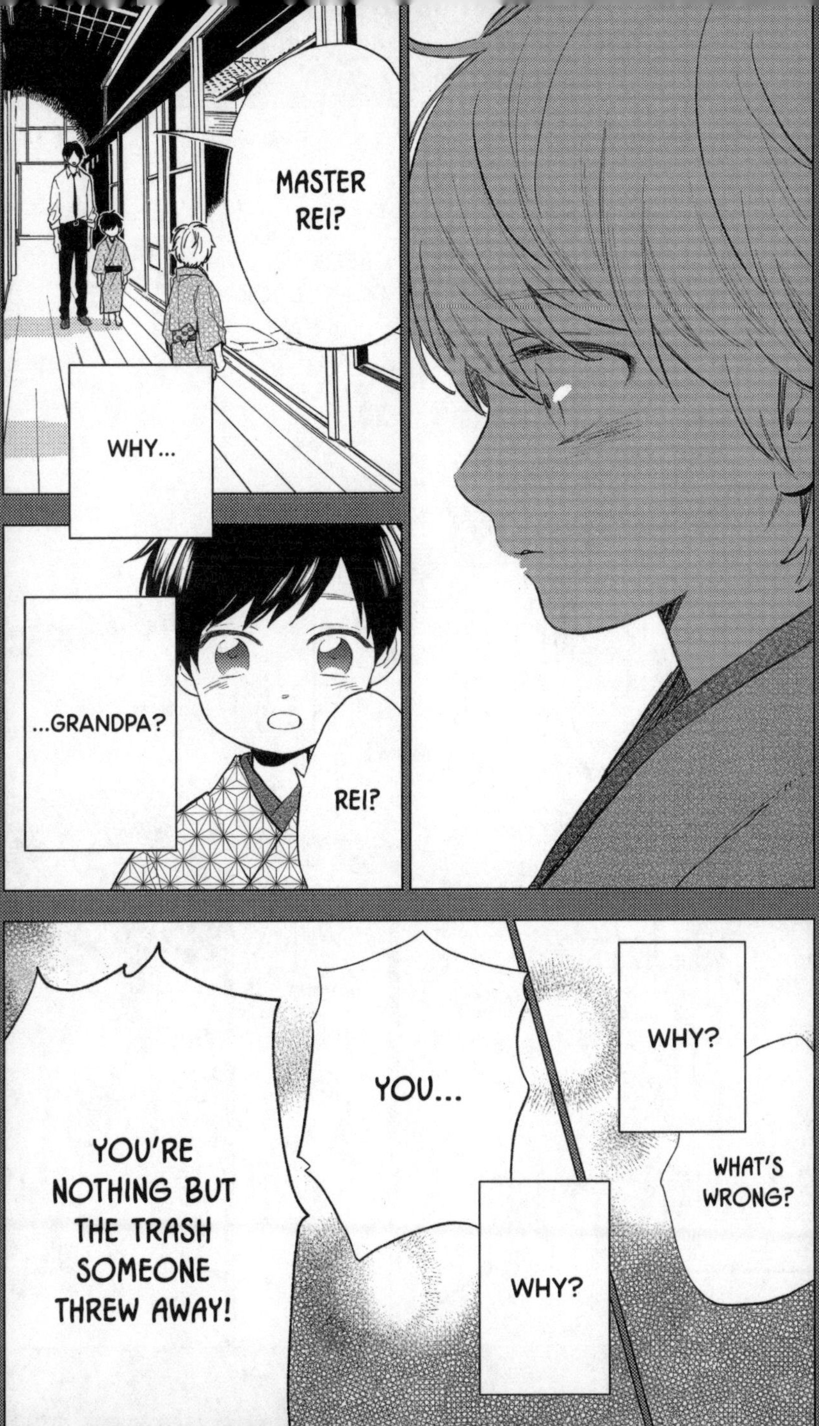
MASTER REI?
WHY...
REI?
...GRANDPA?
WHY?
WHAT'S WRONG?
WHY?
YOU...
YOU'RE NOTHING BUT THE TRASH SOMEONE THREW AWAY!

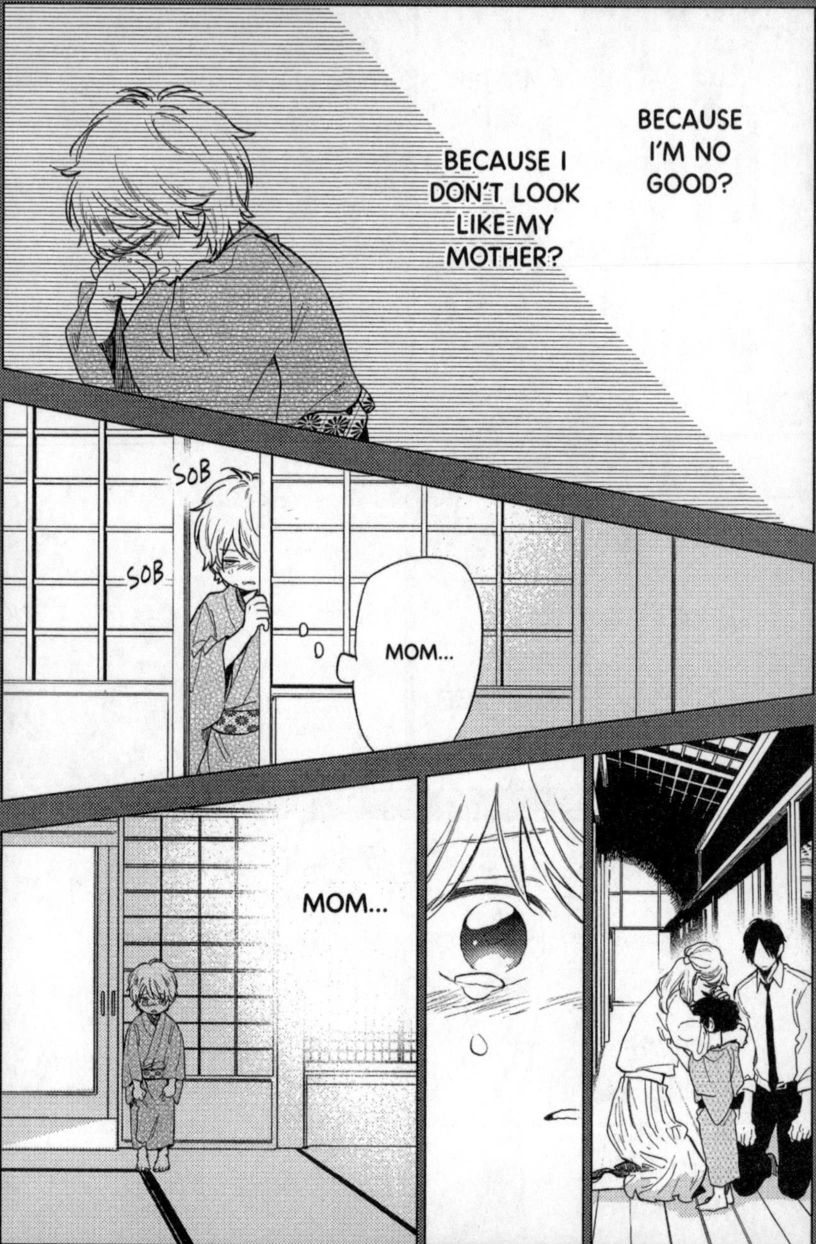
BECAUSE I'M NO GOOD?
BECAUSE I DON'T LOOK LIKE MY MOTHER?
SOB
SOB
MOM...
MOM...

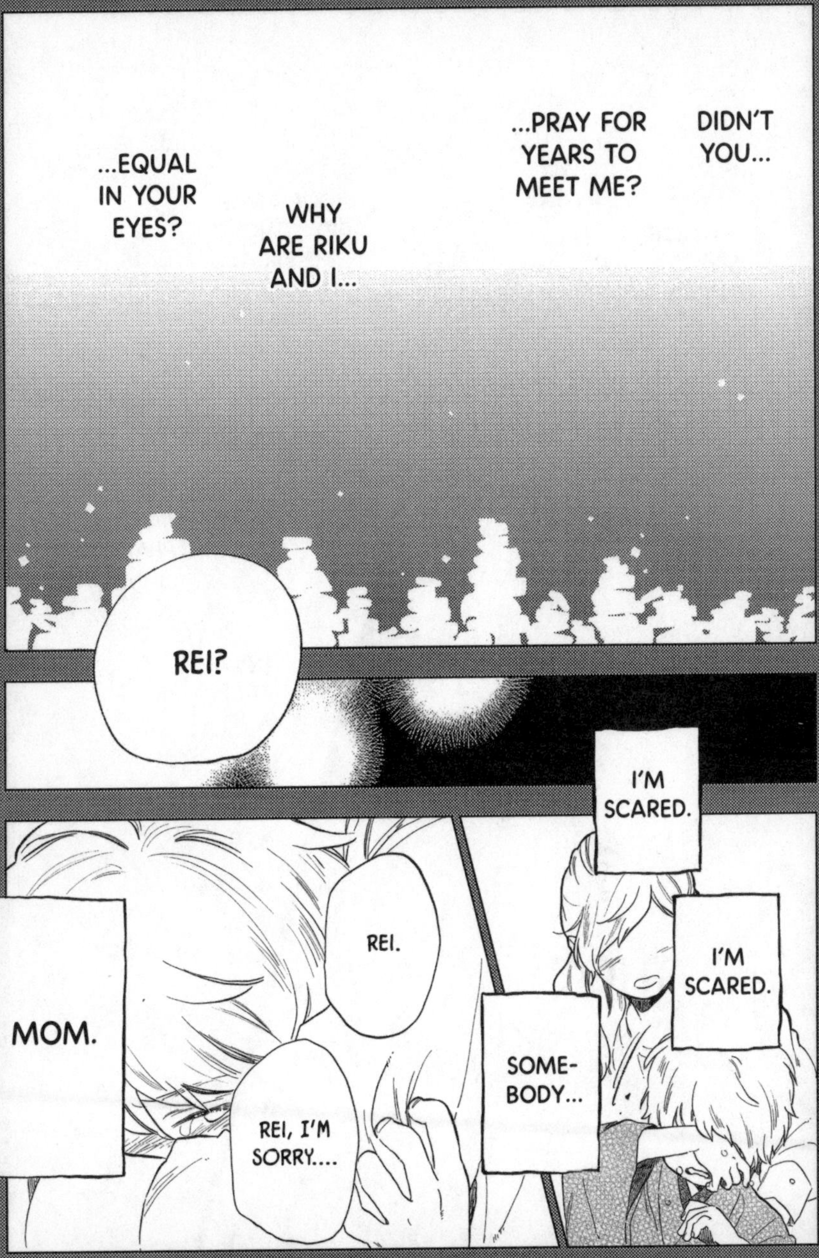
DIDN'T YOU...
...PRAY FOR YEARS TO MEET ME?
WHY ARE RIKU AND I...
...EQUAL IN YOUR EYES?
REI?
I'M SCARED.
I'M SCARED.
SOME-BODY...
REI.
REI, I'M SORRY....
MOM.

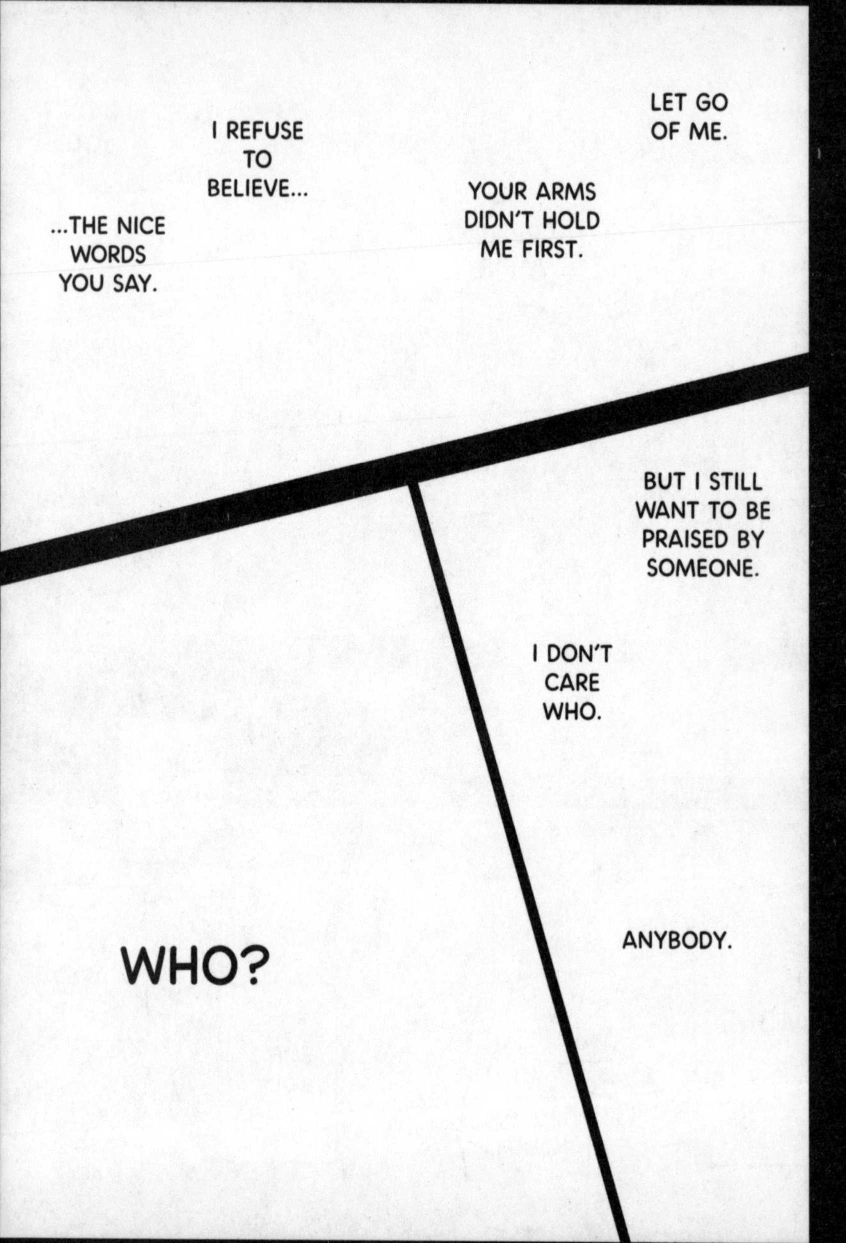
LET GO OF ME.
YOUR ARMS DIDN'T HOLD ME FIRST.
I REFUSE TO BELIEVE...
...THE NICE WORDS YOU SAY.
BUT I STILL WANT TO BE PRAISED BY SOMEONE.
I DON'T CARE WHO.
ANYBODY.
WHO?

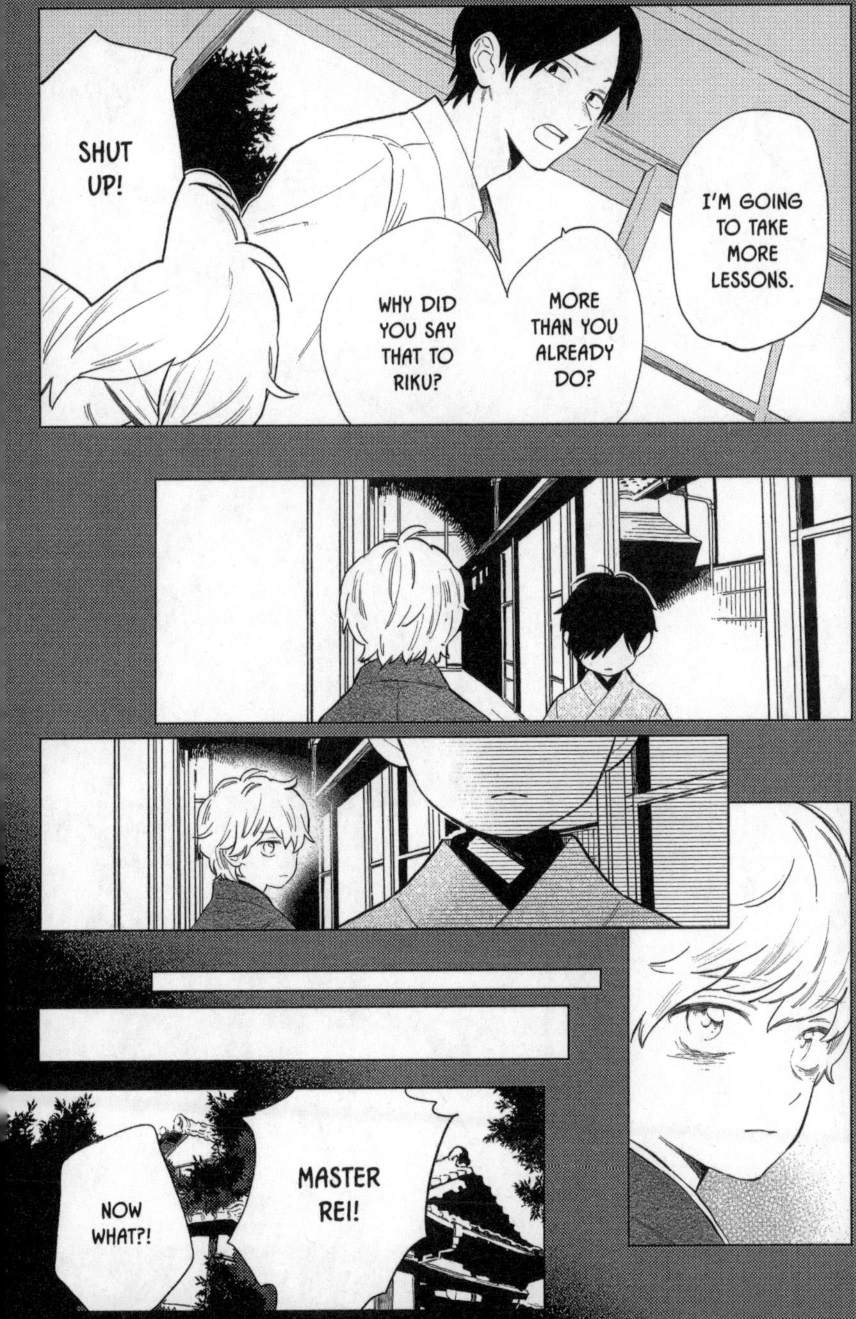
I'M GOING TO TAKE MORE LESSONS.
MORE THAN YOU ALREADY DO?
WHY DID YOU SAY THAT TO RIKU?
SHUT UP!
MASTER REI!
NOW WHAT?!

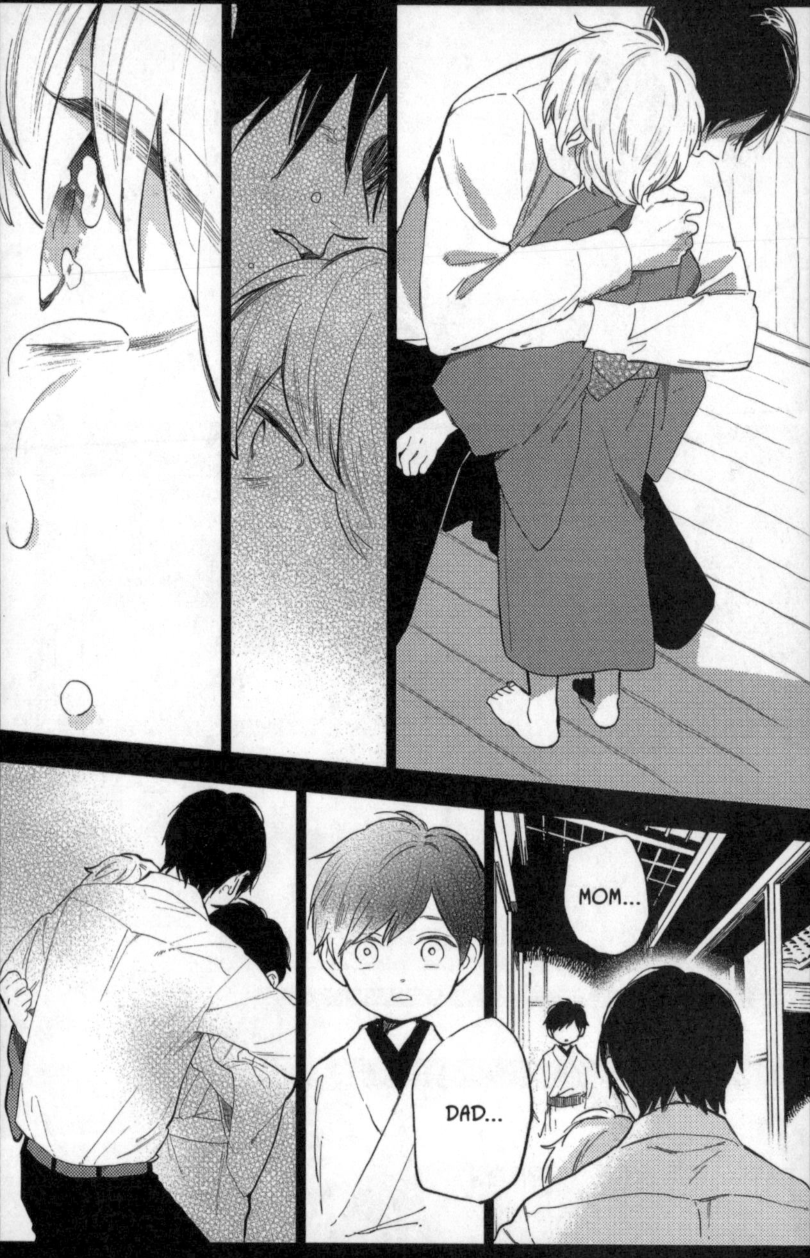
MOM...
DAD...

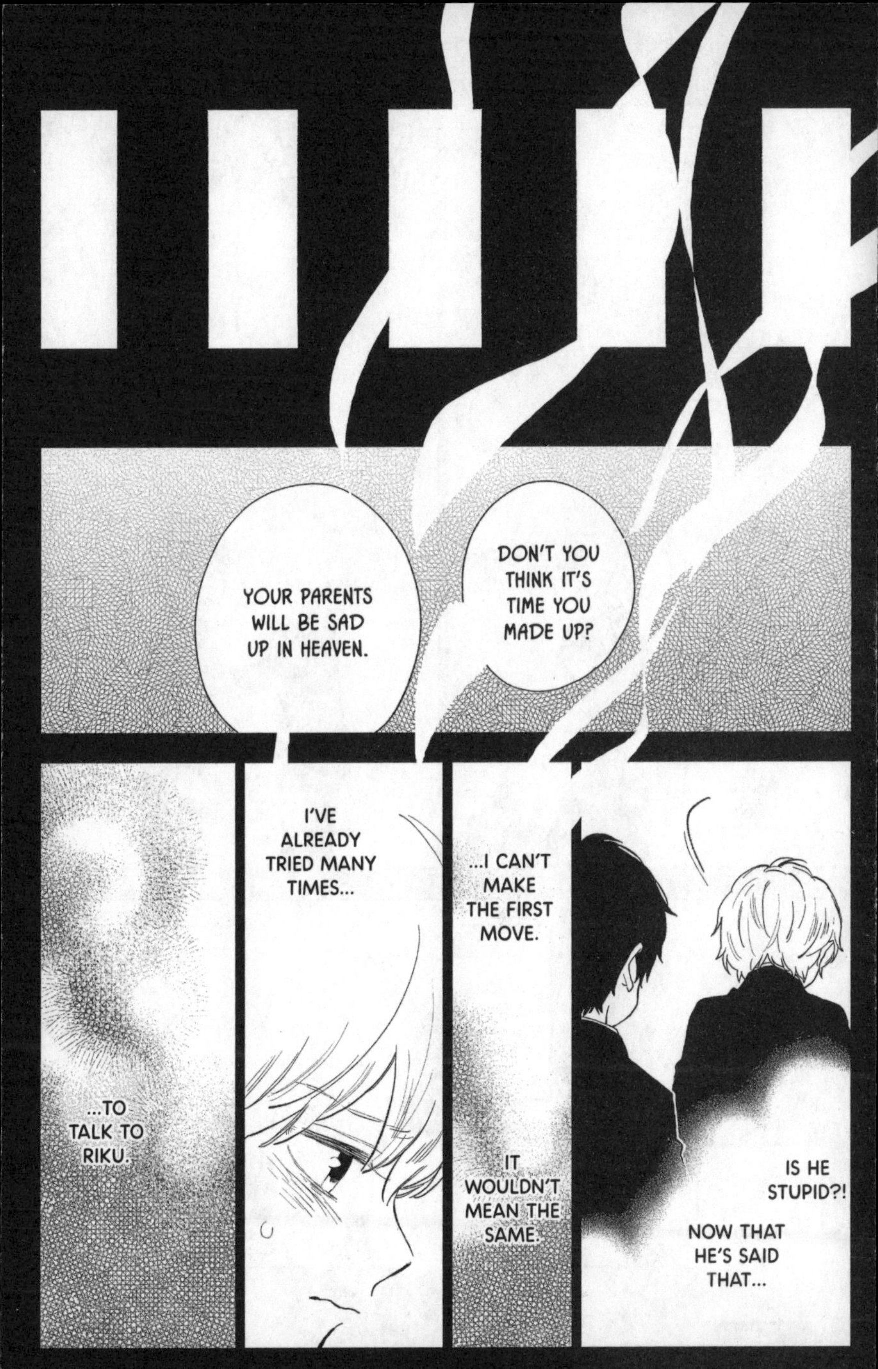
DON'T YOU THINK IT'S TIME YOU MADE UP?
YOUR PARENTS WILL BE SAD UP IN HEAVEN.
IS HE STUPID?!
NOW THAT HE'S SAID THAT...
...I CAN'T MAKE THE FIRST MOVE.
IT WOULDN'T MEAN THE SAME.
I'VE ALREADY TRIED MANY TIMES...
...TO TALK TO RIKU.

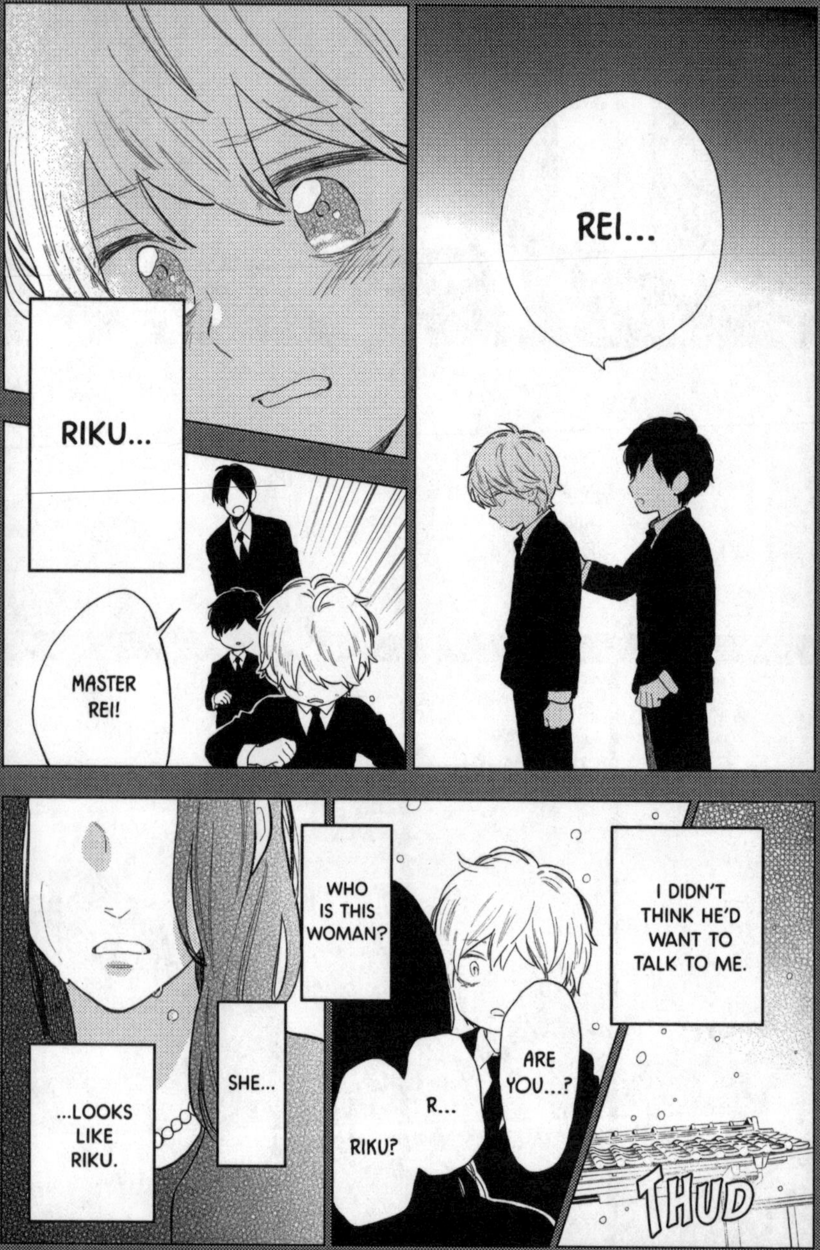
REI...
RIKU...
MASTER REI!
I DIDN'T THINK HE'D WANT TO TALK TO ME.
ARE YOU...?
R...
RIKU?
THUD
WHO IS THIS WOMAN?
SHE...
...LOOKS LIKE RIKU.

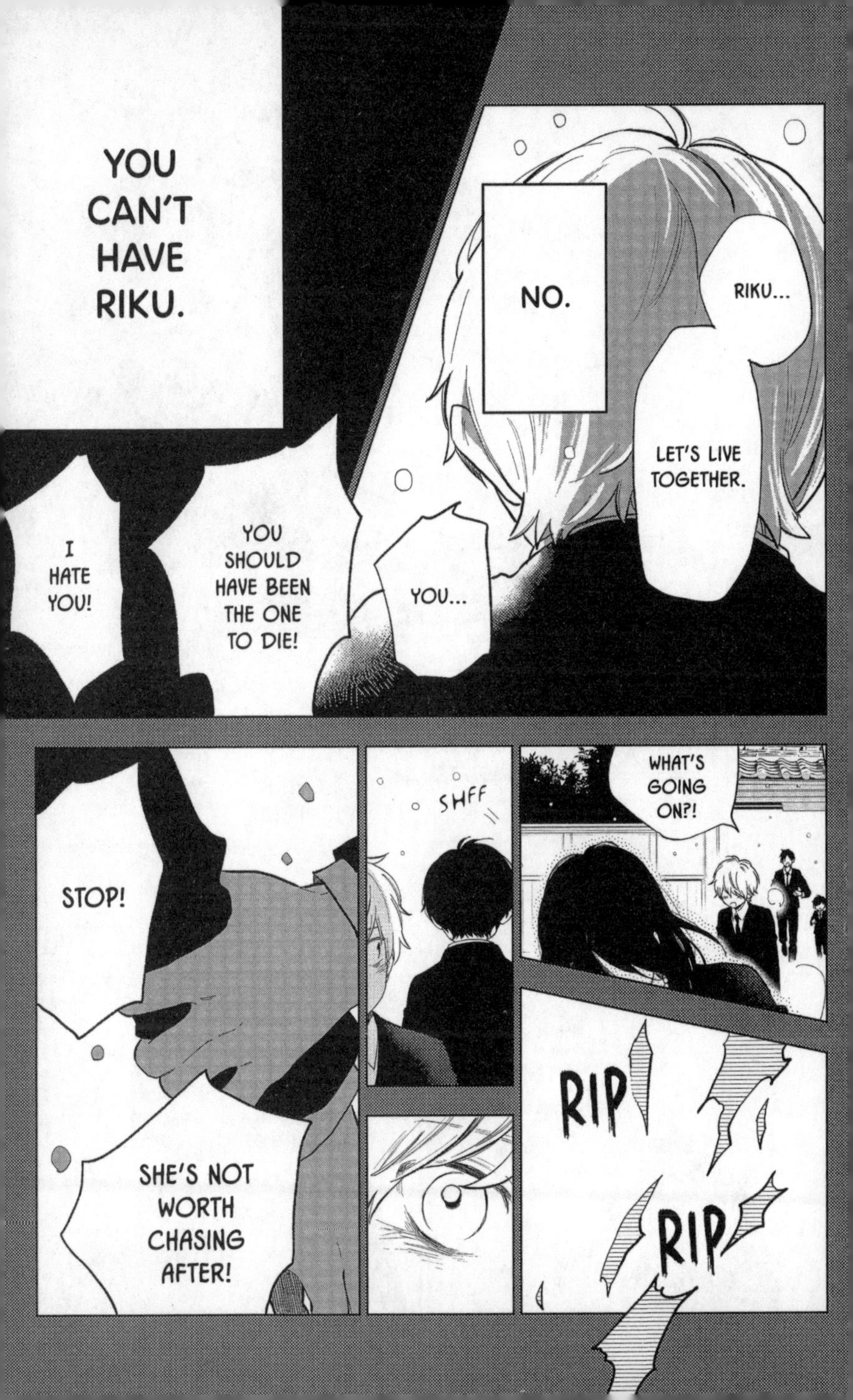
RIKU...
LET'S LIVE TOGETHER.
NO.
YOU...
YOU CAN'T HAVE RIKU.
YOU SHOULD HAVE BEEN THE ONE TO DIE!
I HATE YOU!
WHAT'S GOING ON?!
RIP
RIP
SHFF
STOP!
SHE'S NOT WORTH CHASING AFTER!

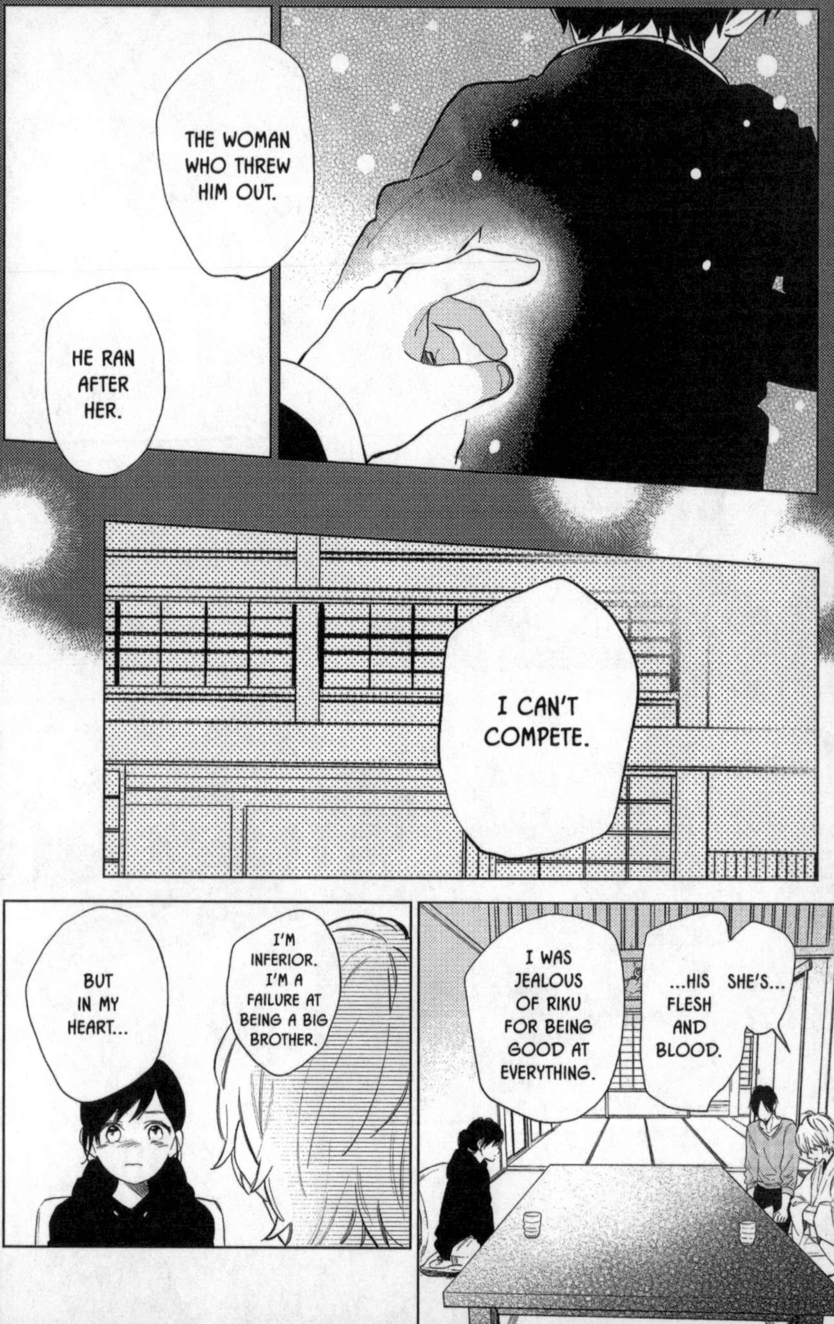
THE WOMAN WHO THREW HIM OUT.
HE RAN AFTER HER.
I CAN'T COMPETE.
SHE'S...
...HIS FLESH AND BLOOD.
I WAS JEALOUS OF RIKU FOR BEING GOOD AT EVERYTHING.
I'M INFERIOR. I'M A FAILURE AT BEING A BIG BROTHER.
BUT IN MY HEART...

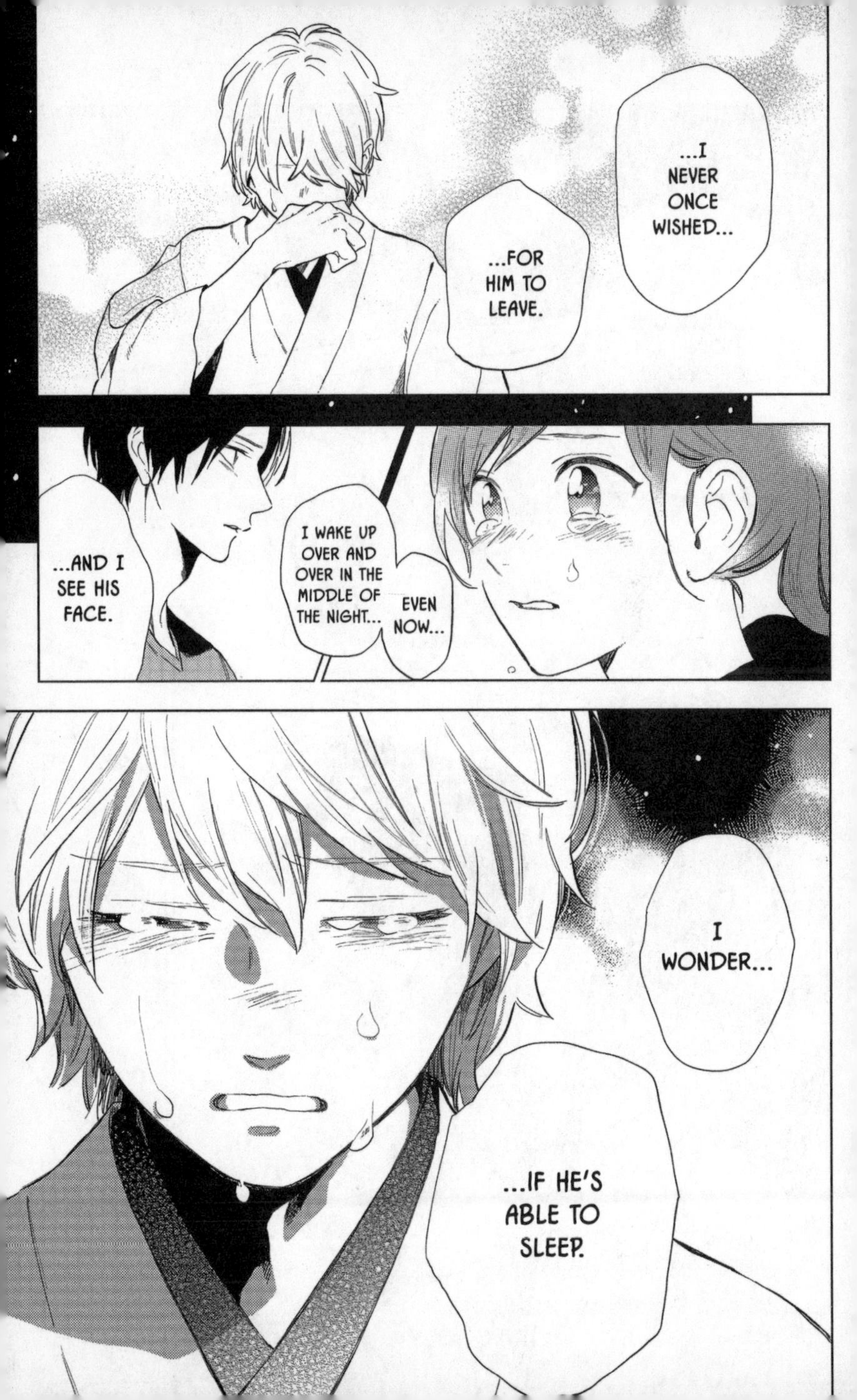
...I NEVER ONCE WISHED...
...FOR HIM TO LEAVE.
EVEN NOW...
I WAKE UP OVER AND OVER IN THE MIDDLE OF THE NIGHT...
...AND I SEE HIS FACE.
I WONDER...
...IF HE'S ABLE TO SLEEP.

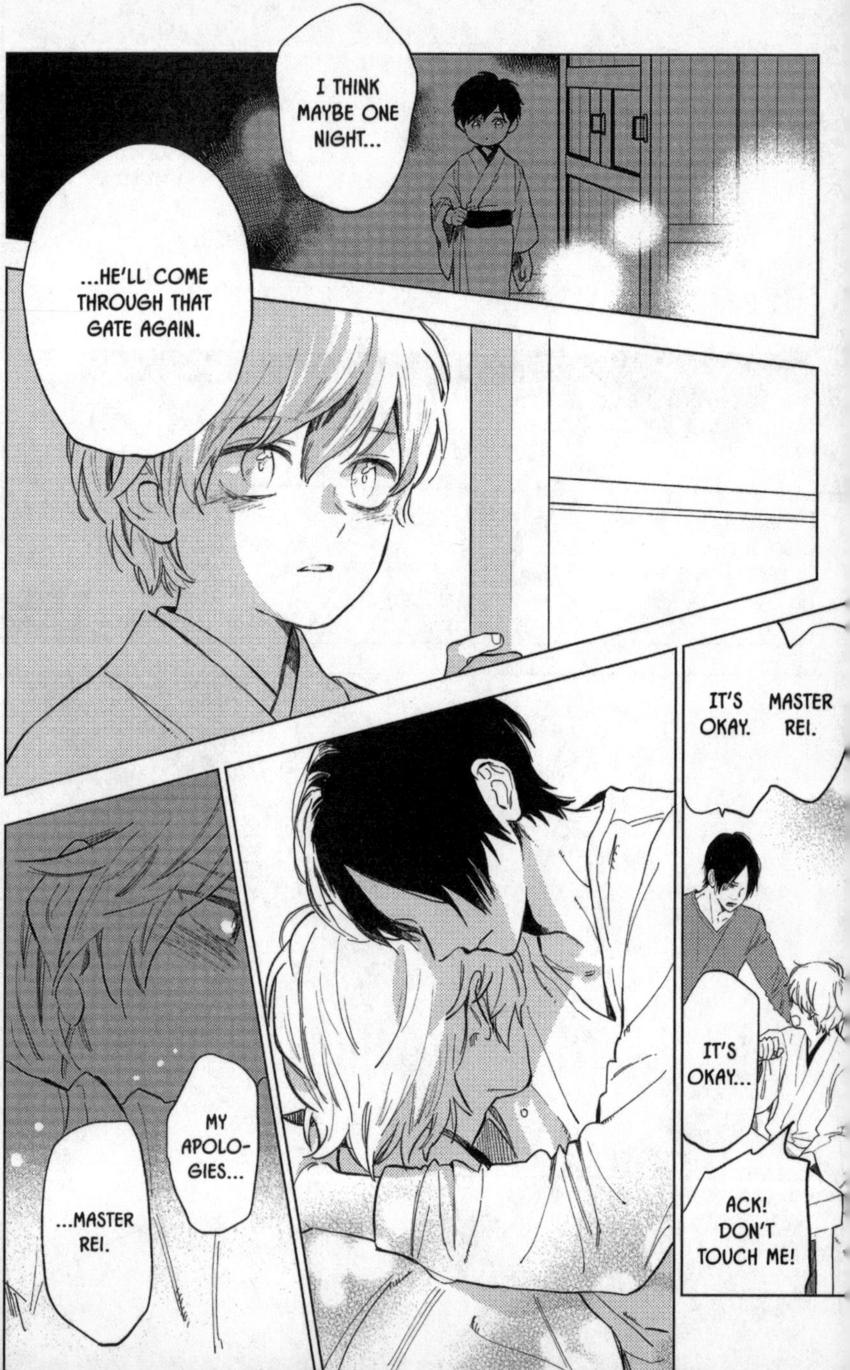
I THINK MAYBE ONE NIGHT...
...HE'LL COME THROUGH THAT GATE AGAIN.
MASTER REI.
IT'S OKAY.
IT'S OKAY...
ACK! DON'T TOUCH ME!
MY APOLOGIES...
...MASTER REI.

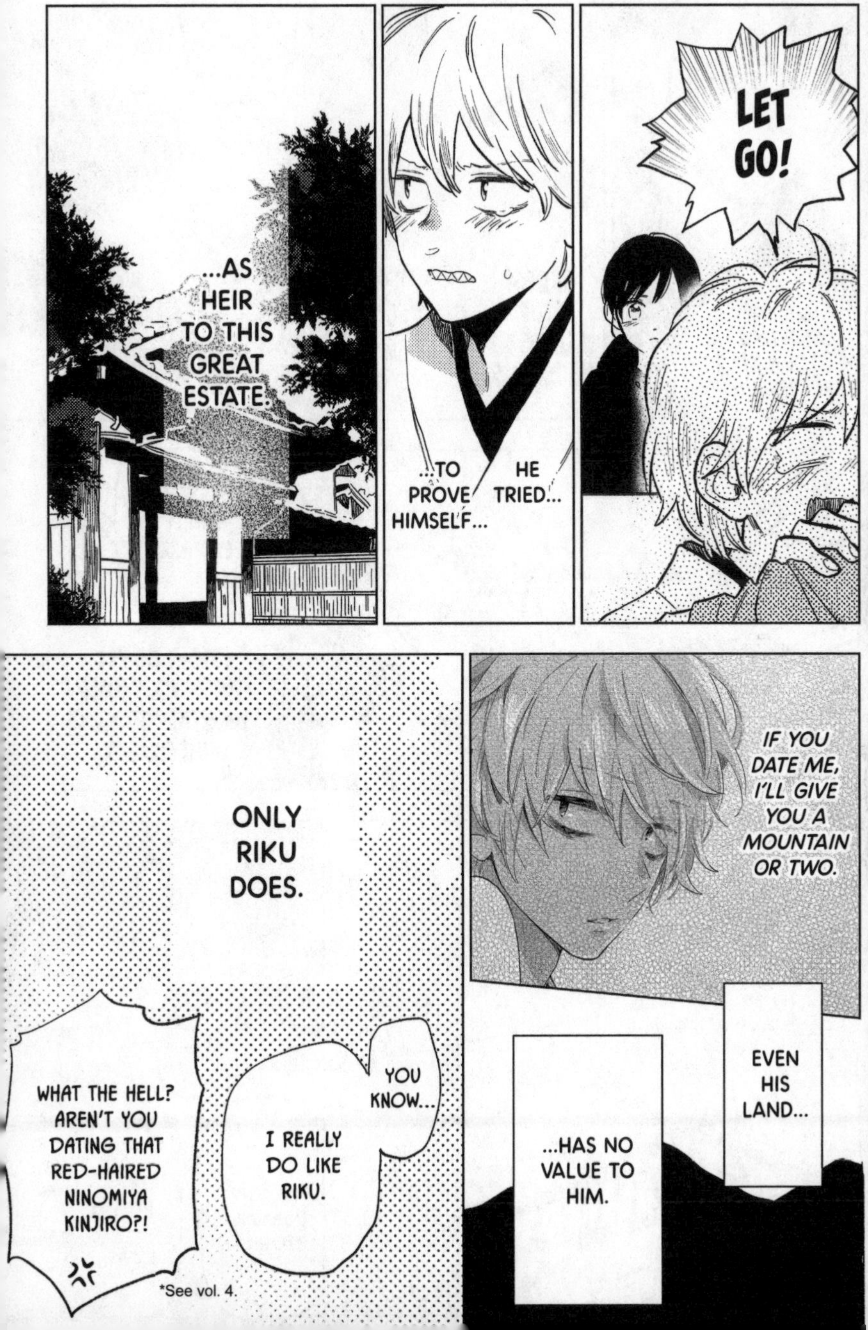
LET GO!
HE TRIED...
...TO PROVE HIMSELF...
...AS HEIR TO THIS GREAT ESTATE.
IF YOU DATE ME, I'LL GIVE YOU A MOUNTAIN OR TWO.
EVEN HIS LAND...
...HAS NO VALUE TO HIM.
ONLY RIKU DOES.
YOU KNOW...
I REALLY DO LIKE RIKU.
WHAT THE HELL? AREN'T YOU DATING THAT RED-HAIRED NINOMIYA KINJIRO?!
*See vol. 4.

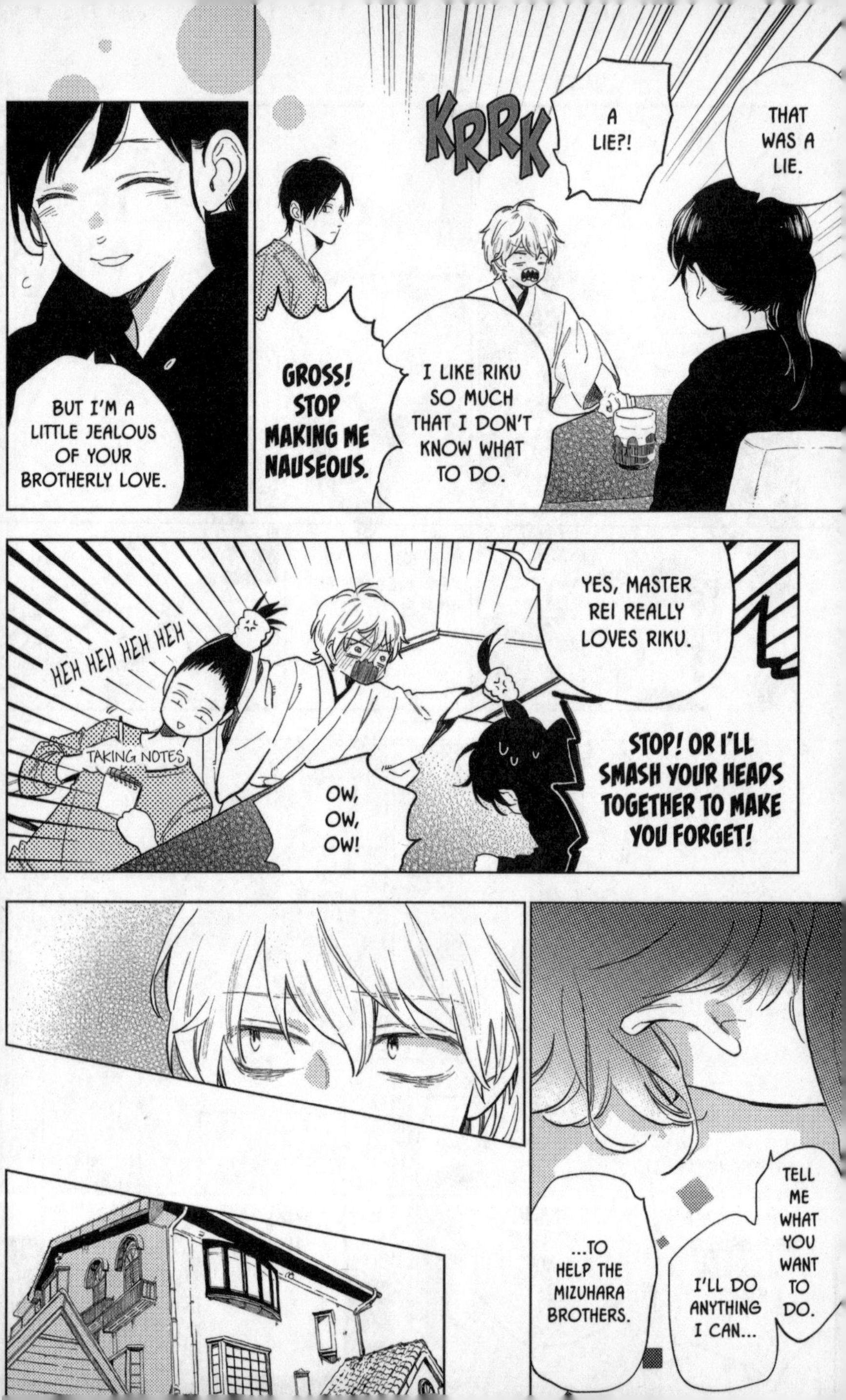
THAT WAS A LIE.
A LIE?!
KRRK
I LIKE RIKU SO MUCH THAT I DON'T KNOW WHAT TO DO.
GROSS! STOP MAKING ME NAUSEOUS.
BUT I'M A LITTLE JEALOUS OF YOUR BROTHERLY LOVE.
YES, MASTER REI REALLY LOVES RIKU.
STOP! OR I'LL SMASH YOUR HEADS TOGETHER TO MAKE YOU FORGET!
OW, OW, OW!
HEH HEH HEH HEH
TAKING NOTES
TELL ME WHAT YOU WANT TO DO.
I'LL DO ANYTHING I CAN...
...TO HELP THE MIZUHARA BROTHERS.

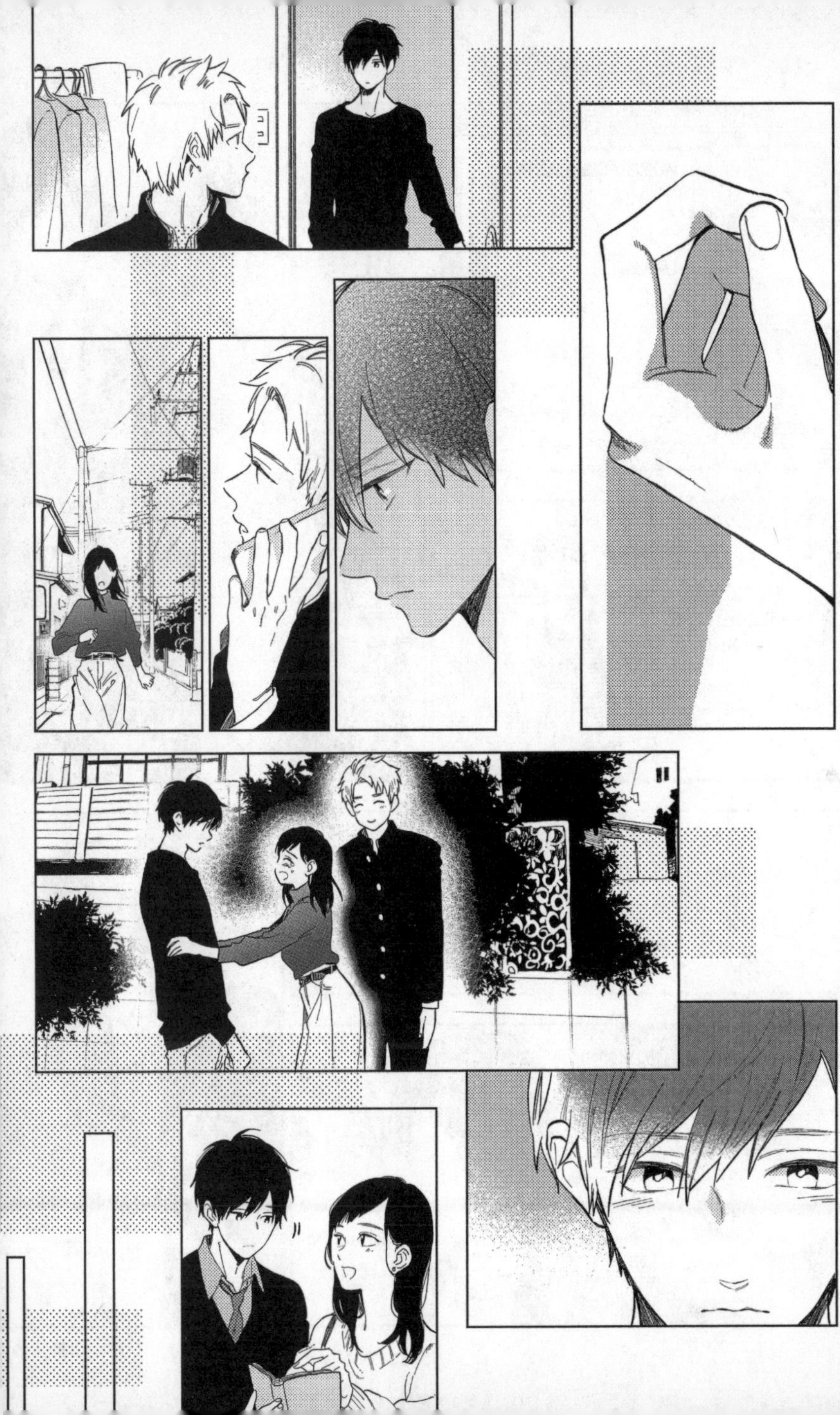
ココ

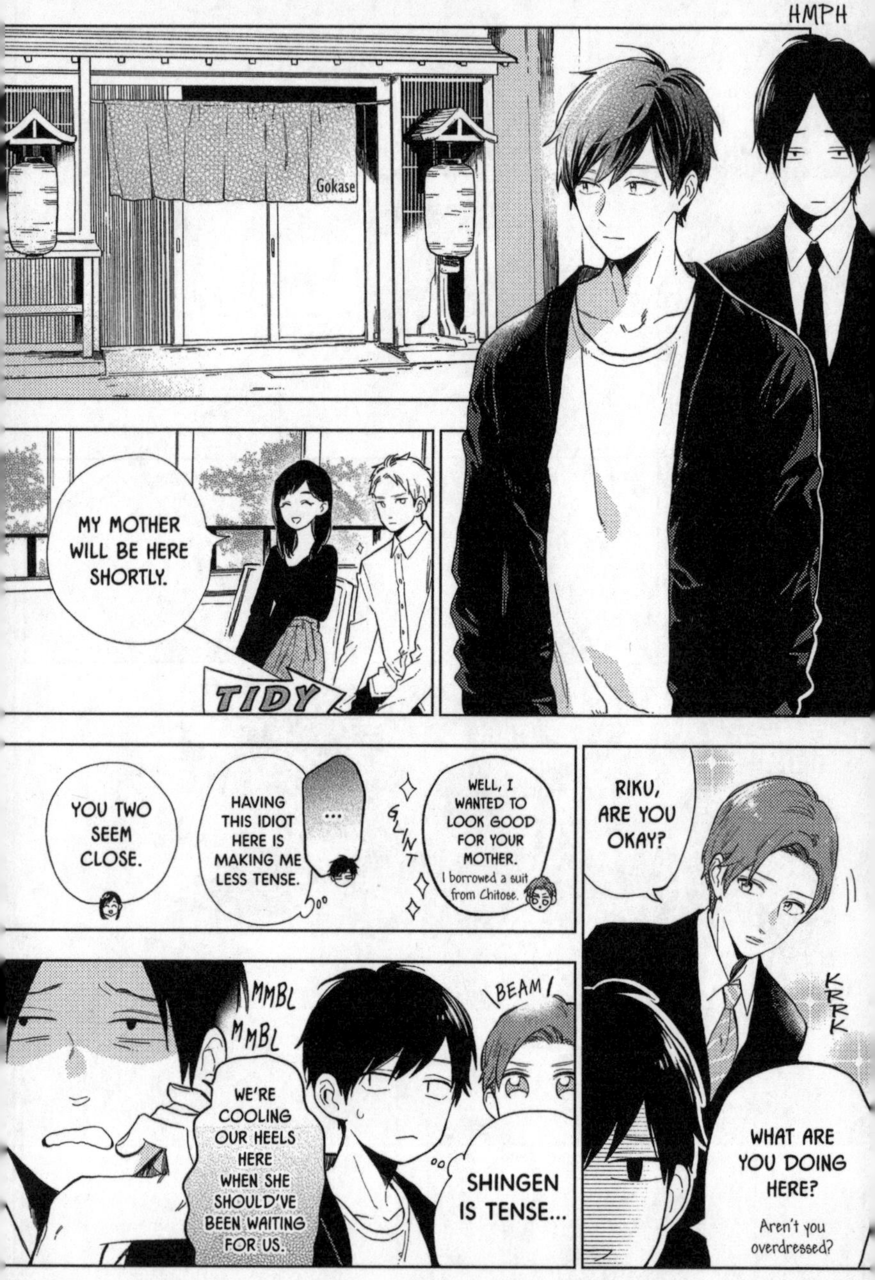
HMPH
Gokase
MY MOTHER WILL BE HERE SHORTLY.
TIDY
RIKU, ARE YOU OKAY?
KRRK
WHAT ARE YOU DOING HERE?
Aren't you overdressed?
WELL, I WANTED TO LOOK GOOD FOR YOUR MOTHER.
I borrowed a suit from Chitose.
GLINT
...
HAVING THIS IDIOT HERE IS MAKING ME LESS TENSE.
YOU TWO SEEM CLOSE.
BEAM
SHINGEN IS TENSE...
MMBL MMBL
WE'RE COOLING OUR HEELS HERE WHEN SHE SHOULD'VE BEEN WAITING FOR US.

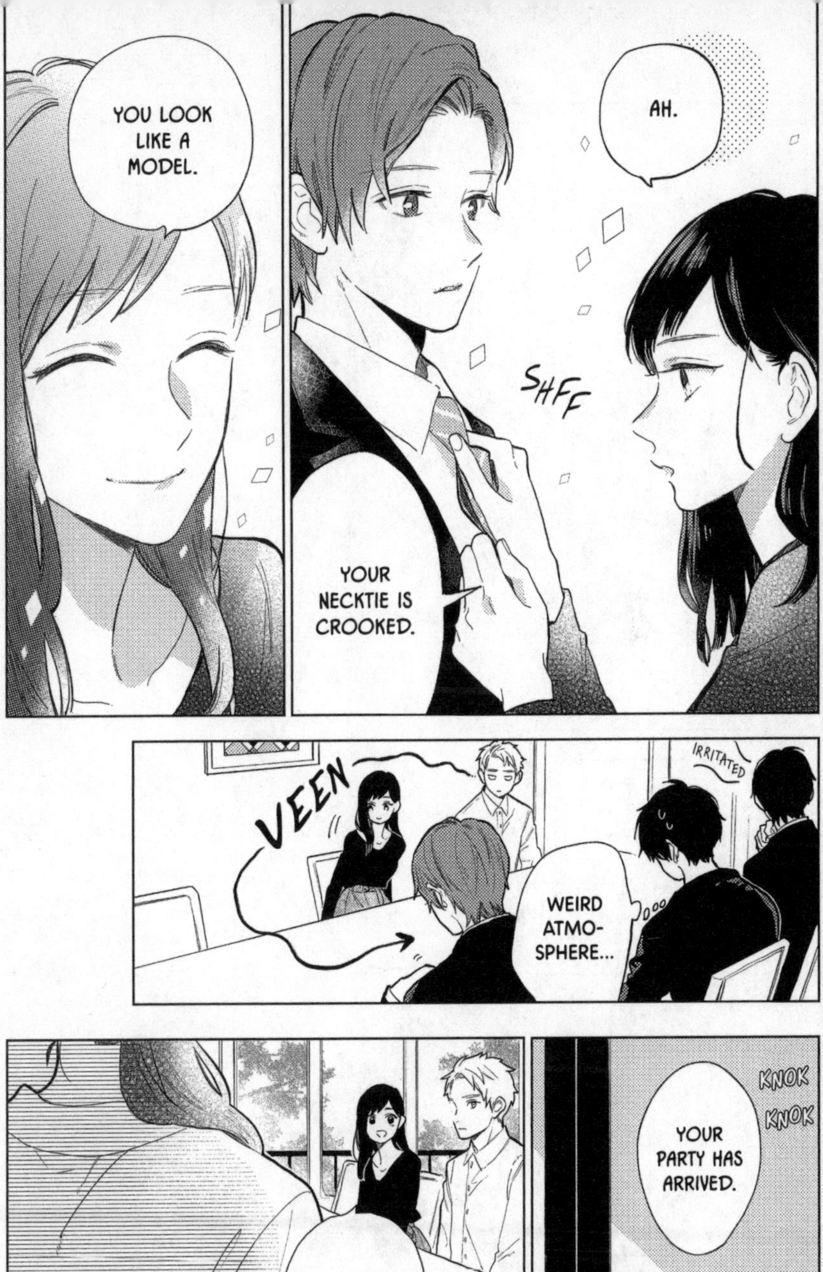
AH.
SHFF
YOUR NECKTIE IS CROOKED.
YOU LOOK LIKE A MODEL.
IRRITATED
VEEN
WEIRD ATMO-SPHERE...
KNOK KNOK
YOUR PARTY HAS ARRIVED.
MOM.

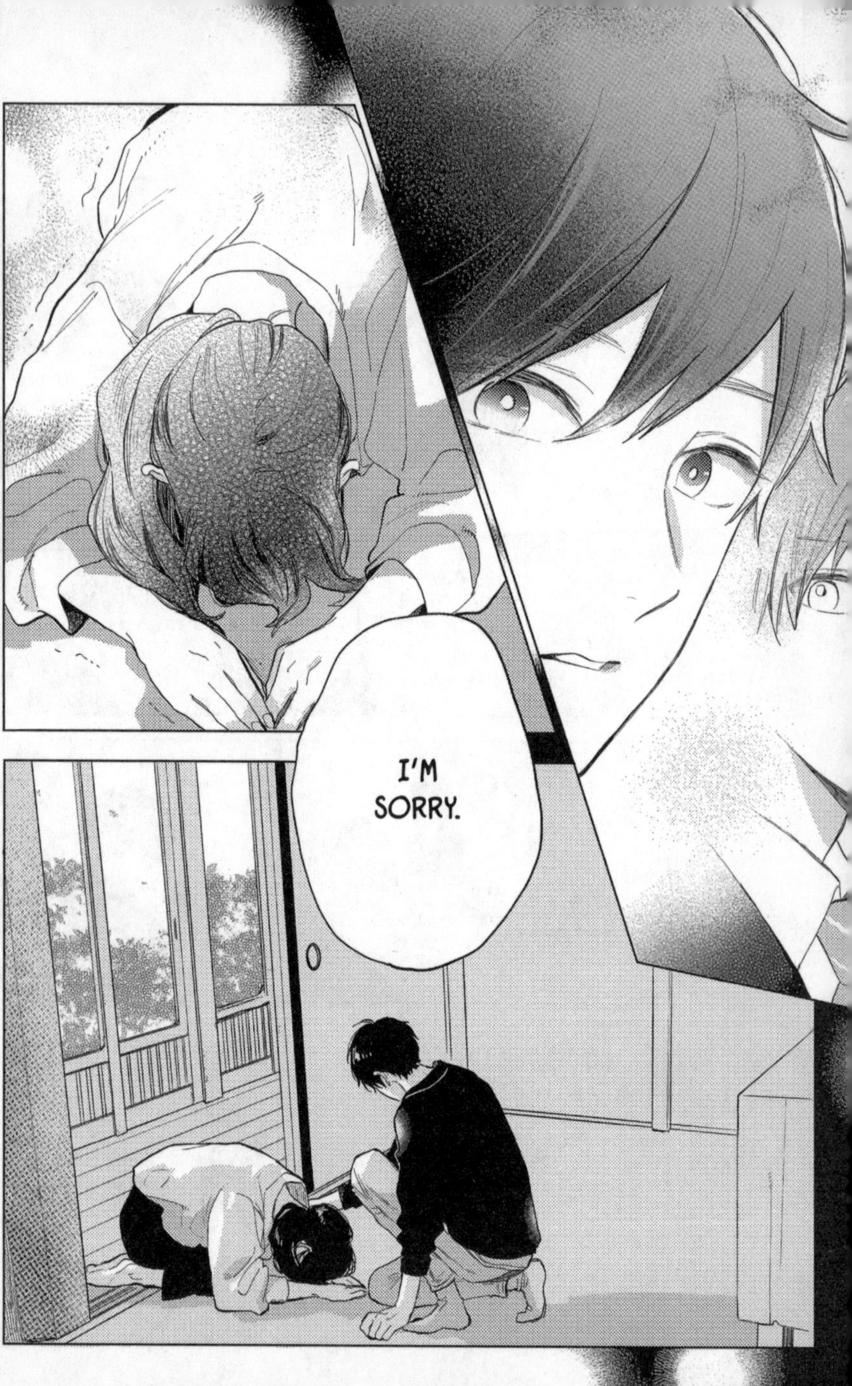
I'M SORRY.

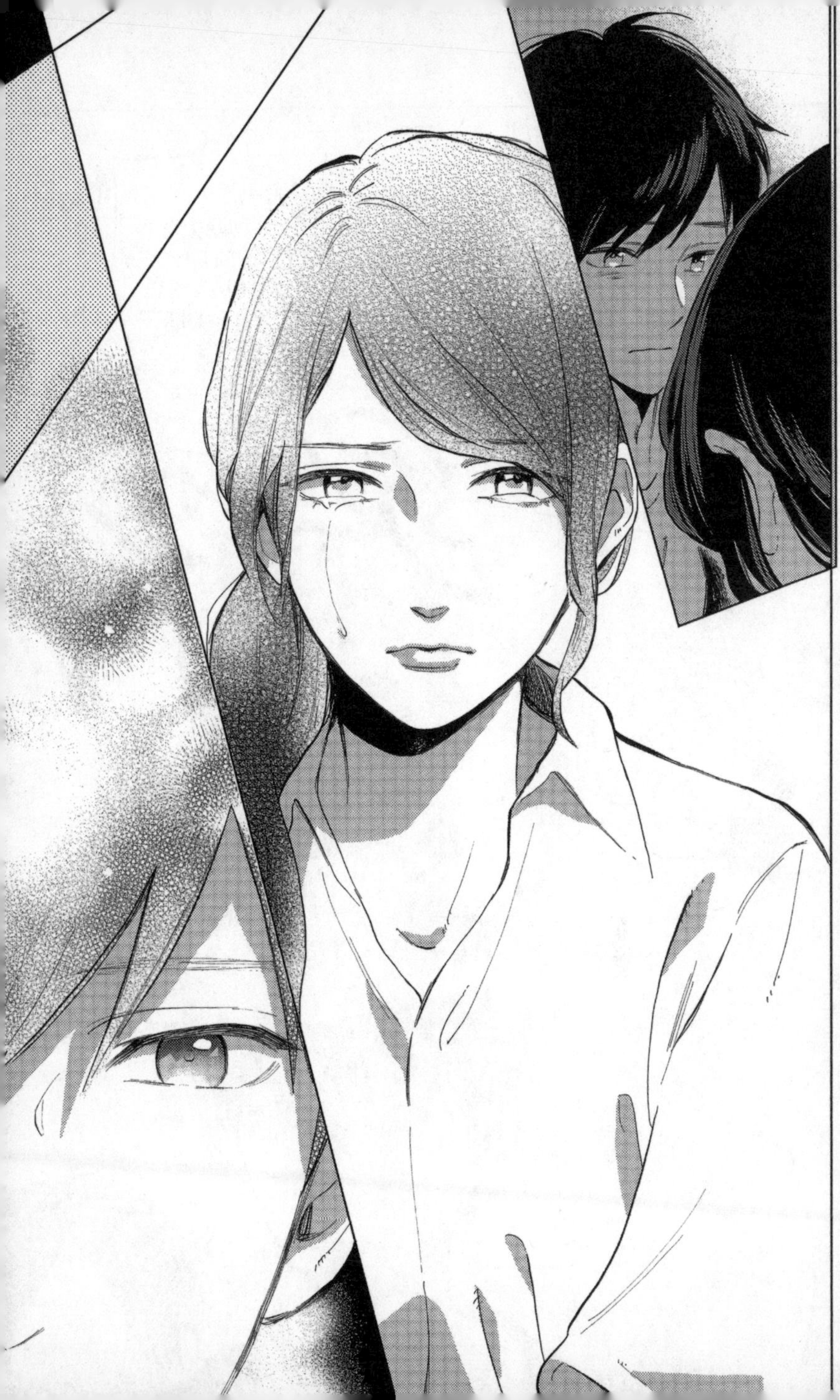

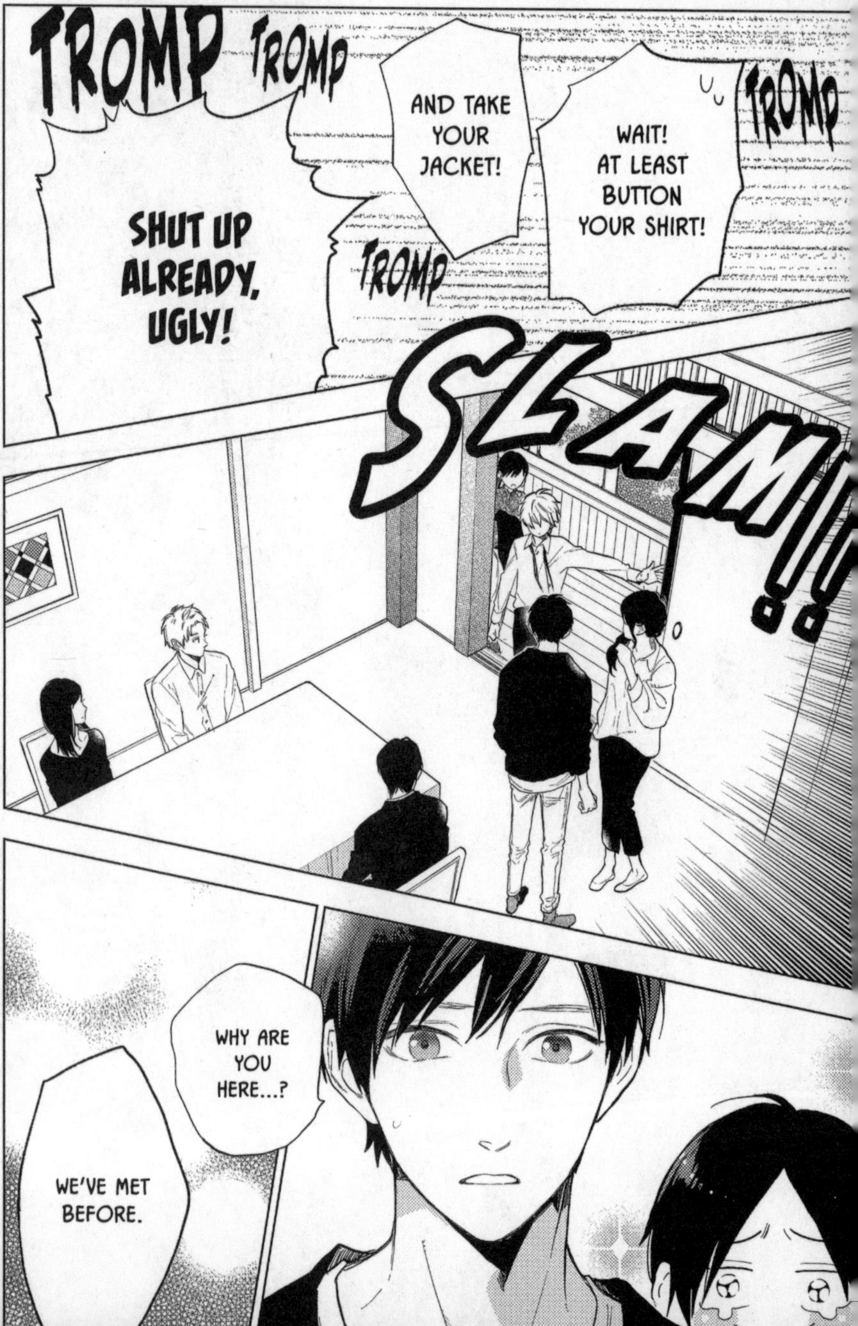
TROMP
WAIT! AT LEAST BUTTON YOUR SHIRT!
AND TAKE YOUR JACKET!
TROMP
TROMP
TROMP
SHUT UP ALREADY, UGLY!
SLAM!!
WHY ARE YOU HERE...?
WE'VE MET BEFORE.

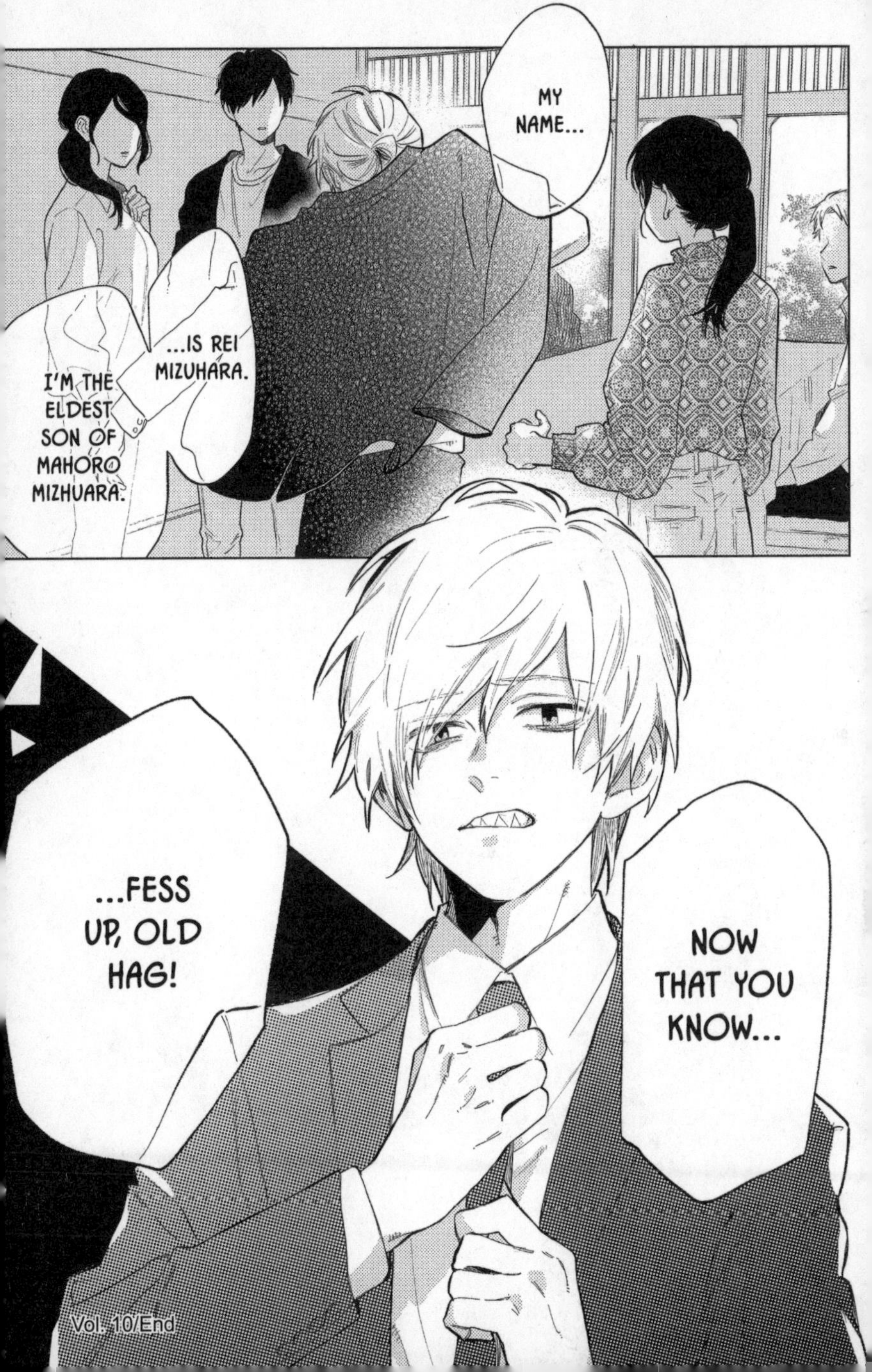
MY NAME...
...IS REI MIZUHARA.
I'M THE ELDEST SON OF MAHORO MIZHUARA.
NOW THAT YOU KNOW...
...FESS UP, OLD HAG!

Vol. 10/End

SHORTCAKE
CAKE

Readers requested to see the character profiles quite a while back, but we wanted to wait until we'd revealed Riku's past. It's a bit late, but here you go!

Ten Serizawa

Birthday: 2/18
Blood type: O
Height: 5' 1"
Favorite food: Anything

Chiaki Kasadera

Birthday: 2/7
Blood type: A
Height: 5' 10"
Favorite book:  Too many to decide

Riku Mizuhara

Birthday: 4/30
Blood type: AB
Height: 5' 9"
Favorite food: Hummus

Rei Mizuhara

Birthday: 3/31
Blood type: O
Height: 5' 7"
Favorite drink: Yoghurppe

Shingen Shiraoka

Birthday: 6/10
Blood type: B
Height: 5' 11"
Favorite food: Japanese

The back story is that before his parents
got divorced, his full name was Shingen
Kai. When he switched to Shiraoka, his
name didn't flow as well.

Bonus

Ran Hoshino

Birthday: 11/5

Blood type: A

Height: 5' 7"

Favorite food: Free-range chicken

The back story is that Ran is embarrassed by her full name, and the track suit she always wears is from Nekochiya High.

Special Thanks

- Editor J
- Designer Yasuhisa Kawatani
- Assistant Nao Hamaguchi
- Helper Kame-chan
- The many people who helped along the way
- And all our readers ♡

SHORTCAKE CAKE
Title Page Collection
Chapter 53

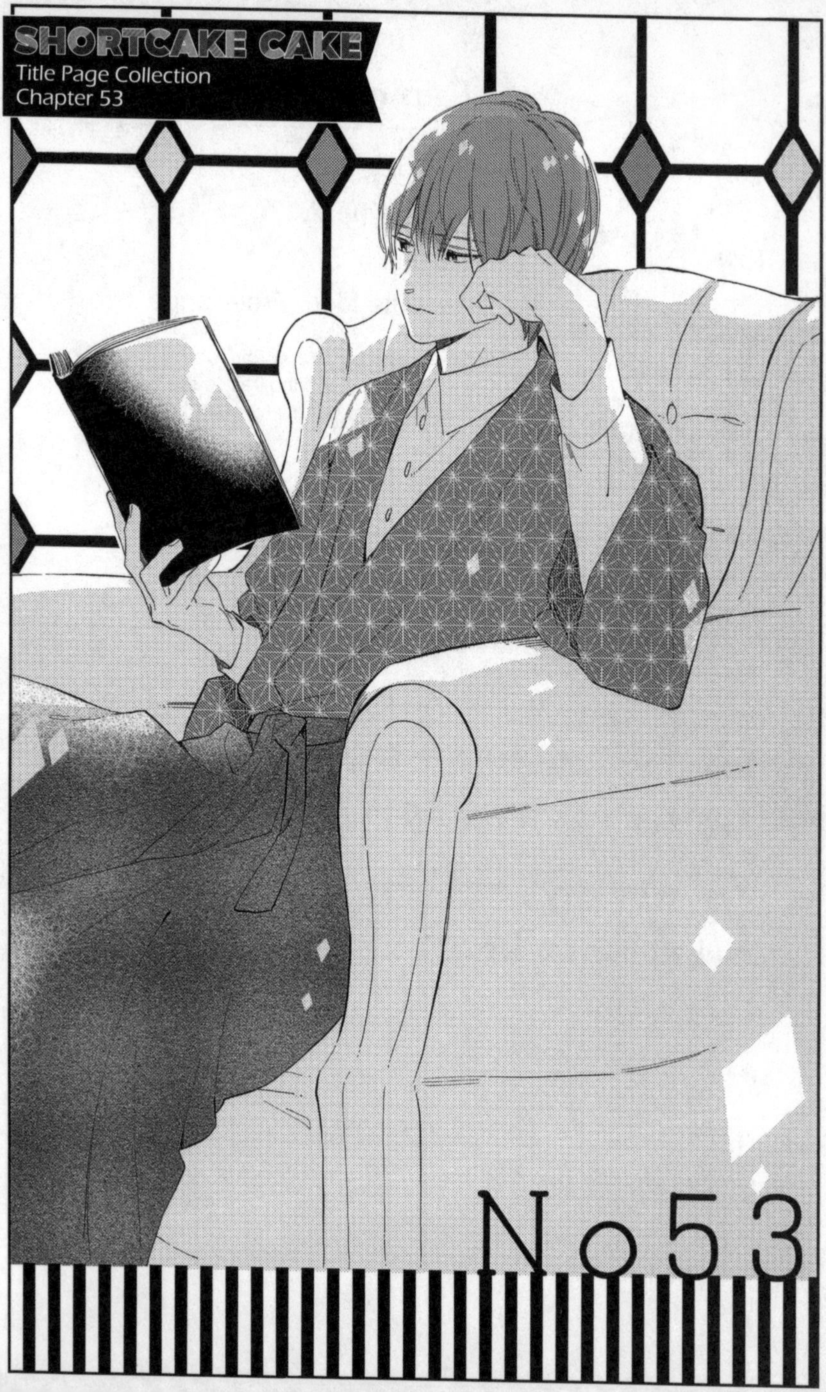
No53

SHORTCAKE CAKE

Title Page Collection
Issue 15 Magazine Cover

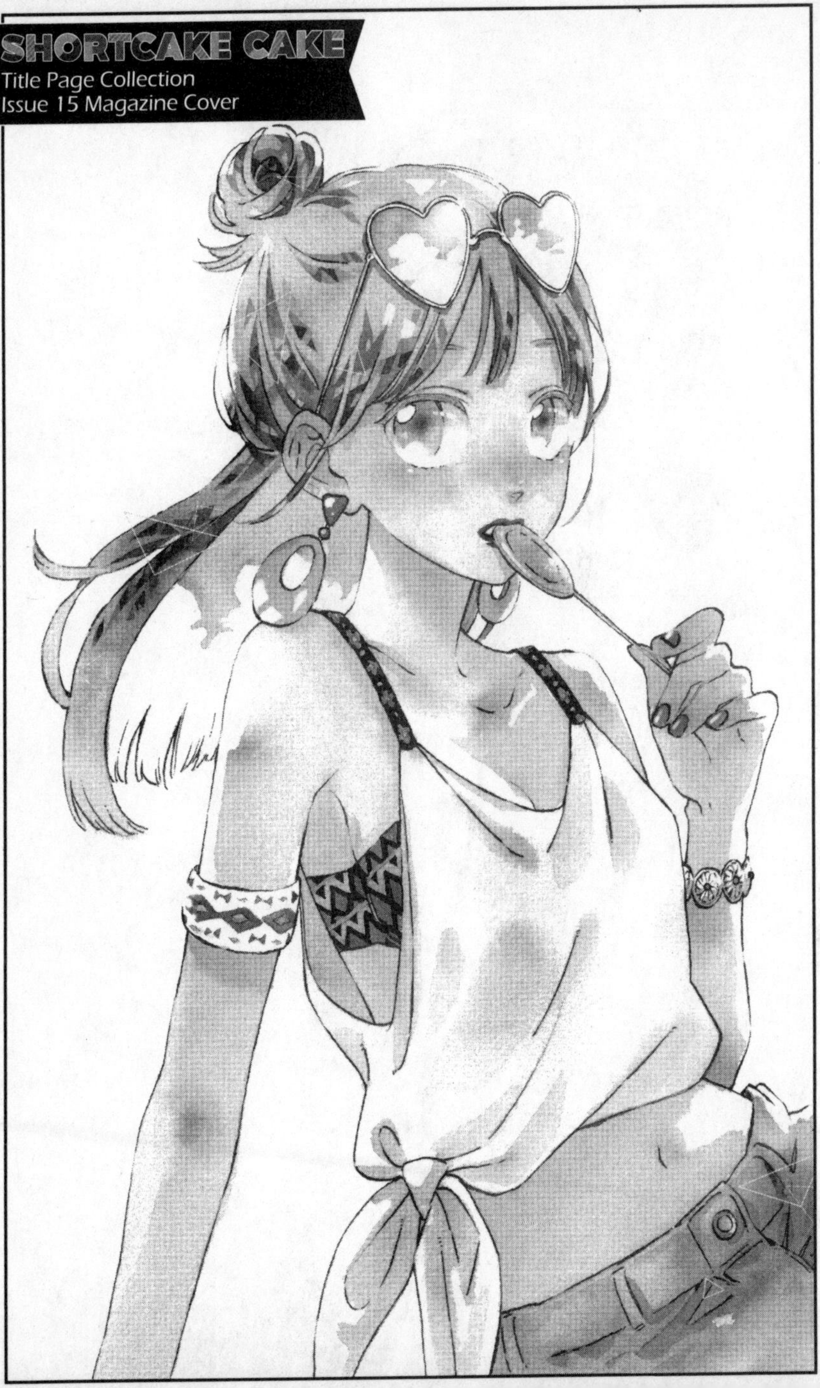

SHORTCAKE CAKE

Title Page Collection
Chapter 54

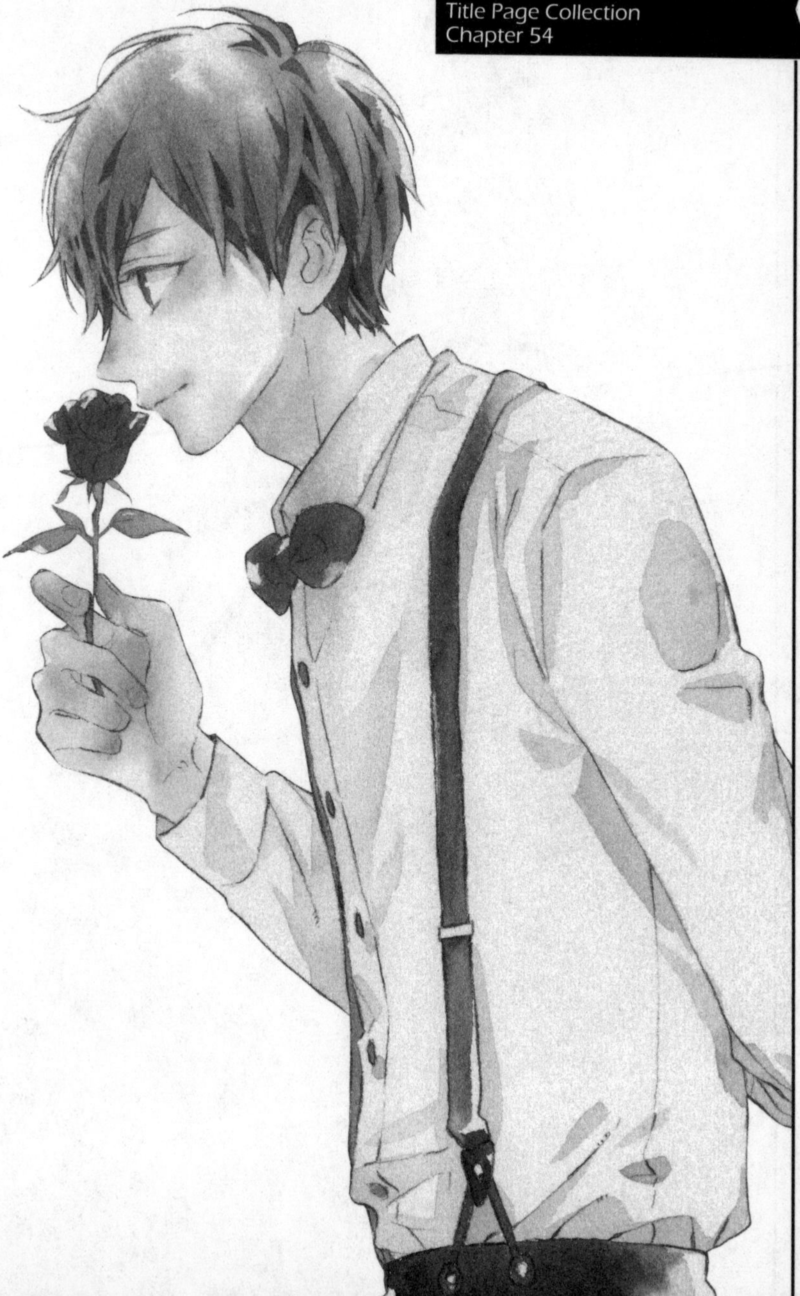

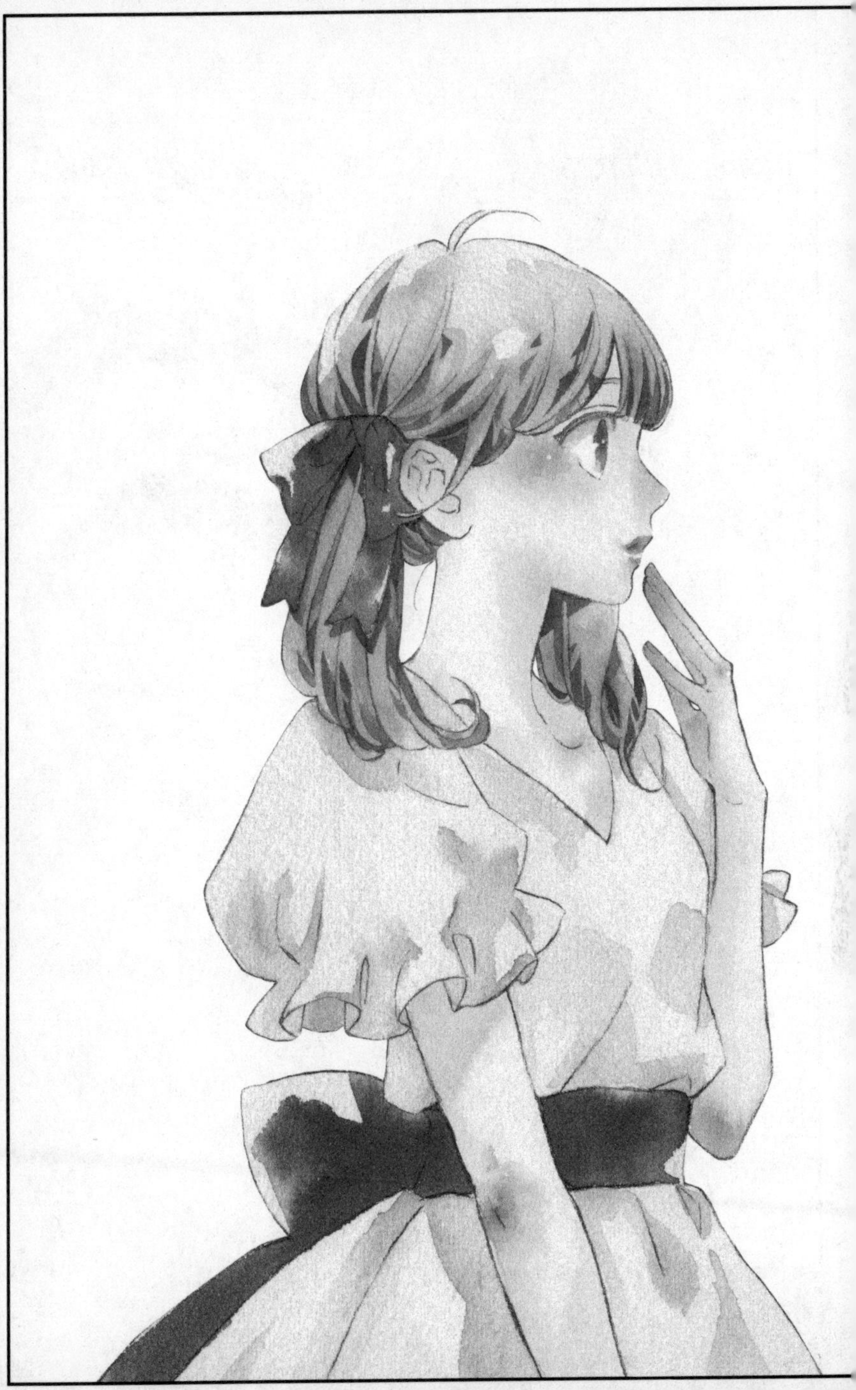

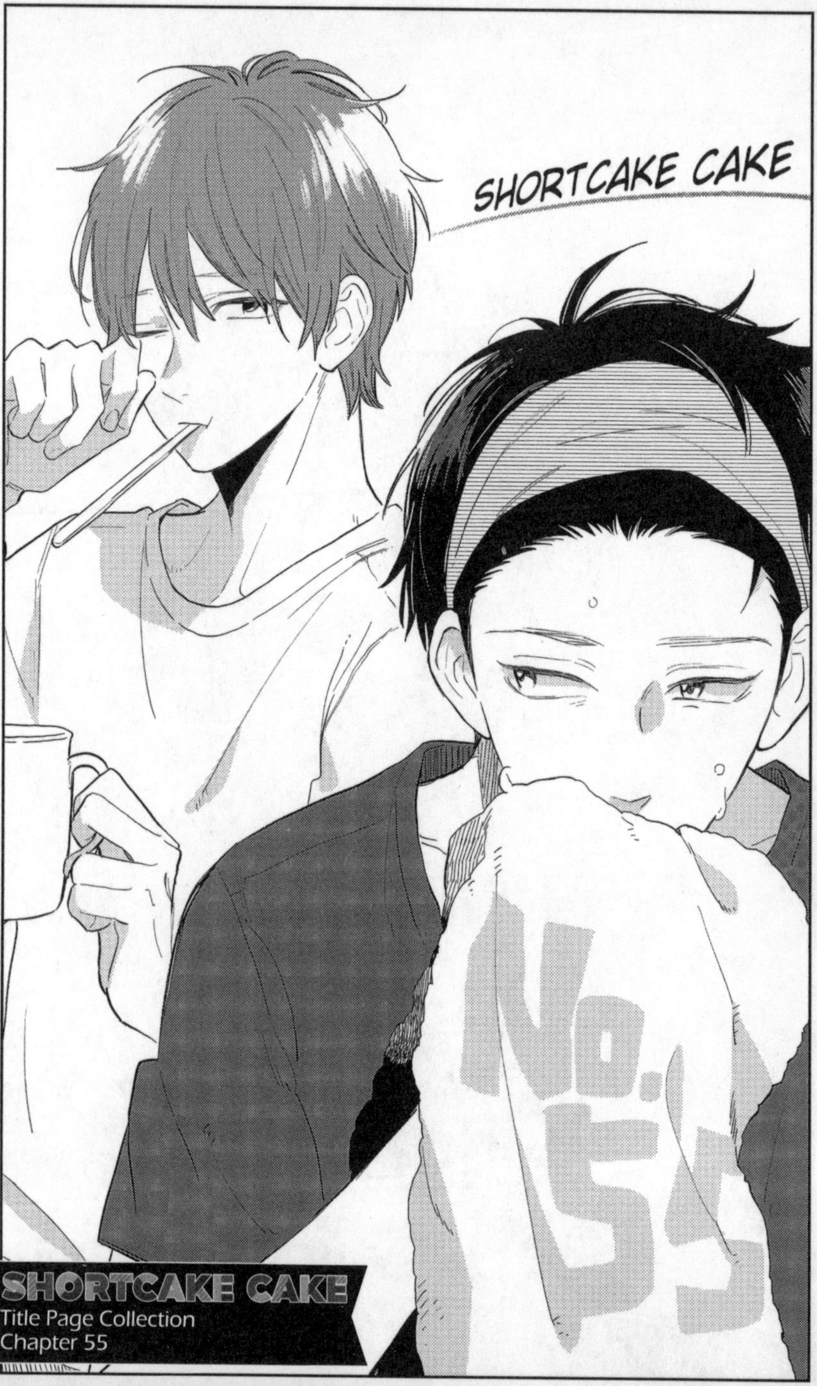
SHORTCAKE CAKE
No. 55

SHORTCAKE CAKE
Title Page Collection
Chapter 55

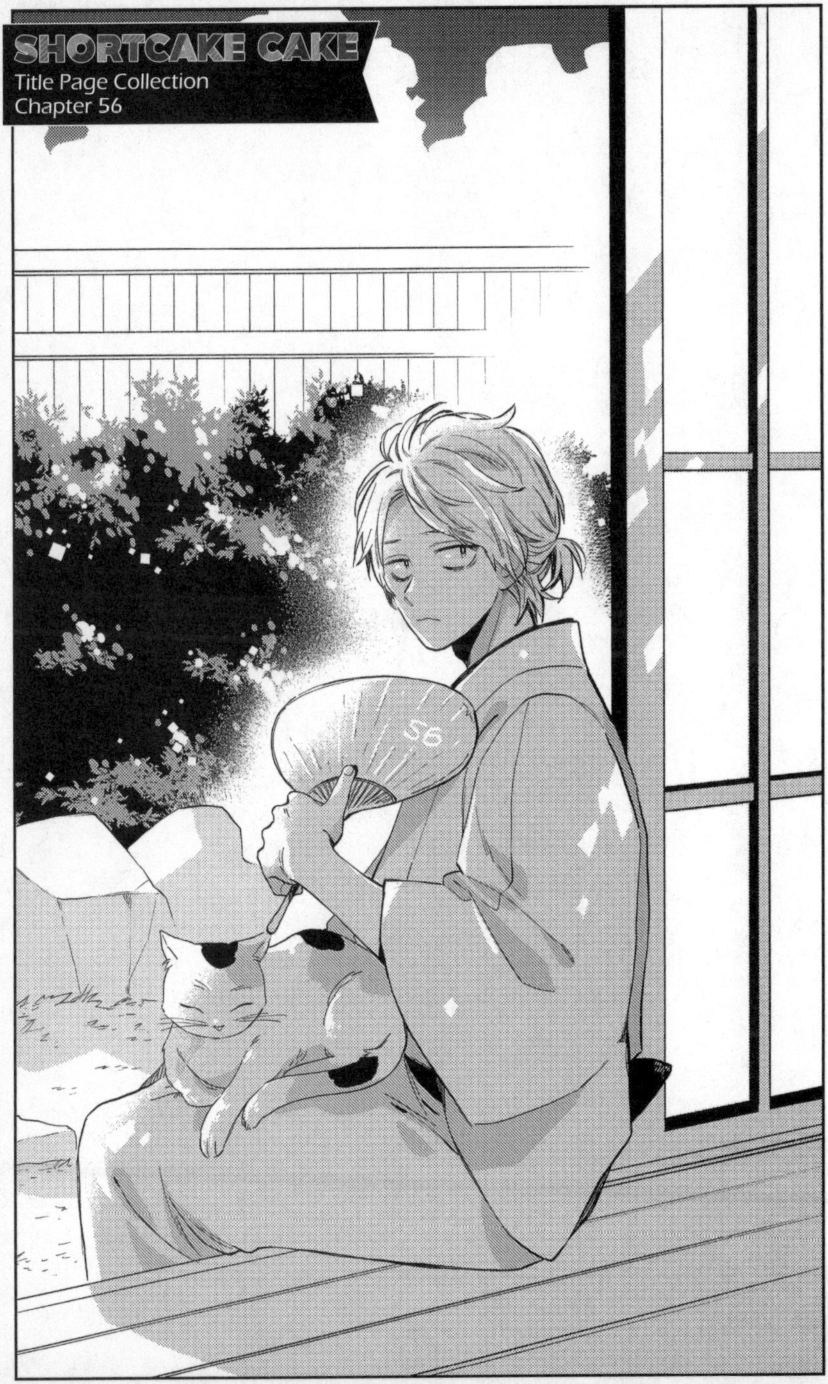
SHORTCAKE CAKE
Title Page Collection
Chapter 56
56

Recently, while reading *Hibi Chouchou* again,
we couldn't help but reminisce about
how peaceful our stories used to be....

—suu Morishita

suu Morishita is a creator duo.
The story is by Makiro, and the art is by
Nachiyan. In 2010 they debuted with the
one-shot "Anote Konote." Their works include
Hibi Chouchou and *Shortcake Cake*.

VOLUME 10
SHOJO BEAT EDITION

STORY + ART BY **suu Morishita**

TRANSLATION **Emi Louie-Nishikawa**
TOUCH-UP ART + LETTERING **Inori Fukuda Trant**
DESIGN **Joy Zhang**
EDITOR **Nancy Thistlethwaite**

SHORTCAKE CAKE © 2015 by Suu Morishita
All rights reserved.
First published in Japan in 2015 by SHUEISHA Inc., Tokyo.
English translation rights arranged by SHUEISHA Inc.

The stories, characters and incidents mentioned
in this publication are entirely fictional.

Printed in the U.S.A.

Published by VIZ Media, LLC
P.O. Box 77010
San Francisco, CA 94107

10 9 8 7 6 5 4 3 2 1
First printing, November 2020

PARENTAL ADVISORY
SHORTCAKE CAKE is rated T for Teen
and is recommended for ages 13 and up.

viz.com   shojobeat.com

DAYTIME SHOOTING STAR

Story & Art by
Mika Yamamori

Small town girl Suzume moves to Tokyo and finds her heart caught between two men!

After arriving in Tokyo to live with her uncle, Suzume collapses in a nearby park when she remembers once seeing a shooting star during the day. A handsome stranger brings her to her new home and tells her they'll meet again. Suzume starts her first day at her new high school sitting next to a boy who blushes furiously at her touch. And her homeroom teacher is none other than the handsome stranger!

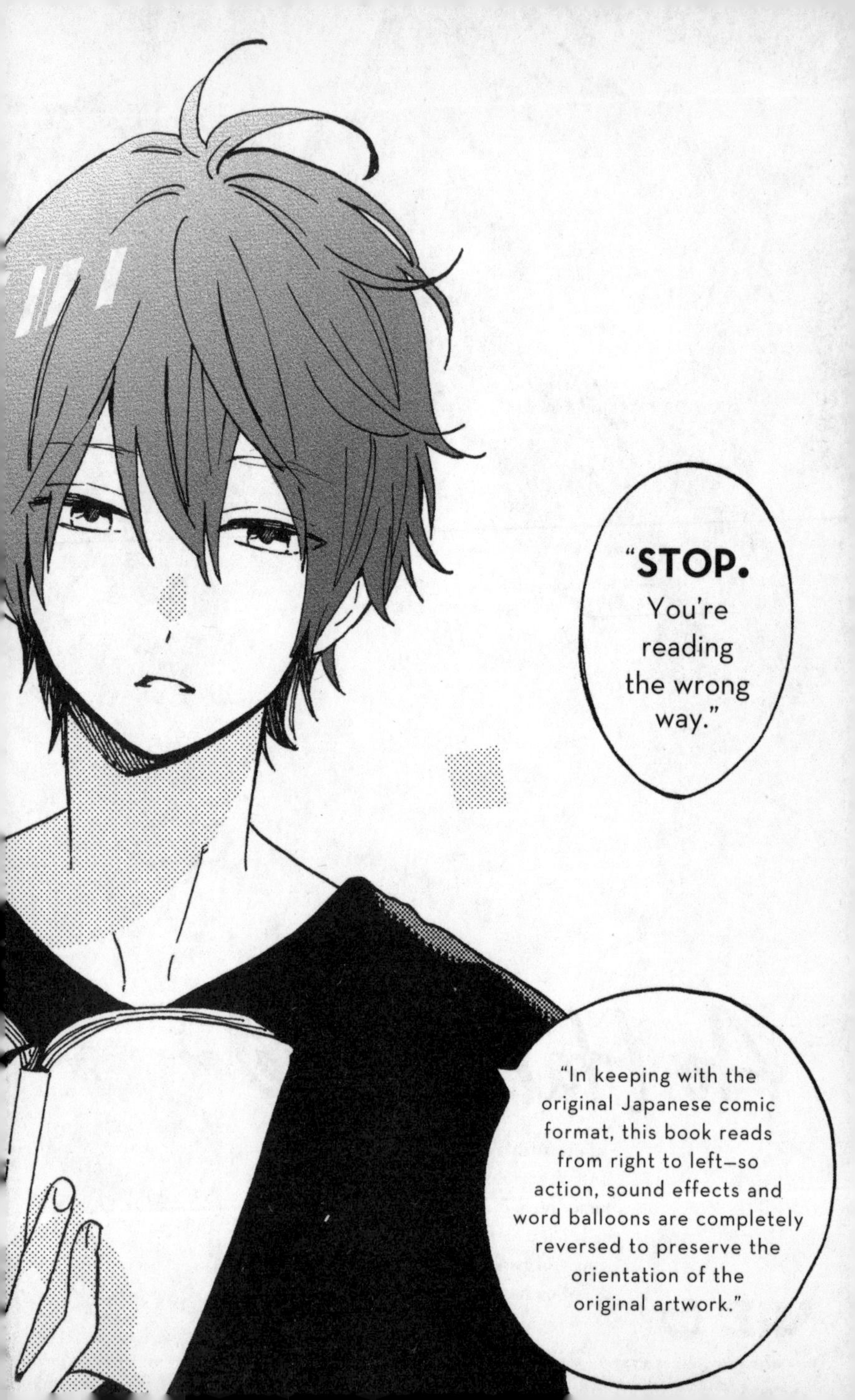
"STOP. You're reading the wrong way."
"In keeping with the original Japanese comic format, this book reads from right to left—so action, sound effects and word balloons are completely reversed to preserve the orientation of the original artwork."